DARRELL CHADIX

^{TO} QUELL THE KORENGAL

To Quell The Korengal, Copyright © 2015 by Darren Shadix

All rights reserved. No part of this publication may be reproduced, distributed, or transmitted in any form or by any means, including photocopying, recording, or other electronic or mechanical methods, without the prior written permission of the publisher, except in the case of brief quotations embodied in critical reviews and certain other noncommercial uses permitted by copyright law. For permission requests, email the publisher at the address below.

DTV Press
www.dtv.press@yahoo.com
Edited by AJ Sikes
Cover Design by Keri Knutson
Formatting by www.formatting4U.com

Dedicated to those who walk outside the wire
and to their families
who wait for them to come home.

CONTENTS

Author's Note   i

I. SUMMER

Prologue	1
Initiation in the Korengal	3
To the Relief of 10th Mountain	7
Phoenix Rising	9
Rest In Peace, Doc Restrepo	13
A typical firefight in the Korengal Valley	17
Belgarde	21
Compton Comes To The Korengal	23
Foreshadowing in Ali Abad Cemetery	25
3rd Squad Gets Their Freak On	27
Secret New Weapon In The War On Terror	29
Phoenix Layout	33
Man-Boy Love Night	37
Hygiene Phoenix Style & the Deployment Dress Code	39
Donga vs. Phoenix	43
Who's the real ass anyway?	47
The Ali Abad 500	51
Days of the Week	53
Prickly Heat	57
Re-fit on O.P. Four: Downtime at its best	59
In The Shit	63
Fun In The Sun On E.A. Killer	65
America On Leave	71

II. FALL

Building Restrepo	81
Vegas Con-Op	83
Sergeant Miller	87
Why my NODs Plate Is Black	89
Korengali Window Treatment	91
The Wayward Sergeant Swoyer	93
Check Please!	95
Campbell	97
Sergeant Major Vimoto's Cameo Appearance	99
Over the river and through the woods, to Hajj's house we go	101
Bottom Guard: Alright by day, not so much at night	103

A Week In The Life—Play By Play	105
The Road to Loot & Loved Ones	113
Mino	115
One September Night	117
Night Attack Aftermath	119
Phones & Internet at First	121
Sergeants Shelton & Blaskowski & Why We Don't Need Reporters In The Valley	123
Anatomy of a Platoon	125
To Christen Or Not To Christen	127
Ambush in Ali Abad	129
Sergeant Hunt's Favorite Deployment Pastime	137
Lightning Never Strikes Twice... Does it?	139
The Unsung	141
Soldiers On The Front Getting Finger Fucked	143
My Debut in the Italian Vanity Fair	145
Plight of the SAW Gunner	149
Rock Avalanche	151

III. WINTER

Voice In The Field	167
Trash Man and the Precision-Guided Mortar	171
In Which The Trails Turn Against Us	173
First trip to Marastana "memorable"	177
Replacements	181
Thanksgiving Kolrengali-Style	185
That's Not Mine!	187
At Odds	189
C.I.B. Ceremony	191
Canned Air	193
The Game of Risk	195
Like Cranking on a Jack-In-The-Box	197
Operation Beanie Baby	199
The Informant Fiasco	203
Sergeant Eddie	207
All I Want For Christmas	209
Merry Christmas, Battle Company!	211
Return of the Anti-Tank Mine	213
Kill Me Please	215
In Recognition Of Our Illustrious Leader	217
An Occupational Hazard Turned Good Riddance	219

What's in your draws?	221
Soldiers Report O.P. Three, "Coldest Goddamned Place In The Korengal"	223
Wintertime Antics	225
The Witch Hunt	229
Fuller Comes To Town	231
Atrium House Firefight	233
She's My Best Friend's Girl	237
Roberts	239
New Plan of Action Raises Eyebrows, Concerns Over Command's Sanity	241
Provided We Patrol	243
What Leap Day Means to a 15-Month Deployment	245

IV. SPRING

The Security Bubble's Great Inexistence	249
New Blood	253
Ali Abad After Dark	255
F.R.G Sends Out Their Bi-Weekly Notices of Death	259
Make Offer	261
Charlie In The Wire	263
Big Hair Band Day in Ali Abad	265
Band of Brothers	267
E.O.D.: Support Gone Awry	269
Pre-Patrol Song	273
Test Fire Gone Wrong	275
You Know You've Been Deployed Too Long When…	277
Five-Five-Six Can Suck My Balls	279
Too Easy	281
Conflicts of Interest	283
Farewell to Phoenix	285
The KOP Life	287
Rattlesnake Appreciation Day	291
PEZ People	295
O.P. Dallas Con-Op	297

V. 2ND SUMMER

The Korengalis	307
Combat Promotion Board	313
Gonna Miss This	317
Replacements to the Rescue?	319

Trouble In The Ranks	323
Boredom: The Ultimate Combat Blessing	325
Of the Atrocities of 2nd Squad and the Resignation to Pop Tarts	327
Officers: Fact vs. Fiction	329
O.P. Paulson	331
Sky Soldier 6 on the High Ground	333
What Happened in Wanat	335
Wanat	343
A Day 15 Months In The Making	355
from "The Light Brigade"	359
Home Psychotic Home	361
Epilogue	365

APPENDIX

Glossary: Acronym, Abbreviation & Jargon Decoder	369
Bibliography	382
About The Author	383

We, the unwilling, led by the unknowing,
are doing the impossible for the ungrateful.
We have done so much, for so long, with so little,
we are now qualified to do anything with nothing.
---Mother Teresa

Author's Note

To all the families of our fallen 173rd Airborne brothers: It is my sincere hope that none of the descriptions in this book either contradict what you have been told nor shed any dishonorable light upon your lost or wounded family member. Please keep in mind that though I might have seen much of the aftermath, in none of these events was I a direct witness. Even in the instances where I might have been in close proximity, I've still relied on what other guys in Battle Company who were there, in that moment, said to me. But even then, the fog of war is such that a guy in the heat of battle can believe he remembers something (and forget other things) contrary to the recollection of another Soldier who was but 5 feet from him. Please believe, I have nothing but the deepest respect and admiration for all who have fought and died or been wounded serving their country.

I. SUMMER

Prologue

In 2007, the focus of the war effort was Iraq. This was during the troop surge that sent an additional 20,000 Soldiers and Marines to bolster that endeavor. Likewise, the media was solely focused on Iraq, to the point that Afghanistan had almost become a forgotten war.

In late May 2007, the 173rd Airborne Brigade deployed for 15 months to northeastern Afghanistan in support of OEF VIII. This was the Brigade's third deployment since the War On Terror began in 2001. Within the Brigade, 2nd Battalion, or, the 2nd of the 503rd (2/503rd), was considered the best the 173rd had to offer. And of 2nd Battalion's five companies, Battle Company was largely regarded as the cream of the proverbial crop. As such, Battle Company was assigned the toughest Area of Operations within the Brigade's footprint. It was called the Korengal Valley. And would later be dubbed "The Valley of Death" by President Bush.

Initiation in the Korengal

I could tell you all sorts of shit. About how nice being stationed in Italy is, about jumping out of airplanes with a machine gun, I could tell you everything about Basic, or I could bitch about some really miserable training rotations in Grafenwoehr, freezing our butts off in the German wood line. But once upon a war, there was this little deployment.

Via commercial aircraft, we had flown from the now faraway comforts of Vicenza, Italy (home to the United States Army's 173rd Airborne Brigade), to a crazy little air base named Manas in the obscure country of Kyrgyzstan, where some Air Force desk jockey held a safety brief in a tent full of combat Infantrymen and preached to us "nozzle awareness." (Obviously he meant "muzzle" awareness, as in the tip of your barrel, and yes it was the middle of the night, but there is no redeeming yourself to us after you interchange the words muzzle and nozzle.)

From there we took C-17s to Bagram Air Field (a former Soviet air strip turned American mega-base) that sits 30 miles outside the Afghan capital of Kabul. After a night's stay, we hopped on a C-130 to Jalalabad (nicknamed J-Bad, and the provincial capital of Nangarhar). We made our final flight through the Kunar Province to the Korengal on a Chinook.

A Chinook is the greyhound bus of Afghanistan. It's a Vietnam-era helicopter which looks like a giant grasshopper, capable of carrying an entire Platoon (about 35 guys), complete with all of their rucksacks and duffle bags packed to the brim with everything one would need for the next 15 months. We also had an escort of two Apaches (attack helicopters as sexy looking as they are lethal).

For whatever reason, my leadership had told me absolutely nothing about where we were going. All I knew was we were going to Afghanistan, which was way safer than Iraq, right?

My understanding is, all the N.C.O.s (Non-Commissioned Officers, which is just a fancy term for Sergeants) were taken aside back in Italy, and had a thorough brief in the Post Theater. This must've included stats such as number of firefights in a year, number of K.I.A.s / W.I.A.s, etc. And those statistics were probably enough to make you consider going AWOL (Absent Without Leave). Why my N.C.O.s didn't disseminate that information down to us, I couldn't tell ya. Maybe they didn't wanna scare us. Maybe they didn't want us booking a flight to Canada, or hopping the next train to Switzerland. They just said vague things like Sergeant Williams kicking back on his cot in Bagram telling us, "I don't think you guys are ready for this." And our dildo Squad Leader saying, "You better not embarrass me." Sergeant Newcomb was always more worried about us embarrassing him than he was in actually training us. And soon enough, he would do a better job of shaming himself than we collectively could ever do.

Anyway, back on the bird, Chinooks have these little round, convex windows that are like looking out of a fishbowl. Through the Chinook's fishbowl windows, we could see the terrain becoming more forested, and steeper. And I mean steep. The Korengal is part of the Hindu Kush mountain range, and lays just 20 kilometers from the Pakistani border. It was a formidable sight. This was my first deployment, and I was getting knots in the ole stomach. The bird hooked a left into a narrow valley, and proceeded high above the riverbed for what felt like another five minutes. The hydraulics inside make this high-pitched whine so loud you have to lean over and scream into the next guy's ear to say anything. "When we touch down, make a chain, get everything off of the bird as fast as possible," was the message being passed along.

Finally, she slowed and began to descend on her big flat belly towards a large gravel covered patch. Several shanty buildings were scattered about. The wheels contacted the ground and we began to unload. But with nearly no sense of urgency. Against the wall of what I would come to know as the Motor Pool, were several Squads from 10th Mountain, waiting to board the bird we were exiting, and finally get away from this godforsaken valley. We must've looked like a bunch of cherries to them in our brand new uniforms and freshly washed body armor. Their gear, uniforms and faces were beyond filthy, and they were visibly nervous, attempting to press themselves into the plywood building they were taking cover behind, as if they expected the entire valley to explode at any second. It didn't take a psychic to tell they were appalled at how long it was taking us to download the chopper.

The rucks and duffles were heavy (anywhere between 60 to 100 pounds), and one after another, they kept coming down the human chain. The temperature was in the triple digits, and standing behind a Chinook entails being blasted by the rotor wash and the brow-tightening heat of its twin turbine engines.

I was thinking, *Welp, we're in Afghanistan, what is up with these bags, this sucks already.* What I should've been thinking was, *These mountains are packed, with nary a tree or rock without a well-armed, American-hating, disciple of Allah behind it, who's not too good to sleep with a sheep or cut your head off on the Internet. So you best get all this bullshit squared away quick like and get the fuck out of the open.*

But we just didn't know no better. And we were goddamned lucky we lived to walk off the L.Z. that first day.

Now that all the gear was downloaded, 10th Mountain rushed past us, loaded their freedom bird, and flew away. Leaving us to try to find our personal ruck and duffle in a veritable mountain of rucks and duffles. This too left us exposed in the open, and no one proceeded with much haste. Finally being reunited with my belongings, I began walking up a winding trail through the KOP (a.k.a. the Korengal Outpost) that led to 3rd Platoon's new hooch. Carrying probably a couple hundred pounds, I wasn't walking for maybe a minute before I was winded. I stopped to catch my breath and looked up at the mountains towering around me. I suddenly felt very small.

Upon finding our tent (the big green dusty variety with plywood floors and bunk beds slapped together out of two-by-fours), Sergeant Miller, my Team Leader, ordered us to clean our weapons, while the N.C.O.s went outside to hold an ironic call for fire class. Ironic because as our guys were adjusting rounds, incoming mortars detonated near their position. Courtesy of the Taliban, I didn't have my gat disassembled more than a few minutes before things were exploding and Sergeants were yelling for everyone to run outside and get in a somewhat underground bunker, which wasn't large enough to hold all of us. I did not arrive in time to get a seat inside.

Our arrival and consequent "enemy contact" certainly fell short of storming the beaches of Normandy. But I suppose it was the best welcome party the Taliban could throw on such short notice. Just their way of saying, "Welcome to the neighborhood."

They did, however, have every intention of seeing to it that our deployment would be a memorable one. Before this was over we'd all go from being cherries to some of the saltiest Paratroopers on the planet. From so charged with adrenaline the rest of our existences would seem too tame, to just not giving a damn anymore. We were in for a gargantuan shit sandwich with an extra helping of recoil and a side of what-the-fuck.

To the Relief of 10th Mountain

    We replaced Alpha Company, 1/32nd of the 10th Mountain Division. We spent about 2 weeks with them doing what the Army calls "Left Seat, Right Seat," meaning they show us around, take us out on patrols for a week with them in the lead, then the next week, we lead the patrols with them trailing us.

    While it is U.S. Army tradition for Airborne units to look down on "Leg" units, I was mesmerized by these guys. When something happened, they immediately jumped to their feet and everyone knew exactly what to do; it was like watching some sort of intensely rehearsed combat choreography.

    I remember we hadn't been there a week when some shit went down (can't remember exactly what) that called for us to send out a mounted patrol, and I mean right the fuck then. Our very own Lieutenant (a.k.a. Platoon Leader, a.k.a. P.L.), could not for the life of him find a CLU, which is allegedly a high-speed piece of night vision gear. (It's a big clumsy piece of shit in my opinion.) But our P.L. refused to leave the firebase till he had this thing with him. The 10th Mountain P.L. rallied his guys in a hurry, jumped in the Humvees, and took right off without a second thought. It left an impression on me. Their P.L. was a combat experienced mo-fo. Ours was a P.L. who didn't have a CLU... go figure.

    As for amenities, or the lack thereof, there was no running water. You only got to take a shower about once a month. The same thing went for laundry. So these 10th Mountain guys had 15 months worth of accumulated dirt and grime on them and their uniforms. Places on their I.B.A.s (body armor), particularly around the neck, were black. They had long hair (for Infantrymen), they were unshaven, and they had holes all over their uniforms. This only made them look more badass.

Another thing of note was how little most of them spoke around us. It was borderline eerie. I almost wondered whether they'd developed some sort of intra-Platoon telepathic capabilities. This place seemed to have done something to them. They all looked like they'd been fighting ghosts nonstop for the last 15 months. They were beyond burned-out. Every single one of them was exhausted and fed-up and projected this numb outrage.

To any Soldier, but especially to a cherry such as myself, this was at once an intimidating fascination. And in all honesty, it gave me a hope that burned hotter than Hades. I realized everything that I'd enlisted for, absolutely everything—every imaginable misery and hardship, every physical and psychological test ever offered in the arena of war, the storied brotherhood only battle can script, every measure of a man, and every test of true combat—it was all on an inevitable collision course with my unwelcome naiveté.

Phoenix Rising

    Third Platoon had spent the first six weeks of the deployment at what I believed to be the lamest place in theater, called Firebase Michigan. Strategically, the existence of the post was justified since it was positioned where the Korengal River fed into the roaring Pesch. The firebase had decent visibility on the two bridges there, one locally built and one constructed (we were told) by 10th Mountain's engineers. And I guess they needed guarding. But little else ever happened there. We'd been in just a handful of contacts and none of them really worth mentioning and none of them anyone could classify as a genuine firefight. Even the patrols were fairly easy and flat, when compared to those that awaited in the Korengal.

    The firebase itself was encompassed in Hescos. (A Hesco is a big wire basket with a fabric lining inside that you fill with dirt. They come in different sizes but the ones used on the perimeter are the 7-footers.) We billeted in hooches made of one giant slab of wood stacked on another. Sergeant Miller said we were living like beavers. We had absolutely no high ground whatsoever. Michigan was on the valley floor. So we were wide open anytime the Taliban felt like taking a potshot.

    One thing Firebase Michigan did have was sand fleas. If there were a worse A.O. (Area of Operations) for sand fleas, I sure wouldn't wanna occupy it. And the Soldiers there to whom the fleas were attracted lost hours upon hours of sleep, scratching in vain. (The closer you are to water the more sand fleas you have to contend with.)

    Meanwhile in the Korengal proper, the very first day that Battle Company assumed command of the valley from 10th Mountain, a patrol from our 2nd Platoon marched south from Firebase Phoenix, past the village of Ali Abad and into Dar Bart (which 10th Mountain told them never to do, and something we would never do again in the daylight, save this little instance). (We walked everywhere. Most of these villages weren't accessible by roads.) From what I was told by Sergeant Bullock whose squad was on that patrol, they knew there were enemy nearby, and Captain Kearney (Commanding Officer of Battle Company) insisted that they find and engage these hoodlums.

Well, sure enough, they did find the badguys, who took the opportunity to shoot one of our guys through the shoulder (Private Pecsek, who was injured bad enough that he'd never return to the valley), and then proceeded to shoot Private Vimoto in the head.

Private Vimoto just so happened to be the Brigade Sergeant Major's son. He'd been with the 173rd only a few months. (Though what a Brigade Sergeant Major's son is doing in the same unit as his dad is a whole other nepotistic story.) This was an enormous deal. There's only one Brigade Sergeant Major and I can only imagine the dread coursing through Captain Kearney's veins at having to tell that Samoan man his son was dead on Day 1, due to officer arrogance.

Then, a few weeks into the deployment, Staff Sergeant Padilla lost his hand to an R.P.G. blast in a nasty assault launched on Firebase Phoenix just after dark. Every day we would hear these, what we call TICs (Troops In Contact) over the Company net. And usually it was twice, even three times a day, sometimes four. My Platoon all talked about it in equal parts jealousy, concern and awe. If ever in that moment on earth there was a place to be reckoned with, its name was Firebase Phoenix.

Some people will tell you that Phoenix was named after the capitol of Arizona, same as similar firebases named Vegas, Michigan, California, etc. But I believe it was named after that bird that rises from the fire and the ash and is a reborn and pissed-off version of its former self.

We got the order to replace 2nd Platoon abruptly, late one afternoon. Rumors had been going around for a couple of weeks, concerning our imminent relocation, but hell, I think at one point I heard someone speculate that Godzilla was wandering the Shuriak (an unruly area to our west with no American presence). Now, it was undeniably on, and we were leaving for Firebase Phoenix at first light.

Everyone scrambled to pack up their gear and belongings. Some of the N.C.O.s weren't as thrilled as I was to be uprooted. And there was a good chance it was just 'cause they better understood the implications. To be sure, it wasn't the kind of place where butterflies landed on your nose. Guys were dying over there. Your odds of survival decreased dramatically the second you set foot on Firebase Phoenix. It was some serious, tip-of-the-spear bullshit. Not something to be taken lightly. But then, I never took any of my desires lightly.

I didn't join the Infantry and come all this way to man some easy-going outpost, when there was a real conflict just seven kilometers away. Had there been no war going on, I'd've never raised my right hand in the first place. I'm not gonna lie; I could not wait to get into the shit.

That was why I enlisted. Combat. I wanted more than life itself to see true tooth-and-nail, blood-and-guts combat. I wanted to be one of those guys—one of those guys out there on the fringe. Fighting for their life and for the lives of their friends. I had to know if I could do it. And too, have you ever seen *Saving Private Ryan*? You know that part towards the end, where the Jewish-American Soldier is about to get run through with a knife by the Nazi, and the interpreter dude, Upham, just sits there crying, and doesn't do anything to stop it? Yeah, well, I needed to make sure I wasn't an Upham. I realize it sounds stupid, but these are things I had to know about myself.

In their previous deployment, 3rd Platoon was in a total of six firefights. We'd have that many under our belts in the next 48 hours.

We loaded our Humvees like a bunch of gypsies (crap hanging off of everything) and began the drive up a road of sorts early the next morning. What we called the KOP Road was very narrow (as in, not constructed with Humvee dimensions in mind), washed-out, and chewed-up 3rd world by-way with a 500-meter sheer drop-off on the other side in most places, which was regularly packed with I.E.D.s and ambush points. It was a long 7 klicks.

Shit was all fucked-up like it usually is. We were told to bring literally everything we possessed, from Michigan, then to download it at the KOP, and from there, just take the essentials to Phoenix. But there was some sort of miscommunication (not enough storage for us to put our stuff, or whatever), the end result being we had way too much crap, and we had to take all of it to Phoenix. It was what we in the Army affectionately call a goatfuck.

So we made the rigorous drive from the KOP to Phoenix with all that we possessed. 2nd Platoon shook their heads as we downloaded the Humvees. "You don't need all that shit here," they told us. Which we already knew. We tried to explain how they wouldn't let us drop our shit off at the KOP and pick it up later. But there we were, on the road which offered no cover, trying to get our belongings into the wire. Meanwhile, 2nd Platoon, knowing the A.O. far better than us, and taking into account the enemy was watching us, and would look upon this as an ideal Target Of Opportunity, was getting very anxious. We did as best we could, but there was just so much stuff. Staff Sergeant Navas (Weapons' Squad Leader) had even insisted on bringing the refrigerator from Michigan. Which was comical 'cause Phoenix didn't hardly have any electricity.

The only guy from 2nd Platoon who said anything to me was Mace. As he walked out of the wire and got in the truck I just exited he said, "When you take contact, fire into the villages. It'll make 'em stop." I nodded as if I understood. 2nd Platoon assumed our trucks, and practically peeled-out making their getaway, en route to go live at Firebase Michigan for some much-needed downtime. Phoenix was all ours. I myself felt a certain sense of pride. At that particular time, we manned the most hardcore firebase in the Middle East.

However, Phoenix has the steepest, most demoralizing stretch of mountain running between the top gate, and the location of the hooches. It sucked the wind out of you every time regardless of how long you'd been in the valley or how many times you'd made that walk. Which made moving all this crap particularly not so fun.

We'd been at Phoenix all of about 2 hours when the first firefight broke out. It wasn't anything overly serious, just 10 or 20 minutes of the Taliban blasting the crap out of the firebase. I ran outside, set my SAW (a light machine gun) up behind a Hesco and went to work. I thought it was fucking awesome. *I'm shooting a machine gun in combat defending my firebase right now*, I said to myself. Smoked a really great cigarette afterwards.

Rest In Peace, Doc Restrepo

July 22, 2007

    Morning in the Korengal Valley. We were doing left-seat-right-seat with what remained of 2nd Platoon at Phoenix. This particular patrol was headed into the village of Ali Abad. "So who wants to get shot at today?" asked Sergeant Newcomb, our Squad Leader. "I only need one guy." I was about to volunteer. I mean I wasn't here to avoid firefights. But then I started thinking, *Well what if...* And before I could finish contemplating the unknown, Belgarde said he'd go.

    The patrol was led by Sergeant Rice and his Squad from 2nd Platoon, along with one of 2nd Platoon's medics, Doc Restrepo. From 3rd Platoon, Sergeant Newcomb and Belgarde, our P.L. (Lieutenant Wells), and our F.O. (Forward Observer), Sergeant Hernandez (or, Hern, as everyone called him), walked out of the wire. Making it into Ali Abad was never a problem. Hell, the Taliban wanted you to come down there. For the simple and sinister reason that it made you an easier target.

    Well, after 2nd Platoon showed our guys the route, and introduced the village elder to our P.L., they began to ex-fill. There are two main routes in and out of Ali Abad. What we called the school trail, and the road. This day, they took the school trail on the way in, and were taking the road on the way back, in order to show our guys both routes. They didn't make it more than a hundred meters or so before rounds started popping off everywhere. And I mean everywhere.

    The patrol was completely pinned down. They were taking fire from about four different places, and these guys had a lot of ammo. Belgarde, Sergeant Newcomb, Hern, and Doc Restrepo all four took cover behind a single tree that was no bigger around than a high school girl's leg. But there wasn't any other cover, and what Belgarde said later was that they didn't even dare move because rounds were landing just inches from them. He told me they could barely return fire.

Back at Phoenix, we had a local who had been doing some excavation on the firebase in a backhoe. He must've been extremely green, and I assume, not from the valley, and as soon as the firefight popped off, he jumped from the backhoe and ran for cover, neglecting to put the parking brake on the backhoe before he did so. The backhoe thus proceeded down the hill through the firebase, and headed directly for 3rd Squad's hooch. Hajj houses may be fairly adept at stopping bullets, but they proved no match for the backhoe, which smashed through the wall, redecorating 3rd Squad's new home for them, and burying all their belongings in a protective coating of rubble. Luckily, none of them were there at the time.

I saw all this, but there were more pressing issues to address. We had every heavy weapon manned and were shooting all over creation. With Bunnell on the .50 cal and Roberts on the Mark, I set my SAW up on a Hesco and started blasting this mountain with a sharp rock spine on it (which I'd later come to know as Marastana), as I'd seen an R.P.G. come from there.

The firebase was only taking minimal fire. The enemy was almost completely concentrated on shooting up our patrol. We were doing what we could to support them, but I believe where the enemy was, our weapons couldn't reach. Hajj is not stupid. As far-reaching as our heavy weapons are (over 1500 meters for both the Mark and the .50 cal) Hajj knew all he had to do was put a mountain between him and the firebase to totally negate our superior firepower.

About a year later, when I asked Belgarde to tell me about that day, he said one burst after another kept coming in. That the enemy knew exactly where the four of them were, and just kept lobbing rounds in. He said one burst came in really close, and he heard something strange behind him. He looked back and Doc Restrepo was grasping at his neck. He told me Doc Restrepo, I guess in an effort to ascertain the severity of his wound, then pulled his hand back, and Belgarde said blood shot out of his neck "just like in a movie." A round had gone in Doc Restrepo's mouth and exited through his jugular.

When you watch a war movie, it's always, oh he got shot in the chest or the shoulder, and it's always a projectile wound straight through that area. In the real world, 3-dimensional battlefield, guys get shot in all sorts of weird fucked-up, anti-Hollywood ways. Because bullets don't watch movies.

Anyhow, Doc Restrepo put his hand back over the wound to put pressure on it, and Belgarde, Hern and Sergeant Newcomb began applying first aid, despite the sheets of seven-six-two raining down on them.

This was a long firefight for the Korengal. A lot of TICs there only last 10 to 20 minutes, but this thing went on for what felt like an hour, hour and a half. We had a Platoon of guys from Destined Company attached to us, who lived at the KOP and did all the mounted operations for us. (Mounted meaning in a Humvee.) They were quickly spun up and drove their Hummvees down to Ali Abad to retrieve the casualty. Still taking heavy fire, they managed to get Doc Restrepo onto one of the trucks and drove him back to the KOP. Doc Sanchez, the head medic for Battle Company, was able to stabilize Doc Restrepo. The problem was, it took the Medevac bird something like 45 minutes to get to the KOP. Doc Restrepo died en route to J-Bad.

I didn't know Doc Restrepo well, since I'd only been with the unit 9 or 10 months and he was in another Platoon and all. (In Italy and during training rotations in Germany, you almost exclusively hangout with your Platoon. You really don't get to know the other guys in the Company till deployment.) However, before we deployed, you get what's called R.F.I.—don't ask me what it stands for, but it's like just a last issue of equipment you'll need (or not) for deployment.

Anyway, both me and Doc Restrepo were on this detail to handout certain stuff to everyone. He was at the table right next to me, and he was doling out something halfway practical and my table was Enhanced Ballistic Sideplates, which you're supposed to attach to your body armor to protect you from getting shot in the side of your torso. Problem was, the damned things weighed about 5 pounds apiece, and adding another 10 pounds to what we already carried was absurd. I bullshitted with him all morning making fun of these stupid sideplates and how no one was ever gonna wear them (which we didn't). He told me he was from Colombia (as in, South America) and had family down there. He had the whitest teeth you've ever fuckin' seen. I spent enough time with him to know he was a good guy and fun to be around. Us joking made the morning go by quick and it was actually kinda enjoyable.

Back on the road to Ali Abad, and after more ado than any of them had in mind when they walked out of the wire, the patrol finally made it back to Phoenix. Belgarde, always jovial and one of the best liked men in the Platoon, wouldn't be the same for months after that. In the hooch, motionless, sitting on his rack, staring at the wall, "If it's your time to go, it's your time to go," was all he said. "And if it's not, it's not. After today, I definitely believe that."

A typical firefight in the Korengal Valley

The typical Taliban S.O.P. (Standard Operating Procedure, if you will—I don't mean to make it sound so formal, like they're over there printing field manuals or anything), was to hit our patrol as we would ex-fill (exfiltrate, or head back home). Which makes perfect sense from a couple of standpoints.

A) They need time to get set up. They're probably drinking some Chai down in Donga or Dar Bart, and ya know, you don't wanna hurry, so you finish your tea, then you flipflop your way up the mountainside, get behind your weapon of choice, and line some Americans up in your sights. And B), they knew damned well after we just got done slogging 60 to 85 pounds of gear for the last hour and a half, we were probably gonna be just a little bit tired.

Hajj likes to shoot when you least feel like it. Hajjs see, don't have a whole lot of better things goin' on, than to hang around, wait till you're good and suckin', then start lobbin' a lotta small arms and R.P.G.s at you. This, to a guy wearing manjams, is the highlight of the goddamned day.

I mean, you gotta put it into perspective: his life is not gonna get any better than this. Look at where this guy's living. He's in a 7-klick long valley, he ain't got no wheels, there ain't no mall, ain't no dance clubs, no alcohol, this guy ain't goin' on vacation to nowhere ever, and he'll probably finish out the entirety of his miserable existence in this shithole valley. By the looks of the females I seen there, he's gotta choose between taking Donkeyface Woman #1 or the Submissive Ogre-Type in the next village. Which might have something to do with why it's socially acceptable to bang little boys over there. It might also explain why they're so hot to get those 72 virgins they vehemently believe they'll receive if they die in a *jihad*.

Now I don't know why the number is 72, but I suspect it's

because maybe 1 in 72 women in the Kunar Province is not a total dog. Added to which, they're programmed by goddamned Muhammed or some fucker, to think anyone who doesn't lay down a prayer mat five times a day, face west and mumble while doing some spiritual calisthenics, is a satan-lovin', Koran-burnin' sonofabitch that's desecrating his sanctuary and is too good to wear pajamas all day long. Hajj is kinda sensitive if you think about it. I mean, Jesus Christ, I'm missing a whole motherfuckin' football season to fight this war and you don't hear me bitchin' 'bout the Twin Towers do you?

So anyway all these pent-up, misplaced feelings in Hajj, result in him blasting the crap out of our patrol as we try to make it home. Now I don't know about the rest of Afghanistan, but in the Korengal the Taliban got their shit pretty much together. More often than not, they used what we call a coordinated (or complex) attack, meaning groups of 3 or 4 boy-lovers, in 3 or 4 different positions (and by positions I'm not talkin' 'bout doggie-style, reverse cowgirl and the Tantra Chair; I mean they got some guys up on the Donga spur, a few more in Marastana, and a good fireteam on Hill 1705). They been doing this shit more than a day. I don't think these guys just got out of basic training from Pakistan or anything. They knew what they were doing the day we got there, and I guess herding goats and planting corn leaves plenty of time to plan attacks.

But it bears emphasizing just how effective a mad pack of inbred cavemen fighting with rifles patented in 1947 can be against the most modern fighting force in the world.

And so as we were high-tailing out of whichever village we had to patrol to that day, and typically, just as we came to the area that offered the least amount of cover possible (which there were no shortages of those in the Korengal Valley) here would come the barrage. We'd run as fast as we could to whatever cover there was, and start blasting the crap out of wherever we thought the fire was coming from.

I can't lie—usually you didn't know where the hell they were. You could hear it coming from Donga, coming from Marastana, coming from 1705, over on Table Rock or maybe Dar Bart. And the rounds were kicking up dust right next to you, but as far as actually seeing a person, or a muzzle flash? Just about never. Still you suppressed them as best you could, while the F.O. called in mortar rounds from the KOP. Our mortar teams received so much experience, they were probably the best the U.S. Army had to offer. So were our F.O.s.

But our mortars normally fired on known targets, and I believe the Taliban knew our known targets, and avoided them. Either way, the mortars did make 'em back off. And finally, on a good day, you might get a little air support. And of course, you can't expect Hajj to sit around sprayin' and prayin' till the next Apache or A-10 arrived. No. They'd ex-fill themselves, slip into the next village or just disappear into a draw we couldn't see into—just vanish. It was particularly frustrating. 'Cause you knew you were probably fighting the same guys every goddamned day.

At that point, you'd think we could go home. But Captain Kearney would usually want us to stay out another 2 hours to draw fire. I'll say that again: Captain Kearney actually wanted us to draw fire. Not go ahead and go home and get back safe. Hey, you been shot at so go ahead and stay out there and see if you can't get your head blown off some more. Well, much like Hajj, we all kinda felt like this was entertainment for Captain Kearney too.

You gotta work with a lotta sick minds when you're at war.

Belgarde

If you asked anyone in 3rd Platoon who their favorite person was, most would tell you it was Belgarde. Cody Belgarde was an adventurous sort, and had spent a good deal of his time working and wandering the woods of Minnesota and thereabouts before deciding to try something a little more hardcore. He'd joined the Army at the more advanced age of 26. He was stockier than the average Paratrooper, and he had himself quite an affinity for eating. The entirety of the space under his cot was devoted to boxes of fat kid food sent in care packages. "Hey Shadix, you ever had a fried Oreo?" he'd ask.

"Why would anyone fry an Oreo?"

"Because that shit's like Christmas in your mouth, dude." Guys will watch anything during a deployment. Slo couldn't get enough of *Rescue Me*. Roberts was addicted to *Smallville*. But for Belgarde, it was *One Tree Hill*.

"Oh my god, you gotta watch this, Shadix."

"No. I'm not watching *One Tree Hill*."

"But this chick Brooke is so hot. It's totally worth watching just for her. You don't know what you're missing, dude. You gotta get some of this."

Belgarde and I were the only two guys who stayed in 1st Squad the whole deployment. He carried the SAW the entire 15 months and hated it. He wasn't the sort who actually enjoyed combat, and I think he probably considered joining the Army to be a mistake. He would have rather been reclining on some porch next to a river in Minnesota eating hot cheese sticks and smoking a fat spliff. But Belgarde was one of those people you were better off for having known. And he normally made whatever shitty situation you were in a helluva lot more entertaining.

Compton Comes To The Korengal

Captain Dan Kearney was Commanding Officer of Battle Company. Like all Officers, he went to college, and he still had some frat boy vestiges about him. Somehow (through MySpace I presume), it was discovered that his fraternity brothers called him "Dirty Dan," which surprised no one. He was definitely a jock and a pretty good-sized guy. Large enough the Taliban would get on their I-coms (walkie talkies) and say, "Shoot the big one." He had thick, dark eyebrows that were constantly ratcheted together. He was the son of a two-star General (deputy commander of SOCOM no less) and so no pressure there.

Anyway, we didn't know it at the time, but this was to be the first of many of Captain Kearney's combat similes. He'd graced our firebase with his presence and gathered everybody oh-so-reluctantly outside the hooches. He started off something like, "Well, I wanted talk to you guys a little about what's going on here. And I want you to think of it like we're in Compton. It's like we're the cops, and the Taliban are the gangbangers. And we need to bust into their little 'hood, and meet force with force. I'm talking about taking the fight to the enemy. We need to show them that this is our turf and take back what's ours. If they want a *jihad*," Captain Kearney loved to say *jihad*, "then we're gonna give them a *jihad*."

After Captain Kearney's departure, no one was quite sure what to make of us being the newly appointed cops of Compton.

"Does that mean we all get badges?" Barnard asked.

"This is bullshit," Sergeant Eddie said. "We ain't got cop cars, ain't no goddamned donuts. I ain't never been to L.A., but I'm pretty sure women don't wear *burkas* there. I can't even get a beer here."

"So do we all get sidearms now?" Barnard continued. "Because I need a Glock. Chico needs a Glock. Chico? Chico, get my Glock, Chico. We gotta go gangbang in Ali Abad, Chico."

Some N.C.O.s would say they thought Captain Kearney seemed like a squared-away officer when we were in Italy or training up in Germany. Some confess, albeit belatedly, that they always had a bad feeling about the guy. Whichever category they fell into, no one fathomed the depths of Dan Kearney's insatiable and demented drive. Some time ago, he'd ordered every Platoon to pull three patrols a day (each), and that shit was really starting to break guys off, bringing Captain Kearney's popularity levels to new lows.

He'll be repeatedly vilified in this book, simply because that's how we felt about him at the time. But after the deployment was over, a lot of things he made us do really began to make sense.

Foreshadowing in the Ali Abad Cemetery

    Once in Ali Abad, we usually set up in this Afghan graveyard. The entire southwest portion of the village was all headstones—the final resting place of every Ali Abad man since time immemorial. An Afghani headstone is just a long, thin, flat rock that they stick straight up in the ground. Only an inch or so thick and maybe a foot wide. And from what I was told, the more important the person, the taller his tombstone (and I say "his" 'cause women aren't deemed important to Pashtuns). There weren't any inscriptions or markings on any of them, but what some of the markers did bear were decorative bullet holes. Because just like the 15 months the 10th Mountain Division spent here before us, going into Ali Abad spelled "SNAP! CRACKLE! POP!" Without a doubt, if you came marching into that village, you were gonna get lit up. Period. At that point there were 500 meters in between you and Phoenix, and any trigger-happy Hajj with a gun on Marastana, Donga, Table Rock or 1705 had perfect line-of-sight on you almost the whole way back. And by the time the P.L. finished talking in circles with the village elder, they'd have had a good hour, hour and a half to set up on you.
    So once again in the cemetery, I'd rotate the ole bipod legs down on my SAW, set in behind a 3-foot burial mound, and ponder the concept of foreshadowing as I scanned the mountainsides for enemy sign. You always had to ask yourself, *Is this gonna be my day?*

3rd Squad Gets Their Freak On

    3rd Squad—in our Platoon, 3rd Squad was synonymous with the following things: 1) Unrivalled leadership (in the form of Staff Sergeant Shelton, Sergeant McDonough, and Sergeant Rozenwald who would not tolerate anything less than Ranger-fied perfection), 2) Possessing the knowledge, discipline and performance that entails, and 3) 3rd Squad's joes (Privates through Specialists—not Shelly, Mac & Rose) were certified freaks. The best example I can think of to illustrate that was this: They had a blow-up sex sheep. Now, not only did they deem it necessary to bring an inflatable sheep on deployment, the entire Squad (minus the NCO's) actually fucked the sheep before we left Italy. Which, it kinda seems to me like, probably there were better options at that time. Why christen the sheep before you get downrange when the town of Vicenza, Italy was full of Romanian strippers and eastern European hookers (if you couldn't coax a local Italian into bed)?

    But allegedly, the joes of 3rd Squad all had protected sex with the plastic sheep in the barracks. Which is a whole lot of plastic for one fucking. Once we got in country, things got even weirder. Bunnell had been tossed out of 1st Squad for antagonizing Sergeant Miller (who thrived on antagonization). No sooner had Bunny been placed in 3rd Squad than they decided to name the sheep Bunnell. Which, mind you, they continued to screw. Now, you can read a lot into that, and none of it makes much heterosexual sense nor is it something you wanna analyze for very long.

To Quell The Korengal

Secret New Weapon In The War On Terror

    The United States Army has unleashed a powerful new load-bearing device to combat the harsh and rugged terrain of Afghanistan's Korengal Valley. While planning an ambitious new Con-Op (a large scale, three to five day mission), Battle Company's commanding officer, Captain Dan Kearney, unveiled this revolutionary idea to the dismay and curiosity of all. "I was expecting something a little more high-tech," said one Platoon Leader who wished to remain anonymous. "Still, it's so crazy, it just might work." As the plan was disseminated down the chain of command, a great buzz began to erupt. "So this is what it's come to. Really?" asked one Squad Leader.
    The series of complications that led to this battlefield innovation, was this: the Con-Op was for two of Battle Company's Platoons to traverse the top of the Talazar (an enormous mountain), from 1st Platoon's A.O., south, to Donga, thus clearing the entire mountainside of evildoers. The problem was, food and water. Primarily water. Because water is heavy, cumbersome even, and a Soldier can only carry so much of it. So how to haul enough water to keep the men hydrated? The answer was obvious: donkeys. The Company would purchase six of the finest asses in the Korengal, load them down with H2O, and proceed on the aforementioned mission. With such sound strategy in place, how could the quest possibly fail?
    The best mules had been identified, and a handsome price had been paid. Members of 1st Platoon had the enviable task of taking the Army's latest acquisitions up the steep and winding trail to Firebase Vegas. Almost immediately, certain glitches were noticed. These vehicles didn't respond well to human wishes and / or prodding. In fact, they seemed to have their own sentient will. And that will did not correspond to the needs of the Army. In fact, their desire to do

nothing anyone wanted them to do could have been seen as insubordination. Punishing them under the Uniform Code of Military Justice was considered. How could it be? That a creature universally associated with stubbornness, didn't want to participate in the hardship of war?

Still, after much ado, the men of 1st Platoon did manage to drag the beasts of burden to Firebase Vegas. Which was when the next challenge presented itself. Unable to acquire any proper saddlebags, the guys had to rig up a way for the donkeys to carry all that water. The word jalopy did come to mind when looking at what the Soldiers and local workers had come up with. It involved a lot of rope, and possibly some ammo crates and wet-weather bags. But nothing better could be found or constructed with the shortage of materials on-hand.

Thus satisfied, they set off on their cross-country mission. Official donkey handlers had to be assigned then rotated out. Because one man was soon fatigued from the constant pulling, cursing and frustration of having to wench the donkey along, while wearing a hundred pound ruck. Worse still, on the second day, the contraptions that held the water on the asses' backs, began to give way. On top of that, Captain Kearney had underestimated the difficulty of traversing such harsh mountains. The climbing was strenuous and the need to hydrate extreme. Everyone was quickly worn out, and as far as the water was concerned, with no way keep it on the donkeys, a carry-all-you-can-and-leave-the-rest strategy was employed.

Day Three: Soldiers out of water. High upon the spurs and draws of Donga, the Con-Op ran dry. Leadership then paused to consider the problem. Because of the logistical difficulties of delivering supplies to the Korengal Valley, provisions were intermittently airdropped from C-130s (cargo planes). However, airdropping is far from an exact science. The gigantic palettes came out the back of the planes, a parachute deployed, and they would then proceed to land wherever the wind and their weight took them.

Sometimes the supplies dropped close to the KOP, sometimes not. They rarely landed inside the wire, requiring a mounted Platoon to drive out and retrieve the supplies before the villagers could get to them. Because once they touched down, pillaging was most certainly in order. It was also not uncommon for the palettes to come down on the other side of the valley. At which point these government issued goodies were a veritable free-for-all. Property of Hajj.

While this may or may not have been a cost-effective means of getting replenishments to the troops, for the purposes of resupplying this Con-Op with some much needed *agua*, it did provide a viable option. Since there was no way Soldiers could drink the river water without becoming seriously sick, Captain Kearney held a *shurra* with the Donga elders. The elders, realizing the severity of the situation, and, quite frankly being better at haggling than some dehydrated American Captain hellbent on continuing this Con-Op, saw a grand opportunity.

It is apparent that if there's one thing Americans have taught the Afghan people, it's the value of the American dollar, and the fact that we have a lot of these dollars to throw around. Battle Company thus purchased their water, back from the Afghans at a scandalous price. The glorious War On Terror carried on!

Phoenix Layout

Tactically speaking, Firebase Phoenix was a spread-out mess. Since there was a shortage of air assets to sling-load supplies in, the original idea had been to build a base that could be re-supplied by truck. Thus, the initial fortifications were built very near to the road. These fortifications included a sort of horseshoe-shaped series of gun positions made out of large pieces of local timber that had been squared off to about a foot by a foot by six feet or so. One was stacked on top of the other to the height of about five or six feet and reinforced in places by sandbags and Hescos.

Phoenix had three gun positions. The one that was manned 24/7 was armed with an M240 Bravo machine gun and faced southwest towards Table Rock (a place from which we took fire near daily). From there the emplacement curved in to form a gathering area we never really came up with a name for, but it was covered with a camo net and was large enough to hold an entire 20-man patrol.

It was from that area we'd S.P. on our patrols that were headed south along the road (to Table Rock or taking the road route into Ali Abad). On the southern end of the emplacement, and accessed from the gathering area, were the .50 cal pit and the Mark pit (the .50 pit faced more southerly, while the Mark pit had fields of fire from due east (Donga) all the way southeast (Honcho Hill and a little bit of Dar Bart).

In addition, up top were three short hooches (which I guess the 10th Mountain guys actually lived in after they'd initially built this place). They were constructed out of that same squared off timber. We only used these for storage. One was solely for water, one was dedicated to ammo, and the third for M.R.E.s (Meals Ready to Eat).

From there it got kinda goofy. Three houses had been leased from a school teacher who worked down in Babyol. The problem was the houses were a good 100 meters from the fortifications up top. Thus, Firebase Phoenix had a large dead space in the middle. The Hajj houses featured luxurious dirt floors, in an electricity and running water free environment. But at least you had four real walls that were fairly bullet repellant, and it did make for better accommodations than stacking a bunch of lumber together and calling it home.

The added tactical advantage of us living in the houses was this: it integrated the firebase into Babyol, which served as a strong deterrent against Phoenix being mortared. The Taliban, known for being wildly inaccurate with their mortar systems, dared not use them against us, for fear the rounds would fall short, land in the village, kill the locals, and thus piss off the elders, whom the Taliban needed on their side to succeed. This was a huge advantage for us.

So as far as lodging was concerned, the northern hooch housed Headquarters (the Platoon Daddy, the P.L., F.O.s, Medics, the radio geek, and the interpreter). Just south of that house was a larger one, which fit both 2nd and 3rd Squad. From there you had to go downhill slightly to where our (1st Squad's) little pad was (two gun positions there), and even down a little farther south to Weapon Squad's hooch (which also had another gun position in it).

Kind of to the southwest of 1st Squad's hooch was the A.N.A. (Afghan National Army) compound. A bunker built out of rocks served as the E.T.T.'s (Embedded Tactical Trainers who took care of the A.N.A.) hooch (with another two gun positions) and a sandbag wall (which allowed a whole Squad or more to fire from). Dug into the ground and fortified with rocks from the outside was the A.N.A.'s living quarters. It was less than lush. The A.N.A. also manned a guard post (and I use that term with the utmost looseness; I honestly don't think the Afghans have a lingual equivalent for the word "guard") on the southern end of the compound.

As for 1st Squad, we lived in the previously stated Hajj house with a dirt floor. There were three bunk beds, which were solid enough but undoubtedly made without a level and without enough wood to thoroughly complete the job so that the portion we slept on consisted of four or five inch slats with several inches in between. It wasn't so bad or anything, I just mean to illustrate the lack of proper building materials we had to deal with. Sergeant Newcomb and

Sergeant Williams had olive drab cots against two of the walls. I beat Roberts in a game of paper-rock-scissors so I got a bottom bunk and he had to sleep above me. Gear was piled all over the room.

I had a gun position at the head of my bed, and another one at the foot of my bed. The latter was manned 24 hours a day by whoever had guard at the time. Sergeant Miller said, "You know when you got gun positions in your sleeping quarters, you're livin' ghetto. This is ghetto."

That gun position was the most coveted, and with two guys on guard at all times, everyone ran for the position in our room first. Partly because it was closer, partly because it was safer, and you also didn't have to man the radio like you did at the upper guard position. Plus, it was constantly in the shade. It also meant there was someone awake 24 hours a day in our room, and if that person happened to be V. (Private First Class Villareal), no way were you getting much sleep with his unending binge eating and constant clearing of his throat.

There was a covered porch outside our place and guys would hangout there during the day and play spades. That's also where most of the cooking (such as it was) took place. A small storage shed sat outside and was immediately christened the "Skeet Shack," where a guy could be "alone."

As for amenities, there was no running water. The KOP sent us bottled water to drink. We had electricity sometimes, depending on whether our generator was working. We had horrible luck with generators, and when they went out, you weren't getting another one for at least a month. When the generator was up, the extent of the electricity was a little power strip in your room that you could use to charge your computer and iPod. We never had light switches, and definitely no air conditioning or heater. When it came to light, you used a headlamp with a red lens. For food, you either ate M.R.E.s (Meals Ready to Eat), or cooked stuff people had sent you in care packages. (We purchased small propane tanks with little burners on top of them from the local workers.) Naturally, there were no phones and no Internet.

Phoenix was so spread out, the perimeter was just a joke. We had Hescos in some places, but the majority of the firebase was protected by nothing but razor wire. I'm talking about something you can literally just step over with enough caution. The threat of the enemy overrunning our firebase was not just real, it was pretty goddamned likely. All the enemy needed was balls.

Man-Boy Love Night

    Little known to the average Westerner, there's a disgusting phenomenon that takes place on a weekly basis in the country of Afghanistan. I'd been told about it by my Team Leader when we were training one day in Germany. But I dismissed it as a combat vet trying to have a little fun with a cherry. Not till we arrived in country and I witnessed it with my own eyes did I believe. See, the Afghan men (and I've been told the same thing goes on in Iraq) have some disturbing ideas about sex. In their culture, women are for bearing children, and boys are for sex. It's called *bacha bazi*, and literally translated means "boy play." Not sure why Thursday is the day, other than Friday is like their sabbath so maybe they figure they better get their sin over with the day before. Whatever the case, every Thursday in Afghanistan, is man-boy love night.
    I think we'd been at Phoenix about a month the first time I saw it. Well, not actually witnessed a gigantic homosexual pedophiliac orgy, but we were coming back from patrol about 1600 local time, walking through the village of Babyol. Then here come all these boys between 10 and 15 years old. Now, the average boy in the Korengal usually wears some haggard manjams and they're all dirty from the fields. But these kids were clean as could be and had on all kinds of fancy garments (like what girls wear over there) laced with embroidery with shiny things woven into them. They even had makeup on. And not just a little makeup. I'm talkin', thick red rougey cheeks, gobs of eyeliner, and lipstick. But they were obviously boys. We started looking wide-eyed at each other like, *What the fuck, over?* And they were all headed towards Ali Abad where I guess the gangbang was. The boys just kinda looked away awkwardly as guys started laughing their asses off. Sure we were there to protect the populace, but I guess intervening in group child rape was outside of

our Rules Of Engagement. That must go back to honoring local customs and courtesies. Or so it would seem. Sergeant Williams, my Team Leader, looked back at me, "See Shadix? I told you, dude. You thought I was lying. Hurt my feelin's and shit."

Hygiene Phoenix Style & The Deployment Dress Code

In garrison (which is to say, when you're at your particular post, be it back in the states or abroad, and not actively engaged in field training), uniform and hygiene restrictions are, well, strict. Even more so when you're a member of an Airborne unit. Uniforms must be new, no strings hanging off them, they must fit properly, with badges clean and precisely spaced, and your pants have to be bloused (via their handy blousing strings around the cuffs) to or into your boots. You had to have a fresh haircut every Monday, and needless to say, always shaved. No exceptions are made, and any joe who didn't comply would be promptly scuffed-up by their Team Leader.

During deployment—especially a deployment such as ours, when you're as far away from the Brass as you can conceivably get—you and your uniform tend to undergo certain downgrades.

Boots were most definitely not bloused. In the 173rd, we were allowed to wear civilian hiking boots rather than our issued "combat boots." (With absolutely no ankle support, and piss-poor traction, combat boots have to be one of the most misnomered military inventions.) Most boots donned flea collars to combat the ever-present sand flea. Whether the flea collars actually helped or not, we still wore 'em.

Pants often got shredded on patrols with either the crotches ripping as one ascended a steep slope, or the ass peeled out as Soldiers descended on their butts. And since no one wore underwear, guys' junk was hanging out in the breeze. T-shirts went untucked, and as for your top, sleeves could be rolled up to the elbows during summer months, which was remarkably more comfortable in the 100°F plus heat.

With no running water whatsoever, showers were obviously out of the question. Staff Sergeant Navas tried to hook up one of those solar showers (a bag you fill with water that heats up in the sun), but we didn't receive enough bottled water from the KOP for fools to be bathing in it. We had a hard enough time keeping the A.N.A. from using it to wash their feet before the 20 of them prayed 5 times a day. So if a shower was in order, you just grabbed a few baby wipes and went to work on yourself.

Baby wipes were one of the most crucial components of our deployment. If you didn't have somebody back home shipping you baby wipes, you were in a lot of trouble. And so was anyone who had to room with you. Finally, no Firebase Phoenix baby wipe shower was complete without taking a handful of hand sanitizer to your balls. The sharp tingling sensation meant that it was working. And that you probably should've used it a little sooner.

Shaving wasn't mandatory. However, depending on your rank and personal preference, probably you wanted to do it every 2 to 4 days. The best way to go about it was to cut a 500ml water bottle so that only about a third of it was left, and use that as your wash basin.

Laundry was accomplished once a month when your Squad rotated back to the KOP on refit. Not good considering we each had about 10 pairs of socks, 6 t-shirts, and 4 uniforms. Once when we were all chillin' in the hooch, and Sergeant Slo took his A.C.U. top, held it at the very bottom, and said, "Look at this shit," as the jacket stood straight up in the air like a piece of cardboard. Every article of clothing we had was dirt-brown, filthy, crusted and so drenched with salty sweat. So when you did finally make it back to the KOP to do laundry in one of its two Hajj washers, it turned the water in the washing machine practically into mud. You had to wash everything twice and the only reason you didn't wash it three times is because you didn't have the time.

You took a crap into a sawed-in-half 50 gallon steel barrel. Commonly, a couple of 2x4s were placed on either side so you could sit. It was enough to make even the most defiled of public restrooms look like a sweet place to shit. The number of flies this attracted could not easily be counted. The shit barrel filled up every 2 to 3 days, requiring the joes to take turns burning it with diesel. What I called "cooking the poo stew," was about an 8-hour ordeal (depending on how full the barrel was). You poured some fuel in the barrel, stirred it with a metal picket, waited a few minutes, then repeated the process. It was pretty gross at first, but you got used to it.

You did not pee in the shit barrel as that would make burning it take too long. What we had were piss tubes. A piss tube consists of a big P.V.C. pipe about 4" in diameter. What you do is, you dig a hole a couple feet deep, throw a bunch of little rocks in there, then bury your P.V.C. pipe at an angle and height suitable to pissing in. This too had its own aroma and share of flies.

Some guys thought brushing your teeth was optional. But I go insane if I don't brush twice a day. Especially since I was smoking cigarettes as fast as I could get them into my mouth. I bet Bunnell and Mino didn't brush twice the entire deployment. Which I consider sick. But, in the far-away life of the deployed Soldier, to each his own I guess. Except when it comes to smelly feet that wreak in your hooch like 12 year old cheese every minute of every day... But you couldn't very well just kill Roberts. And even if you did, that'd just mean more guard.

Donga Vs. Phoenix

The first few months we were in the Korengal Valley saw an almost daily battle between Firebase Phoenix and the village of Donga which sat due east of Phoenix on the other side of the valley. They'd hit us out on patrol, sure. But just because you were back on the firebase didn't mean the fight was over.

Often the fire would come from a landmark on top of the Donga spur, dubbed Nipple Rock (because it was melonious at the base and arched oh so carefully into a nubile point, which, to the Soldier who hadn't been in the company of females in several months looked decidedly like...)

But besides Nipple Rock, there was this one house in particular—a really long house. The southern quarter was two stories, the northern three-quarters was some weird "multi-purpose" sort, which had a wall about chest-high and almost everything in between being one gigantic glass-less window. And when I say gigantic, I mean it was narrow, but it stretched on for a hundred feet, maybe more, with supports few and far between.

What never ceased to amaze me was people actually lived in this house. This was someone's home. And this dude had kids too. A girl maybe 5, and a son even younger. Three years old maybe. Now if it were me, and especially if I were a father of two, and someone was both shooting from and at my house on a daily basis, I would seriously consider moving to another neighborhood. Preferably one with no line-of-sight to an American base or with any strategic value whatsoever.

Maybe the real estate market in the Korengal was soft at the time, I don't know. Even if it wasn't, it's probably hard to show a house that gets shot every day.

Regardless, this guy's 2 kids, and sometimes his wife, and

maybe her friends or sisters or whatever too, would be hanging out, on the roof, her doing laundry or some sort of chore; the kids playing around. Which would be all fine and good were it not for the copious exchanges of projectiles that broke out constantly. But I mean, you had to know they were in on it, to whatever extent. 'Cause one minute, that little girl would be on the roof kicking around a lime green ball. Then she'd be gone. Next thing ya know, oh goddamn here comes a buncha gunfire from that same house. And afterwards, and I'm talkin' not 10 minutes after cease fire, that little bitch is back on the roof playing soccer by herself.

    I cannot stress the resiliency of these houses they build over there. To build a house in the Kunar Province, you take 1 fairly flat rock, maybe 10, 12 inches long, a few inches thick, and you stack another next to it, and another on top of that. And you keep stacking till you have something that remarkably resembles a goddamned house. They didn't use any mortar, and no concrete for the foundation. Maybe Frank Lloyd Wright wouldn't be overly impressed. Maybe there wasn't a true right angle in the whole edifice. But these people could stack rocks so well, some of these places were 3 or 4 stories tall, if you count the goat apartment. (The goats live inside the houses with them. They're tight like that.)

    If you or I attempted to recreate one of these homes, and on the extreme off-chance it managed to stand straight and by the grace of God we got a roof on it, it would ultimately (and by ultimately I mean in the first 48 hours) cave in, killing us all. But not only do the houses there not cave in, they're probably the most bullet resistant structures known to man. Or caveman. Or any kind of man. You could shoot the shit out of these places and, nothing would happen. Never saw one collapse. And I'm talking SAWs, 240s, A.T.4s, Mark-19s, .50 cals... We even dropped bombs on them sometimes (if it was a domicile perpetually used to attack American troops from), and a lot of times, this rock house withstood the bomb.

    Let me clarify before all the anti-war enthusiasts go crazy—we shot at a house only if we received fire from the house. We didn't just go lighting into somebody's circa-Flintstones flophouse with no good cause. The place was constantly being used as an enemy fortification. It was a menace that under our Rules Of Engagement, we could totally shoot the shit out of.

At first all these firefights weren't so bad. At first, hey this is what you signed up for. You were in the fight. You were maybe not kicking ass, but you were doing your job and so you felt a small sense of accomplishment. But eventually, that gave way to, "Oh man, not again," or, sigh, "Why can't they just leave us alone?" You'd be at long last chillin' on your cot, taking a much-needed nap or maybe, watching a one dollar knockoff of *Transformers* on your laptop, then the whole firebase just starts gettin' lit up and you gotta throw all your shit on, haul ass outside, take up a position and return fire; it got to be a real hassle. There was never a time, where you could say, "Alright, now I don't have to worry about nothin'. I can just kick back and have me some me-time."

The threat was always there. The threat was always real. And the threat was ready to give you the business. Especially if you were in the midst of that coveted downtime.

Eventually, we'd stop taking fire so often from this House of Insurrection. Come early winter, we'd even send patrols in that same house, and we'd survey the detritus of our profuse battles. But in the Summer and Fall of 2007, it was nothing but on.

Who's the real ass anyway?

    In July, we had some intelligence that the insurgents were using donkeys to transport weapons and ammunition. I guess you could call that intelligence. I kinda call it common sense. I mean what the hell you expect 'em to use? They're a bunch of destitute hillbillies with all the resources of Cro-Magnon man. They're not gonna be ridin' around on quads or flyin' shit in on helicopters. They don't exactly have access to FedEx do they? I don't work at the Pentagon or anything, but I'm pretty damned sure they had to move everything either on their backs, or with donkeys or with Toyota Hiluxes or jingle trucks. Because those are the only modes of transportation in Afghanistan.

    A jingle truck is the Afghani semi, though much, much shorter so they can navigate the mountain roads. They're so-named because all of the metallic decorations that hang from their carriages, which make a jingley sound as they drive. A Toyota Hilux is the equivalent of a Tacoma pickup in the states. And since we had a T.C.P. (Traffic Control Point) at the KOP that searched all vehicles, that left hand-carrying or donkeys.

    So yeah—donkeys. This one hot afternoon on Firebase Phoenix, somebody somehow (down in Headquarters I think), spotted this donkey up on the mountainside, way the hell out there. I happened to be on guard at the time, sittin' at the top of the firebase behind a machinegun, got the ole radio right there. And that was the gig: for 2 hours, you sat there, answered the radio if anyone called, and if somebody shot at you, you shot back.

    Well, our Platoon Sergeant, Sern't Hunt, called me up and told me to holler at Battle Base (the KOP), apprise them of the situation, and get permission to assassinate (Get it?) this southbound burro. So I got on the ole ASIP (which is this heavy clunky looking green rectangle of steel, that I guess scrambles your message a million times a second or something). Beep, "Battle Base, Phoenix."

Beep, "Battle Base, go ahead."

Beep, "Yeah roger, we got this fuckin' donkey up north of Donga, like way up high on the Talazar, looks all weighted down, and uh, Three-Five wants to, wants to fuckin' take it out. Over." (You can't use to many "fuckin's" when you're talking on the radio in a combat zone.)

Beep, "Wait one, over." Maybe a minute and a half goes by, beep, "Firebase Phoenix, Battle Base."

Beep, "Battle Base, Phoenix."

Beep, "Roger, you are cleared to engage target, over."

Beep, "Rodge." (Rodge as in rhymes with dodge, as in, I'm too lazy to say roger.)

We had little walkie-talkies (only the Army calls a walkie-talkie an I-Com) that we used on the firebase just to like, if you were on guard you could call down to the Headquarters hooch and be like, "Hey. Battle Base needs so-and-so on the radio." Or, "Hey. Where the fuck's my relief?" was a common one. Anyway.

"Headquarters this is top."

"Top, headquarters."

"Battle Base says you are cleared to engage ass, over."

"Roger. Engaging ass, time now."

None of us had been to sniper school and this donkey was a good thousand meters away, maybe more. Hitting something with an M4 at just 500 meters is somewhat of a feat. A SAW can suppress up to 1,000 meters, but suppressing and hitting a point target are two entirely different things.

I don't really know why, but nobody at Phoenix at that time had a properly sighted M14, which would've been the ideal weapon with which to eliminate our evil ass problem. All the heavy weapons on Phoenix faced south, southeast or southwest. 'Cause that's where we took fire from. And since the perpetrator was to the northeast, there was no hitting it with the heavies. Which was unfortunate 'cause a Mark-19 (automatic grenade launcher) would've worked well in said situation. That brought us to everybody's favorite machine gun, the M240 Bravo.

It has a greater range than the SAW does, and also fires a larger round. Weapons Squad started going to town tryin' to wipe out this mule. They even got one guy workin' as a spotter to try and adjust rounds. "Oh you're hitting too high. Oh now too low. A little to the left. Now right just, just a tad," and so on. They fired I don't know how many rounds at the damned thing, and I'm totally confident they'd've gotten it except, at that point in time, the whole Korengal Valley was low on seven-six-two (the type of bullet the 240 fired). So they had to stop. We couldn't waste more ammunition 'cause we were in this "economy of force operation", which essentially means you can't get the resources you need to win, but you have to stay out there and make do with what they give you. We'd only been out there a couple of months, but I guess we'd already gone over budget.

However, one thing we did have plenty of then was mortars. So Sergeant Coffee, one of our F.O.s (Forward Operator, the guy that adjusts mortar rounds and calls in bombs and shit) radioed up to the KOP, and told 'em he wanted to drop some mortars on our little donkey dilemma. So, here came all these mortars, blowin' up all over this mountain, and I guess they were gettin' close, but all of a sudden, a TIC broke out at Vegas.

Beep, "Phoenix, Battle Base. How're you guys coming with that donkey thing?"

Beep, "Negative. Ass is not neutralized. I repeat," (mostly because I knew I'd never get a chance to seriously say that again as long as I lived), "Ass is not neutralized."

Beep, "Alright. Battle 6 says he wants you to cease fire, over." (Battle 6 being Captain Kearney's call sign.)

So I called this down to Headquarters, but Sergeant Hunt said he thought he could take it out for sure now and to call Battle Base back and tell them we wanted to take another shot at it. Beep, "Battle Base, Phoenix. Three-Five says he has a clear shot at the donkey. Request permission to fire, over."

And then Six got on the horn. You could hear the sheer annoyance and frustration in his voice. Operation Die Donkey was clearly getting to him. It was actually taking its toll on us all. Beep, "Okay, leave the damned donkey alone!"

I found this pretty fucking amusing. I mean, here's the most powerful military the world has ever known, versus a jackass. A literal jackass. And this whole time, the burro continued plodding along. Still goin' south. Bullets and mortars impacting all around him. The guy who was leading it had long since vanished, but if that donkey ever sped up while he was under fire, I never noticed it. If that mule had been an American Soldier taking that kind of a barrage, he'd be either hauling ass, or crouched down behind the best cover he could find.

But this ass refused to waver. It just kept coming. Either astoundingly brave, or completely oblivious that it was on the business end of a direct and indirect fire engagement—that the world's greatest superpower was hot on its heels. I mean I didn't think we necessarily needed another donkey full of R.P.G.s and seven-six-two in the valley but, towards the end there I kinda started to root for the donkey. You had to hand it to 'im—that was one resilient ass. It oh-so-slowly hoofed its way south, and finally out of view.

The only thing our Company had that could've made quick work of this situation was, the Scouts had a Barrett (a .50 caliber sniper rifle capable of tearing guys in two from well over a thousand meters). One round from that and the beast of burden would've been done. Except, then you have a dead donkey on the side of the mountain supposedly laden with ammunition. It was already mid to late afternoon, and nobody could get up to that particular location before dark—not without taking a couple of W.I.A.s and maybe K.I.A.s. And once night fell, Hajj would most assuredly pour out of the mountains and strip everything off its carcass. So really, killing the thing would've done us exactly no good whatsoever. As it was, that donkey lazily lumbered off into the sunset. Probably delivered some weapons, maybe that jack used the money to meet some jenny and raise a couple of foals. I mean, goddamn, surely somebody deserved some slice of happiness in this shithole valley.

We had fired enough munitions at it to obliterate a small village. But hitting a target that tiny from so far away with the weapons we had, was simply not an easy thing to do. Thus, Operation Ass Be-Gone was not such a success. And if there was ever a metaphor for why America will never win in Afghanistan, it was the mighty U.S. Army trying to kill that ass.

The Ali Abad 500

As I've said before, that first summer in the Korengal, any trip into Ali Abad was accompanied by an obligatory firefight as you attempted to leave said village. This was always bad news because there were only two types of cover between Ali Abad and Phoenix: shitty and none. I don't know if it was just tradition handed down from 10th Mountain, to 2nd Platoon, to us, or what, but someone along the way had decided the best way to make it home was to run. Whether the P.L. chose to take the road or the school trail home, the distance between Phoenix and Ali Abad was about 500 meters. And that's how this little race against speeding bullets became known as The Ali Abad 500.

Now, running 500 meters in a wife-beater and a pair of shorts isn't much of a feat. But doing it wearing full battle rattle in 100° heat was a little much. As a SAW gunner with 85 pounds on, I'm suckin' after 100 meters, and after 200 meters, I'm halfway hoping I do get shot. It's not like you're running on a track either. The school trail is a series of uneven rocks and roots, while the road is comprised of one pothole after another concealed by moondust.

Why, once I was running behind Sergeant Williams who didn't quite clear one of the potholes, and proceeded to do summersaults forward. I was kinda happy, too. Not because my Team Leader had taken a spill, but because it slowed his tall ass down a little bit so I could catch my breath.

Truth be told, I never cared for this running business. Seriously, what's your enemy to think when he sees you running out of his village? He's gonna think you're scared, that's what. And one of the last things you want in war is for your enemy to think you're afraid of him. It had to give Hajj a swelling sense of satisfaction to see us tear out of there like that. I always thought we should've at least waited till they started lighting us up to run. But at the time I was just an E-4 and no one cared what I thought.

Days of the Week

Mefloquine Monday

    Though days of the week might seem irrelevant to guys working 7 days a week for 15 months straight, there were a few that did have some significance. Mondays were a double. First, it was Mefloquine Monday—Mefloquine being an anti-malarial pill that everyone was supposed to take, obviously on Monday (someone in the Army must've had a thing for alliteration). Most guys didn't even use the pills, the majority complaining they caused some very disturbing dreams. I ate mine—what the fuck? I rarely remember my dreams and didn't get to sleep more than 4 hours at a time anyway.
However, I might should've not taken it. A few years after we got back, the Veteran's Administration published a public health warning that Mefloquine can cause cardiomyopathy—a weakened heart condition. Symptoms include shortness of breath, fatigue, high blood pressure, chest pains, and I know one guy that passed out while driving down the road. Of course, the Army's always been really good at poisoning its Soldiers—a tradition likely to continue.

H.A. Mondays

    On Mondays, we took H.A. (Humanitarian Aid) to the village below our firebase, called Babyol. Every Soldier would hand carry about 3 bags of beans, rice, and flour—though I avoided the flour, as flour tended to seep out of the bag and get all over my SAW. And I was not authorized a flour-coated light machine gun. So I went with the beans and the rice. Each bag probably weighed about 5 pounds and in my mind could keep a family of Hajj on their bony feet for at least a week. It was severely untactical. If we took contact while we had our hands full of those bags of food, we'd be fucked. But not so curiously, I can't recall ever being attacked on an H.A. run.

We'd pull aside the high-speed log that propped against the door that served as the lower entrance to the firebase (that was what we in the Army call "Force Protection" and that's how the most advanced military in the world locked their back door) and began the steep descent to the Babyol mosque. (Hey, at least it was downhill. Believe me, there were objections enough to delivering staples to the Taliban like we were goddamned Domino's, without having to lug their food up the side of some sheer-faced cliff.)

Upon arrival at the mosque we'd lay the food down, then setup security. What always killed me was, the guy we gave the food to was a known insurgent. If you went to the TOC (Tactical Operations Center—where the C.O. hangs out and they have all their computer screens and shit) at the KOP, you would see this guy's picture hanging up, along with a lot of other bearded pirates in pajamas.

He was classified as an H.V.T. or, High Value Target. Well if this chode was such a threat, why didn't we nab him instead of issuing him enough food to feed the Taliban for another seven days? The guy was a school teacher on top of that, which no doubt gave him ample opportunities for both Taliban recruitment and instructing all the young ones in the finer points of anti-Americanism. He was a real weasley-looking character with tiny round spectacles, and it didn't take a military intelligence officer to deduce, this was one shady cat. He exuded contempt.

The P.L. would sit down and bullshit with the guy for a good half hour, achieving absolutely nothing, other than giving oldboy the satisfaction of having his ass kissed by an American officer. Amazing: here we were trying to placate a recognized terrorist. And in a way, validating the guy by putting him in charge of food stores. Make sense?

And when I say we were feeding the Taliban, I mean, once we dropped the food off, it was theirs to do with what they wished. We didn't oversee the villagers-in-need coming by and receiving their welfare. It was just, oh here's some food, oh how ya doin', oh okay, gotta go now, shoot at ya later. Here in the United States Army, we like our enemies well-fed.

TIC Tuesday

A clear indication that our H.A. Monday program was a bang-up success was a phenomenon known as TIC Tuesday. So on Mondays we fed the Taliban and on Tuesdays, they repaid the kindness by lighting us up at least twice a day. I'm not making it up, and I wasn't the one that coined the term TIC Tuesday, but sure as the sand flea bites at night, every Tuesday you could expect absurd quantities of incoming lead.

They might hit us 3 times on a Tuesday. Even 4 firefights wasn't out of the question. It was ridiculous. I guess once Hajj gets his beans and rice, he's ready to rumble. If you went out on patrol, you were definitely gonna get hit. If you stayed on the firebase, you were still gonna get hit. If you started to watch a movie in between patrols or guard shifts, or if you were asleep, it was only a matter of time...

Resupply Truck Thursday

Thursdays were for resupply trucks. I doubt the God Of War, Sun Tzu, Rodger's Rangers, or even Private Pyle would approve any more than we did of Company sending us resupply trucks on the very same day every week. The Taliban kinda caught onto that pretty quick. They tend to notice things like a whole Platoon of Americans standing out in the open with their hands full of crap and their backs turned. So when a truck was coming down, you took your full kit (body armor, weapon and all) up to the top of the firebase to download the supplies. Naturally, the truck was never loaded with anything light. I'm talking about dozens upon dozens of cases of bottled water, food, fuel, sometimes concertina wire, sandbags, Hescos, and you formed a human chain and began the process of getting the supplies off the truck which always took forever. The jingle truck almost always came in the afternoon too, so all Hajj had to do was head up the mountain after lunch, get behind his P.K.M. and wait a little bit. Which they did. It was not at all uncommon for a resupply truck to kick off a TIC.

Sand Flea Recognition Day

    Lastly, sand fleas could be had any day of the week. And in fact, mandated every day of the week. The way one celebrated Sand Flea Recognition Day was by squandering at least a quarter of your precious sleep by scratching at these insatiable beasts, then in the morning and afternoon, paying homage to the work done by the sand fleas the previous night by scratching at about a billion little bites. Chico was the master of this, as the sand flea seemed to have a thing for our Platoon's sole representative of the Philippines. He scratched so much, his legs were constantly covered in scabs, scars and blood.

Prickly Heat

According to Wikipedia, Miliaria, or, "prickly heat" as it is called by us Soldiers, "is a skin disease marked by small and itchy rashes," which "may itch or more often cause an intense 'pins-and-needles' prickling sensation." The condition is due to sweat gland ducts getting plugged. Wikipedia goes on to say that it "can be prevented by avoiding activities that induce sweating, using air conditioning to cool the environment, wearing light clothing and in general, avoiding hot and humid weather. Frequent cool showers or cool baths with mild soap can help prevent heat rash."

So let's see here: Avoiding activities that induce sweating? Impossible. Using air conditioning? Didn't have none. Wearing light clothing? Uh, is 85 pounds of shit constantly strapped to me considered light? Avoid hot and humid weather? Ever been to Afghanistan? Frequent cool showers? Is once a month good enough?

So, no. You could use baby wipes to take a "shower," put hand sanitizer on your chest when you were through, but it wouldn't do a damned bit of good. Prickly heat was just unavoidable. And once you had it, it wasn't goin' away till winter, and it'd be back in the spring. Every time you moved, it felt like you were being stuck with about a thousand needles. And nothin' to be done about it.

Re-fit on O.P. Four: Downtime at its best

About once a month, one Squad per Platoon would rotate back to the KOP on what was called re-fit. Re-fit was your much-welcomed break from patrolling and significantly lessened your chances of dying. Your only job on re-fit was to man one of the KOP's four O.P.s (Overwatch Positions). Each O.P. was designed a little different, but could be thought of as a bunker with a large gunpit complete with heavy weapons, and an attached living quarters (which was just a small room with either cots or impromptu bunk beds).

So say you have a Squad of seven, the Squad Leader and one joe would stay in our Platoon hooch on the KOP, which gave you five dudes to pull guard on the O.P. Thus, two hours of guard, eight off. This afforded you the opportunity to catch up on the ole sleep debt, actually do your once-a-month laundry, take your monthly shower, and offered multiple liberties with the phones and Internet.

You also got hot chow as it was served once a day for lunch on the KOP. The food probably wasn't that great, but compared to what you'd been eating it tasted like goddamned five-star gourmet morsels from God. Aside from that, you could read, watch movies, lay around—it was a tremendous and essential break. Of course the KOP would usually find some annoying details for you to do from time to time, but at least none of them resulted in any fatalities.

For the first several months of the deployment, 3rd Platoon was responsible for manning O.P. Four—the choicest of all the KOP's O.P.s. For starters, it was the closest, which thus made it easy to go down to the M-Dub (M.W.R.—Morale, Welfare & Recreation) to use the Internet or phones. It wasn't an O.P. that was in the fight as much as O.P. One or O.P. Three; O.P. Four's primary purpose was to guard the KOP against this blind draw and thus theoretically keep it from getting overrun. It was goofy though, 'cause you couldn't see into the draw from the O.P. either. We just had a Claymore mine placed down there. (Which we'd come to learn later, the Taliban are very familiar with Claymores and so they cut the wires before they attack. Not to mention, if the wire's not buried, the goddamned crows will eat the crap out of your detonation wire. I don't know if they make that wire out of crackers or what, but 10 out of 10 crows in the Korengal find it delicious.)

O.P. Four's bunker was made of Hescos and sandbags, and the living quarters was so cramped all of the cots had to be lined up side-by-side, touching each other. But the crowning jewel at O.P. Four, was power. We'd run an extension cord all the way from the KOP, so you could power a small oscillating fan, and any and all of your portable electronics.

The worst thing about O.P. Four was pulling guard at night. Especially for the first few months (when the thought of being overrun was, if not very real, at least frequently imagined). The design of the O.P. was particularly poor when it came to being able to see out of, and I swear to God there were more noises out there than you'd ever thought imaginable. Of course it was always monkeys or wild dogs, but that didn't make it any less unnerving.

Out there, something stirred every few minutes and it began to make you paranoid. Half way through your two-hour guard shift, you were probably hearing and seeing things that didn't exist. There would come a noise over to your left. And the genius who designed the O.P. decided you didn't need to be able to see in that direction. So you'd listen harder to see what it was.

Monkeys maybe? Or a whole Platoon of Hajj creeping silently up to slit your throat with a *gurkha* so they can slip down into the KOP and annihilate everyone as they slept in their hooches?

You'd think you saw something, and then you'd start focusing on it as hard as you could. Wait! Did it just move? Did that goddamned thing just move?! And you kept watching it but you weren't sure. Then you'd hear another noise over to the right.

What the fuck? Are there really people out there? Is something going on? You fumble in the dark for the Claymore clackers. You make damned sure the cord's plugged in. You feel for your rifle. You know where it is, but it's comforting to touch it. You hope the .50 cal doesn't fail if you need it.

You keep watching. You keep listening. You keep imagining you see and hear things. You wonder if your lack of competence could cause the entire Company FOB to be overrun.

Your stomach sinks and you consider waking someone else up. But maybe this is all bullshit. Maybe it's just a bunch of monkeys and dogs fucking around, and if you wake someone up, not only would you look like a chicken-shit, they'd also be pissed that you robbed them of some sleep.

You sigh. You keep scanning. The noises continue. You cover your watch with the opposite hand, and hit the illumination button so that the glowing face can't be seen. Fuck. Thirty-three more minutes. Then you can finally go to sleep while your friends hangout in the gunpit worrying about whether or not the noises they're hearing are a prelude to an all-out attack.

In the shit

(Troops In Contact out on patrol)

And my Squad Leader's running through a shower of lead and bullets are kicking up the dirt all around him and he's yelling something indiscernible. An R.P.G. explodes just a few meters away. Then another one, but it comes in too low this time. I switch out the 100-round nutsack on the SAW for a full 200-round drum. We're taking just an immense amount of fire. We're getting hit from three different directions.

The thigh-high rock wall I'm crouched behind blocks the bullets from two sides, but the Taliban element on Donga I'm wide open to, and they fire on me again and again and the bullets are but two or three feet from me. I concentrate the SAW on 1705 but I don't see a goddamned soul. I know they're there 'cause that's where the largest volume of fire is coming from, but it's like they're ghosts, or just some very violent trees. I walk my rounds up and down the spur and I think to myself, *Where would I be if I were them?* and show those areas extra love.

Another R.P.G. blows up behind me close enough that I feel it in my teeth and get peppered with rocks. I remain focused and pull the trigger. Just three to five round bursts. I don't want the motherfuckin' barrel to overheat. I think about how much ammo I'm goin' through and what's the least amount of ammo I think I can make it back to the firebase on.

The mortars from the KOP begin to plug away at the mountainsides. It makes a lotta noise but effective fire it ain't. The onslaught continues. Roberts is just a little bit above me popping off every two-oh-three at his disposal. But the weapon can only shoot about 350 meters. It just doesn't have the range we need.

I hear nothing but machine gun fire provided by Weapons Squad and my own SAW and Belgarde's, and the intermittent pop of M-4s. I wouldn't exactly say we're pinned down, but ain't nobody moving out from behind what little cover we have either. I squint into the reticle of my scope and lob another three-to-five at Hajj, frustrated I don't even have a human target. The rounds coming at me from Donga I could still reach out and touch. If they move that P.K.M. barrel up just a hair I'll be shredded by seven-six-two. I try not to think about it and keep blasting away at 1705. We're obviously not gonna get any air support else it would've been here already.

I see Roberts pop back—I think for a second he's been hit, but I guess he was just reacting to some close fire. Sergeant Miller's barking orders in between squeezing off rounds. His radio's goin' crazy. Sergeant Slo's crouched down behind a tree with about a 6" diameter, pulling back on the trigger and working mag changes. I can't see Sergeant Eddie and I can't see Mino. Everything just looks like a really twisted slow-mo version of the 4th of July.

The badguys up on Donga land a few right on the rock wall I'm fighting behind and not but a foot or so from my back. Just then a barrage impacts the rock wall in front of me from the 1705 side. Shards from the rock fly up in my face. Somebody knows I'm here. In any intelligent modern military, you always try to take out the opponent's most casualty-producing weapon, and in this case that means me. I got somebody's attention but I hunker down and fuckin' let out big ole long blast. "Motherfuckers!" I yell, 'cause goddammit nothin' pisses me off more than sons-of-bitches tryin' to blow my head off. I fuckin' let loose on the SAW. "You wanna piece of this, motherfuckers?! Come get you some of this!" I light that whole godforsaken mountainside up.

But still it does next to no good. We ain't takin' not one bullet less than we were 2 minutes ago. I pull the SAW down behind the wall, switch out to my second 200-round drum. I jam that shit in there, pop open the feed tray cover, and lay in the rounds as I shake my head a little bit. *This shit don't look good at all,* I said to myself.

In the back of your mind, there's always this unwanted thought: *Someday, man, someday they're just gonna get lucky. Just gonna get lucky on my ass. They can't shoot that many bullets, and you expect to never get shot. My time is comin', man. That shit is comin'. Fifteen months. Fifteen months. Ain't no way. Ain't no way any of us can expect to survive fifteen months of this shit.*

Fun In The Sun On E.A. Killer

August 2007

The patrol S.P.ed way before dawn. Our objective was to reach E.A. (Engagement Area) Killer before the sun came up. We called it Engagement Area Killer, 'cause it was a location commonly used by the Scouts to set up and snipe some Hajj. The purpose of this particular patrol was to recon the area and ascertain whether it would make a suitable spot for a brand-spanking new firebase. (Later it would be known as O.P. Restrepo.)

There was undoubtedly a better route to take than what we took. In fact, the direct route (the one we'd use later), you could get from Phoenix to Restrepo in about 20 minutes. But at the time we'd never even attempted to climb up there in the daylight which made endeavoring it at night all the more difficult.

Someone from another Squad had suggested we walk the road north towards the KOP a few hundred meters, and then cut up. Someone who had no idea what they were talking about and should've been shot upon our patrol's return. If one were to take a topographic map, plot both Phoenix and E.A. Killer upon this map, then devise the absolute longest, windingest, most unnecessarily grueling route available, it would match exactly, the path we took.

It was times like these I was thankful my Squad Leader was in such shitty shape. I might've had more kit on, but Sergeant Newcomb certainly had more "Nuke" on him. He was mostly bullshit and blubber and I once joked in front of the whole Squad that the guy could be his own T.R.P. (Terrain Reference Point—a natural or manmade terrain feature large enough to direct mortar fire off of). He called for breaks and often, which didn't offend most of us. The climb was punishing. The brush seemed to maliciously reach out and hook onto uniforms and gear. And if it wasn't the brush, it was the shale. Often, taking one step forward meant sliding back four feet.

Sergeant Newcomb's frequent breaks were starting to take their toll on what was originally drawn-up as a night mission. Soldiers began to raise their NODs. Bob was on the horizon.

The going didn't get any easier towards the top. It was a get-on-all-fours-and-climb-for-your-life scramble to the summit. And towards the summit, we were scaling a small cliff. The SAW gunners and the Two-Forty Gunner had it the worst when it came to tight climbing. I believe there's an adage in the rock climbing community that goes something like, "Hug the rock," or, "Stay as flat to the rock as possible." You can't really do that with a machine gun in between you and the wall. Which is probably why the best rock climbers don't scale cliffs with machine guns swinging from their guts. Not to mention half your body weight in gear. I honestly didn't know but whether my next handhold would fail and send me tumbling 500 meters or more down the mountain.

At long last, the patrol reached E.A. Killer. We were smoked. We all knew better by then, but everyone reached the top and just plopped down, damn near in a straight line—sat on our asses and caught our breath. No one pulling security (much less 360° security), or taking adequate cover. Everyone just sucking down water and smoking butts. A lot of us (me included) had taken our helmets off.

Some guys were digging through their assault packs for a protein bar. We weren't neglecting our true duties more than three minutes when a burst of A.K. fire brought us to our senses. It no-shit sprayed less than a meter from my feet. My eyebrows raised and I grabbed my SAW and assault pack (which I'd taken off), and (same as everyone) was leaping over this short spine of rock we were leaning on to our east side. I had to reach up and over the rock wall to secure my helmet, buckled the damned thing, charged the SAW and opened up on where I thought the lone gunman was. We had just gotten so goddamned lucky—everyone was okay.

Guns were blazing till finally someone called cease-fire. The F.O. (which was Specialist Ricky Viets) called for fire and a number of mortars exploded, but whoever had shot at us was long gone. Well-reminded to take our jobs and this valley very seriously, we spread out and pulled 360° security, while I guess Sergeant Newcomb and the P.L. surveyed the new firebase site. Or so I assume—I had a position facing southeastward down the mountain a little ways and couldn't tell you what they were doing up above. I can imagine they were getting measurements and taking pictures, but my job was to suppress anything that popped-off.

However, we received no further fire. We were all but ready to head back down the hill, when all of the sudden we heard a very distinct WHOOMP, WHOOMP, WHOOMP! come from the southern end of the valley, followed by explosions a few hundred meters short of the KOP. Then it came again: WHOOMP, WHOOMP, WHOOMP! Each round detonated a little closer to the KOP. All of us were looking at each other like, *What the fuck was that?!* It wasn't a weapon we'd ever heard Hajj use before. It sounded almost the same as one of our MK-19s (pronounced Mark-19; a 40mm automatic grenade launcher, and a very deadly weapon). It continued to fire and walk its rounds closer to the KOP.

We were then ordered by Battle 6 (Captain Kearney) to dig in and try to get eyes on this weapon that the Taliban were ultimately gonna use to blow the KOP all to hell. I can imagine the panic on the KOP: everyone being stirred from their sleep or hurried out of the M.W.R. and ordered into bunkers... Well, if we were staying here, I didn't like my position much. I stood and began stacking rocks to do a little fortification. I had been in country long enough to learn from Hajj the bullet-stopping ability of some good old-fashioned rocks. The 240 was positioned just to my south and the really awful thing about where we were was the absence of shade. We had none and the sun was rising higher and higher.

It was August. Temperatures were in excess of 100°. The Team Leaders, Squad Leaders and Headquarters were able to take at least partial shelter under a few scant trees. But myself and the gun team had nothing between us and the brain-baking sun. I heard Sergeant Willie say, "E.A. Killer. It's in the suck."

Each time the weapon fired, we heard it for sure, but could see no muzzle flashes and could do nothing but ascertain that it was coming from somewhere way down south. As in, south of Dar Bart even, towards the Taliban-owned village of Qualaygal. We had absolutely no way to get eyes on this thing. Still, with the KOP getting hammered by this grenade launcher, the C.O. insisted we stay put; we had the best vantage point even if our best was inadequate. The only thing the KOP could do was lob mortars almost indiscriminately down that direction.

This went on all day. We rationed our water, but we were already over 6 hours in to what was supposed to be a 3-hour patrol, and what with cooking in the Afghan sun, everyone was running next to dry. My camelbak was sitting at less than a third. I inventoried my water (I had brought along some extra bottled water too) and came to the conclusion that if we were out here till 1600 local time (worst case scenario in my mind), I could drink a quarter of a 500ml bottle every hour. It wasn't much, but I checked my watch and maintained my ration schedule.

   By now our skin, dark as it already was, began to sunburn. No one had shot at us since that initial gun burst, and we all believed the enemy didn't know where we were. We speculated the guy who'd shot at us was just some goat herder looking to take a potshot at some Americans.

   Every 15 to 30 minutes, the Taliban grenade launcher went WHOOMP, WHOOMP, WHOOMPing at the KOP—us all but resigned to not being able to see it, yet Captain Kearney adamant that we sit put while we ran out of water in the relentless sun. Everyone was angry and increasingly dehydrated. It was much worse than I can describe. Just let us come down already. There's nothing we can do for you from here.

   And then, in the very late afternoon, it just stopped. Either the Taliban ran out of ammo, or their weapon system broke. Either way, we still stood fast. Our primary concern had now shifted: how were we gonna get back down off this mountain and home safe? Of course the obvious answer was to wait for the sun to set and head back under the cover of darkness. Obvious to everyone except Captain Kearney that is. He ordered us to pullback, not 30 minutes before dusk. Apparently, he wanted us to draw fire.

   It was after 1700 local when Willie told me to get ready to pickup. *Thank God*, was all that was going through my mind. I almost didn't care that we were being used as bait again. "Let's move!" someone yelled, and I grabbed the SAW by its handle, tossed the sling over my head, and folded the bipod legs up. "Why are we doing this in the daylight?" I whispered to myself. To Captain Kearney's credit, an A-10 Warthog was called in—two of them actually. They soared in with Gatling guns blazing. Those things make the most awesome, comforting sound in all of combat. It's like a gigantic, violent belch. BRRAAA!, BRAAA!, BRAAA! It had to scare the shit out of Hajj. However, we knew the air support wouldn't last. We hauled ass down those steep slopes. Half skiing down the shale with full combat loads. (Minus water of course.) We took the most direct route down (the same one we'd use to get to Restrepo from then on) which probably didn't take us ten minutes.

The A-10s diddied out when we were a couple hundred meters from the road. Which was fine; we weren't accustomed to, nor expectant of, constant air support. If you came out and covered us at all, we were thankful beyond belief. We scrambled down fast as we could, everyone cotton-mouthed as hell, till we finally reached Firebase Phoenix.

The patrol had left at 0300. It was now almost 1800. We'd been out for 15 hours with 3 hours worth of water. The first order of business I thought, was to consume as much H2O as humanly possible. But not 7 minutes after we'd been back I was informed to pack all my shit, as I had to take off with a patrol from 2nd Platoon (who'd been covering down on Phoenix for us), that was headed back to the KOP. See, I was going on leave. They'd been threatening to send me on leave for several weeks now. But this wasn't what I would call good timing. I had a headache from hell, and even though we'd been just sitting since our fatiguing ascent, I felt like I'd been marching uphill all day.

This was such bullshit. I threw all my things together—there was no way I could've seen this coming, and humped up the goddamned hill running through the firebase to the upper gun positions. These guys were fresh and ready to go home. I was burned out and ready for bed. So when they stepped off, they went at an ungodly pace. I brought up the rear (me and Roberts, the Battalion Chaplain in front of us), and I was getting pissed. "Tell 'em to fuckin' slow down!" I said. "These motherfuckers been sittin' on their asses all day while we been up there suckin' and now they wanna haul balls back? Fuck this goddamned shit!" I don't think the Chaplain approved of my language, but he knew better than to say anything.

Yea! Thanks to Sergeant Newcomb being the last Squad Leader in the Company to submit our leave requests, I was going on "mid-tour" leave 3 months into a 15-month deployment. I'd come back and have to do a year straight here. What a goddamned day.

America On Leave

 Despite me being all but drug back to the KOP for what I assumed was an immediate evac for leave, I had to hangout there for 2 or 3 more days. Haircuts were in order, as was appearing for inspection in front of First Sergeant Caldwell in new boots and new A.C.U.s. Being all clean and wearing this new uniform made me feel like less of a Soldier. Dirt and filth during a deployment has a way of becoming a badge of honor. And though I sure as hell didn't choose to go on "mid-tour" so soon, this was the slot I was given. But it just felt all wrong. I didn't wanna leave my Platoon.

 On my morning to takeoff, I gathered down at the L.Z. at the specified time. My assault pack was carefully packed with my civvies, computer, beret, and most importantly of all, my C.I.B. (Combat Infantryman's Badge). Staff Sergeant Martin was in charge of loading those of us departing on leave (only me from 3rd Platoon, and a couple from 1st and 2nd). I front-loaded my assault pack and when the Black Hawk landed, we all hauled ass through the rotor wash and all the dirt and debris it kicked up, to the bird. Everyone understood getting on a helicopter in the Korengal was a dangerous proposition. I expected R.P.G.s to start flying in at any moment.

 The other guys were bringing home about twice as much as I was (they had rucks, even duffle bags), and it thus took longer to get off the ground than it should've. As soon as I loaded, I tried like hell to fasten my goddamned seatbelt, which is what I'd been trained to do, but through the noise of the Black Hawk, Sern't Martin yelled, "Don't worry about that bullshit." There's a definite difference between what you do in training, versus what actually takes place in a combat zone. This, I learned, was one of those differences. It was a fast reminder that, though I wasn't a cherry anymore, I still had a lot to learn.

The bird lifted off. I had this anxious feeling the bird would get shot down and we'd all die. It only took a few minutes to get to the end of the valley, and as the Black Hawk took a right at the Pesch River, I exhaled and felt a helluva relief.

In my mind we were safe now. The other occupants in the helicopter were some Major and his entourage. He was getting a tour from a Lieutenant who kept yelling in the Major's ear about where exactly we were. Both the Black Hawks (there were two of them) set down at Asadabad to refuel. It was an interesting experience, 'cause it really gave me a better feel for where the Korengal was relative to everywhere else. A-Bad (as it's called) looked pretty civilized, and we were told by the flight crew we could unload if we wanted to smoke or whatever and pointed us to a suitable spot away from the fueling equipment. Myself having turned into a pack-a-day smoker, I took advantage.

We reloaded the bird, again with difficulty due to the excess baggage. From A-Bad it was maybe 30 minutes to J-Bad. There I got quarters in an almost vacant transient tent, which blew cold-air constantly. For the first time since we deployed, I was actually wishing I was warmer.

Compared to the Korengal, J-Bad was paradise. They had a full-blown chow hall, with a Salsa night on Tuesdays for God's sake, phones, something better resembling the Internet than we had, and a real concrete wall surrounding the perimeter with guard towers. It didn't appear that anyone here was doing anything save the helicopter pilots and medical personnel. This was the closest place where a bird could be safely stored and also the most immediate, adequate Aid Station for the entire Kunar province. J-Bad wasn't exactly in the war, but it was on the cusp of it. At least from here you knew there was a war.

As I was told, I checked in every morning with the flight manifest to see when and how I would catch a ride to Bagram Air Field (BAF), and finally on the third day my name was on the flight roster. I helped load baggage on, then took off in, a civilian turbo-prop, which was sweet if not a little strange. It was akin to taking a flight from one small American town to another. The other passengers were an interesting mix of Soldiers and contractors. I do not believe this was the normal mode of travel for guys goin' on leave and wondered just how much the civilian pilot was making. Undoubtedly, it was a significant chunk of change. But I was just thankful to have a peaceful seat on an almost normal airplane.

The flight from J-Bad to Bagram was maybe 45 minutes. It wasn't long before we landed, and as we disembarked there was little organization as to where I was to go afterwards. I checked in with the flight accountability office (for lack of proper terminology). I was told not-so-specifically (as in a finger-pointing that way) where the 173rd was setup.

We came through Bagram on our way to the Korengal. However, we only stayed a day or two, and almost all of that was consumed with prepping to go downrange. They had these orientation classes for us to try to stay awake through while we battled jetlag. For maybe 20 to 30 minutes each day our Squad Leaders said, "Hey you can go use the phones or whatever." The rest of the time we were pretty much on lockdown. So this was my first real exposure to Bagram.

Never were the inequities of war so blatant as they were between Bagram and the Korengal. You had about as much chance dying on BAF as you did in a small town in middle America. No one had on body armor, a lot of people didn't carry weapons and those that did didn't have magazines in their wells. Everyone was clean and fresh-shaven with immaculate uniforms. And you've never seen so many officers in your entire life. You had to salute no-shit every third step. The officer to enlisted ratio must've been about 27 to 1.

The place was enormous. So large they had shuttle buses to take you from one end to the other—down paved roads no less. Paved roads, actual cement sidewalks—it looked just like any Army post back in the states. They had Burger King, they had Dairy Queen, Popeye's, Pizza Hut, Starbuck's, Green Beans, Air Force chicks, clothing stores, a P.X., even massage parlors (sans happy endings). Not to mention the scale of the chow halls—those places had everything. Ice cream even. And they even paid somebody to scoop it for you. Best of all, they had hot showers and a/c.

People actually did their deployments here. And got paid just as much as we did fighting for our lives in the Korengal. I swear to God, Bagram is not a deployment. You may be away from your family, but this place was a goddamned 15-month trip to Disneyland compared to what we were going through.

I found our Battalion Headquarters—a small little stall with a couple of desks, a couch, and tv with Xbox, where I'm sure these guys spent all their time. Some bored E-7 took my information and told me where to billet. He said roll call was at 0700 and 1700 daily over by the gazebo and not to be late.

Our billeting was a tent big enough to hold a circus in. It had a plywood floor and four very long rows of olive drab Army cots inside, with an immense fan-driven air conditioner. *Sweet*, I thought, *I'm not gonna have to sweat myself to sleep.* Oh, little did I know. About four hours into the night it got so goddamned cold in there I couldn't quit shivering. This was preposterous. Maybe a little ironic. From having no shirt on, no blanket, but still just pouring sweat as you lay in your hooch in the Korengal, to wearing everything you brought (which wasn't much), wrapped up as tight as humanly possible in your poncho liner in Bagram and still freezing your ass off. The God Of War has an interesting sense of humor alright.

I awoke the next morning, to the sound of cadence. This place was so goddamned backwards, guys had to do P.T. (Physical Training). And they actually ran to cadence here. I was in utter disbelief. I went outside to brush my teeth and shave, then smoked a cigarette in the rising sun. So this is how the other half live, huh?

I could continue to bore you with the nuances of Bagram Air Field, but aside from the free Internet and getting to talk to my wife twice a day, there were only two noteworthy incidents.

On my second day there at our 1700 formation, I was told that I had a 12-hour guard shift. *WTF?!* There had to be 10,000 people on this base at least! And I had to pull guard? You gotta be shittin' me.

But sure 'nough, at 2100 I had to report to this dog-and-pony-show formation. These fatass M.P. dudes even made us open ranks, and had us clear and present arms. It was unbelievable. Like we were in basic training or something. In the Korengal, not only is your weapon always loaded, if you have an M-4, it's always got a round chambered—one in the pipe ready to deliver some death. These guys gave us one box of live rounds a piece. Twenty bullets. No way would I go on guard at Firebase Phoenix with but twenty bullets.

I got in a van, me and some others, and we were driven way out to the perimeter, to this guard tower. Myself and this other Specialist were told to dismount. The guard tower was 3-stories high—it looked like an air traffic control tower. They even had a/c in there. And a mini-fridge. Which was good for the Red Bull I'd bought and brought.

This kid I was on guard with was a straight-up POG (pronounced *pogue*—meaning person other than grunt). He was an admin clerk or M.I. (military intelligence) or finance or something. I could tell in the first two minutes that he was going to be annoying.

He dropped his stuff and immediately got behind this wild thermal camera system in the tower called the SPIDER. You could see out for over a kilometer with this thing. What it was doing here and not some place useful, I couldn't tell ya. It was fun to fuck with for about 10 minutes. But this POG was all about the goddamned thing. He was constantly scanning with it even though there was no one out there but some Hajj with hoes and shovels walking around.

I wanted to slap him. He kept talking about how there was this purple pickup truck that tried to drive along the perimeter (which consisted of a 20-foot concrete wall) and how he suspected it was a V-BIED (Vehicle Born Improvised Explosive Device—which is Army for car bomb). And how he hoped they came back tonight so he could see some action. He'd been here almost 12 months and never fired a shot.

If you wanted to shoot your gun, why didn't you join the Infantry is what I wanted to ask. I'd been in thirty-some-odd, maybe forty firefights in the past 3 weeks and the last thing I wanted was to get in a shootout in goddamned Bagram of all places, with this cherry and only 20 rounds. We didn't have any ammo for it, but they had this SAW in the tower that looked like it belonged in a museum.

"I didn't know they made those things new," I commented. The thing was pristine. I was well aware that 2nd Platoon's SAWs were crap. And here was a brand new SAW that would never get shot. You just can't help but think about how the Army needed to reallocate some of its assets. Well, after about 12 hours of exactly nothing happening, the van pulled up at about 0945 local (just a little late), and I got a ride back to my billeting.

Later that same day, I saw Sergeant Miller stumble into our circus tent. Very surprised to see him there, I asked him what was going on and he told me Phoenix had been violently attacked the night before—tons of R.P.G.s and small arms. He said he was fine, but that an R.P.G. blast had caused him to lose his vision for a spell and they insisted on medevacing him. Johnson on the other hand, was not all right. An R.P.G. had penetrated Weapons Squad's hooch and the shrapnel had ripped into his abdomen. He was in the Bagram hospital. I went to see him of course, but I doubt he remembers it. Johnson was in a bad way. He'd never be back to the valley as he had dozens of surgeries to look forward to. They flew him to Landstuhl, Germany the next morning.

The whole Bagram ordeal went on for no less than five days and left a very bad taste in my mouth. Every day I went to formation, every day they read the flight manifest, and every day I wasn't on it. Until the last day on which I was. I could not wait. The next morning I was shuttled to the air strip at about 0400 where I waited in a hangar for about three hours before my beautiful bird (a jet-propelled C-17) at long last took-off. Destination, Kuwait.

For those of you who've never had the pleasure of visiting Kuwait in August, I recommend not going to Kuwait in August. Or maybe just not going to Kuwait ever. Probably it wasn't on your Top Ten List of Dream Vacations anyway. You could say it was a little hot there. Had to stay 2 or 3 days. Mostly indoors with air conditioning, thank God. When it was finally my time, we boarded civilian buses, escorted by guntrucks, to the Kuwati airport. It was an all military flight bound for Atlanta if you were going to the east coast or thereabouts, and Dallas if you were headed out west, which was my case.

One really cool thing was, when we touched down at D.F.W., they had a fire truck out there and it ceremoniously hosed down our plane. (They did this for every single flight coming in with Soldiers on mid-tour—remarkable really.) When we disembarked the bird, there were rows of guys from the V.F.W. and guys and gals from the U.S.O. and the whole airport gave us a standing ovation. That was a little overwhelming, and I felt humbled and not deserving of the attention.

This isn't a book about my vacation to America, so I'll just say, naturally leave was nice and it's good to take a break from a combat zone. Got to spend time with my wife, with my family, and all that sweet stuff.

But, the whole trip, I was suspended in disbelief. I mean, you couldn't even tell there was a war on when you were home. And I thought Bagram was bad. Here, everyone went about business as usual. People conspicuously went to movies, went mindlessly shopping, habitually went to work, repeatedly ate fast food—normal people shit to be sure, but at the same time there were twenty-five to thirty thousand of us in Afghanistan and about four or five times that many in Iraq.

Guys sucking and dying everyday. And for what? Yeah they volunteered for it. But it's true what they say: America wasn't at war, America's military was. Aside from a couple of yellow ribbon bumper stickers on random cars, you wouldn't know it.

Everything in my so-called homeland felt so surreal, alien even—I couldn't figure out which world was true; this one, or the raucous life we were living in the Korengal. But I was already convinced that the war in Afghanistan was my reality, and that this continuance in America was some sort of sheltered, docile dream world.

I had nothing but silent contempt for it. To voice these matters to people who've never experienced combat, just wouldn't do much good. Either everybody was oblivious as to what was really going on over there, or they just didn't care. Whichever, both my sand flea bites and prickly heat had time to heal. So I guess that meant it was time to go home.

Due to our 15-month deployment, we were given 18 days of leave versus the 14 days you get for a 12-monther. But it's the fastest 18 days of your life. Before I knew it I was back on a plane headin' the other way. I got good and loaded on my flight to Dallas and the flight attendant was really hooking me up.

Going back, logistically, was much the same as when you were headed out on leave. Takes about as long. The only real difference is, once you get to Kuwait and start hookin' up with guys from your Company, you start hearing the rumors. "They built O.P. Atlanta." "Sern't Loza got shot in the shoulder; he's alive, but he'll never fight again." "3rd Platoon is patrolling to Donga now."

I was damned glad I wasn't there for Atlanta (later to be renamed O.P. Restrepo)—I knew that must've been enough to make you wanna suck start an M-4. But as for the other two pieces of information, I wasn't sure which was worse. Sern't Loza was a fun guy to have around and a smart Squad Leader besides; he'd be missed. He turned 2nd Squad from borderline turd-dom into Soldiers that rivaled Sern't Shelton's (3rd Squad). Loza was one of those guys you just couldn't replace. But the very thought of patrolling across that river and into Donga sent my anxiety into overdrive. It sounded dangerous beyond my capacity to describe. I didn't even see how that patrol was possible. I'd soon find out.

II. FALL

Building Restrepo

While I was on leave, the Con-Op to build O.P. Restrepo (originally dubbed O.P. Atlanta) came down. Despite what anybody says, Restrepo was initially built by 3rd Platoon, not 2nd. I believe 2nd Platoon had some blocking position down south (around Dar Bart somewhere), which isn't exactly a fun place to be, but from what I was told, the enemy focused its fire on those that were digging (3rd Platoon).

Most of this is coming from Belgarde, who was there. He said they got in 15 firefights the first day alone. He said they'd dig, and when they took contact (which was about every hour or less for 3 days), they'd drop their shovels and picks and grab their guns. As soon as the firefight ceased, they'd lay down their weapons and resume filling sandbags and Hescos.

Belgarde said it was miserably hot (late August in Afghanistan and all) and they were only getting about 2 hours of sleep a day. "Captain Kearney was up there calling for fire watching us dig," he told me. "I asked him, I said, 'Hey, Sir, you ever fill a sandbag?' Guess not." I told Belgarde I was surprised Captain Kearney was up there at all. Usually on Con-Ops he did go out, but normally he'd place himself just outside the edge of the actual fight.

At one point Sergeant Loza took a round to the shoulder. I was told he was laughing as they put him on the medevac. "I'm outta here, pussies!" he yelled.

The onslaught continued. After one firefight Belgarde turned to Sergeant Rozenwald and said, "Hey Rose, you know why I joined the Army? My wiffle ball career wasn't taking off."

"Are you ever serious?" Captain Kearney asked him.

"No. There's no time for it up here, Sir."

After the 3-day Con-Op concluded, 2nd Platoon (having

relinquished Firebase Michigan to Chosen Company) then relieved 3rd, and were chosen to man the new O.P. There was plenty more digging and firefights to be had for them.

Vegas Con-Op

    1st Platoon's A.O. had been heating up for a while. There was this H.V.T. (High Value Target) operating over there by the name of Juma Kahn. We'd been hearing this guy's name since before we even set foot in the valley. I don't know exactly what the purpose of this Con-Op was, but it had something to do with him and at least limiting his capabilities.

    I had literally just gotten off the bird from leave, went to the Platoon hooch on the KOP, and was told I was going out on a Con-Op later that night. We'd had a few personnel changes in my absence. Lieutenant Wells' time as a P.L. was over. He'd done his mandatory year and so he got a cush job at Camp Blessing (Battalion Headquarters) and we got a new P.L., Lieutenant Gillespie. He looked like Napoleon Dynamite with a haircut, and you had to wonder if he cringed when he found out he was assigned to the Infantry. (As officers don't get to choose their branch.) He looked like he'd be better suited to commo, or maybe quartermastering something. I called him Sir all the same.

    Another interesting development, as I was told by Sergeant Miller, who re-introduced himself as my new Squad Leader, was that Sergeant Newcomb had refused to go on patrols about the same time I went on leave, and that he was still hiding here somewhere, but that he was for all intents and purposes, dead to us. I wasn't especially upset as I never liked that guy or considered him anything resembling a good leader to begin with. It was still startling news though, when one took into consideration how much shit he talked. I can still hear him goin' off about how badass he was in Iraq, sprayin' down towns and cars with .50 cals and shit.

    I honestly had no idea it was even possible to quit in combat. But Newcomb wasn't the only quitter. A Staff Sergeant from 1st

Platoon quit, two or three E-5s, and one E-4 (from our Company alone). I don't understand why the Army tolerated it. I mean, if somebody refused to do their duties, I think they should've been put in handcuffs, court martialled, and promptly locked up in Leavenworth. Or at least stripped of all rank and sentenced to a year cutting grass with a ruler and scissors. Hell, in Stalingrad the Russians shot their own Soldiers for retreating. But we didn't seem to have the same policy. They placated the quitters by reassigning them to some easy-going job far away from any action.

I couldn't fathom any of it. Combat, in its purest form, is supposed to be about selflessness. You're supposed to be willing to give your life to save your buddies, or to accomplish the mission. But quitting, that's like saying your life is more valuable than ours. It was the very antithesis of what we were about. In my mind, it was unforgivable. Not to mention, how do you live with yourself after you pull something like that? How do you to go through the rest of your life knowing you are a complete coward? Anyway, I guess we were better off without those pussies, but it still felt like we'd been betrayed.

This was all very interesting, but me and the 15 pounds I gained whilst on leave needed to prepare for the forthcoming Con-Op. (Everyone put on a lot of weight during leave. I heard something about how, when your body is starved and over-exerted for long periods of time, when you do get a chance to chill and actually eat real food, your body starts storing fat like it's going back into combat tomorrow or something.)

I had concerns that this going to end poorly for me. I'd never heard of a guy literally walking off the bird from leave and going straight onto a Con-Op. I had done exactly zero exercise since I left. Intentionally. But I wasn't gonna be a little bitch about either. It was time to man-up and get this Con-Op on.

My Squad wasn't going. Nor would this be the last Con-Op I did while 1st Squad was chillin' on the O.P. But by the grace of God, whoever's decision it was to make me go, had the foresight to send me as a Grenadier instead of as the SAW gunner I was. I would've really been suckin' with the SAW. I took Roberts' 203 off of him, adjusted my RACK accordingly, and went onto the business of prepping (field-stripped M.R.E.s, grabbed enough (probably too much) water, took like half a carton of cigs and whatever else and stood by).

1st Platoon's A.O. was most notable for its brutal walks. 1st Platoon's patrols were longer and steeper than anything the A.O.'s of 2nd or 3rd Platoon had. And we'd all heard the stories of these death marches. Added to which, we didn't know that area to save our lives. And as the Taliban can attest to, knowing the terrain is an enormous advantage. So leaving a place we knew, with an extra 40 pounds of shit on (not counting my vacation fat), to go hump up 1st Platoon's Mystery Mountains of Ultimate Suck, was not so appealing.

I got attached to 2nd Squad, whom Sergeant Willie (my former Team Leader) was now a member of, since you couldn't have Sergeant Miller and Willie in the same Squad. (There was this incident at Firebase Michigan where Sergeant Miller had tried to choke Willie to death.) Likewise, Bunnell had gone to 3rd Squad in exchange for Mino (which was a good trade for us). Bunnell and Sergeant Miller had had several similar run-ins dating back to 2006, and I suppose segregation was in order. Sergeant Miller was an angry 240-pound black man. No one ever accused him of being the easiest guy to get along with. He was however, much more likely to bring you home alive than Newcomb.

Anyway, we S.P.ed from the KOP at zero-dark-thirty, and began slogging our way towards God knows where. Usually on a Con-Op you have 100% lume (meaning, a full moon), but I think we had way less than 50% on this one, and maybe it was more like 25%. All I know is, it was dark. The trail we took was so hard to see that guys kept falling off of it. Captain Kearney fell off, Sergeant Navas fell off, and so did I. I fell about 6 feet but landed upright and scrambled my way back onto the trail. This little midnight hike went on for hours. I was suckin', but not as bad as I thought I would.

This Con-Op turned out to be really lame. I must've missed the part where they put out what we were attempting to accomplish. We set up in this defensive position and were presumably waiting on Hajj to just waltz on into our fields of fire. I found a shallow cave to chill in and I just sat there and smoked and poured some grape drink mix into my water, which I thought brought out the flavor in my Pine cigarettes.

About the only action was when the Scouts got eyes on some

fool. Me, Sergeant Willie and one of the Scouts had to go chase him down. We apprehended him, but after he was questioned, it turned out he wasn't a badguy after all. Well, right about when temperatures in the Korengal peaked, Captain Kearney decided we should all just go back to the KOP.

The Scouts took off first, and next in order of movement was 2nd Squad with Sergeant Oquendo (we called him Q) on point. I have no idea why, but Q thought it would be a good idea if we could all keep up with the Scouts. Now, these guys are Scouts for a reason. They are hand selected because they're in outstanding shape (even by Paratrooper standards), they're all at least 6' 2", and most of them are really thin, or at least especially lean. They are not someone you wanna tag along with particularly if you're carrying 110 pounds of crap.

But Q took off after these jackrabbits. And even though we were mostly going downhill, by the time we got to the river, both Q and Barnard were on the verge of unconsciousness and required I.V.s. We then climbed our way up to the KOP road and began walking home. At one point we took a brief halt on the road, which offered not a lot of cover. As such, me and Sebastian Junger took cover behind the same large rock. Him and his cameraman, Tim Hetherington, were there making a documentary about 2nd Platoon. It was interesting to hear him and Tim evaluate us. "They're just carrying too much weight," Junger said. My sentiments exactly.

Sergeant Miller

    I believe Sergeant Marcus Miller came from South Carolina. He never really talked much about where he was from, or his family, which led me to believe it was something he'd like to forget. When it came to his personal life, he was normally aloof. He would make mention of some girl he was seeing in Spain named Samantha, but you got the feeling it would be inappropriate to ask about it, just leaving it at him saying, "That bitch is bad." I believe it was Sergeant Mac (McDonough, formerly a Team Leader in 3rd Platoon, 3rd Squad, but now with 2nd Platoon), who gave Miller the nickname "Darkness." Though I'm pretty sure Mac meant that as a reference to the shade of Miller's skin, it also worked on a personal and professional level.
    The man lived to workout. He was about six-two, six-three, and I can only guess he weighed in the 220-240 range. Though he wasn't particularly cut, he definitely had the mass part down. Back in Italy, when not at work and not at the gym, he would be beating on these goddamned drums in the barracks. It was incredibly loud, and he possessed a poor sense of rhythm. Problem was, Sergeant Miller was so large and intimidating, and, being one of the few E-5s who resided in the barracks, he out-ranked all of us, so no one ever really said anything to him about it.
    As far as soldiering went, he was not the best teacher. He knew what he was doing, but he wasn't about to explain it. He just expected you to know things. And he had a terrible temper. It was not unlike him to physically threaten anyone at any time. He could be very difficult to deal with. You often had to swallow your pride to be with him.
    I honestly don't mean to portray him as being all bad. Compared to Sergeant Newcomb, he was a goddamned blessing. 'Cause Miller

definitely had balls. He never cowered under fire, he never backed down from anyone or anything. And though he yelled incessantly, and was adept at making things harder than they needed to be, like Belgarde said, you'd rather have him on your side than not. And in his own psychotic way, I really do think he cared about his Squad. He was just a little dysfunctional, that's all.

Why My NODs Plate Is Black

So I'd just gotten back from leave a few days ago, and I was down at Phoenix, waiting to go out on patrol. It was mid-morning and I was on my second cigarette when I noticed everyone had painted their NODs plate tan. (A NODs plate is a piece of metal that attaches to the forehead of your helmet and it allows you to mount your NODs (night vision) onto it.) I was like, "Did we get a shipment of spray paint while I was gone? Yall just felt like painting some shit or what?"

My new Team Leader, Sergeant Slomiak, or "Slo" as everyone called him, said, "No. They made us do it. Some order came down, somethin' about how the Taliban are aiming for NODs plates."

"And the tan somehow dissuades them from shooting at the NODs plate?" I asked. "Like tan's harder to hit than black? Who comes up with these things? I swear to God sometimes I think there's a paranoid room full of retards with a lotta rank and no practical experience that just sit around and dream up dumb things for us to do."

"Shit, I don't know. They said do it, so we did," said Slo.

Viets nodded, "I think we still got some paint left in Headquarters if you want it."

I thought about it a second. It sounded stupid as all hell to me, as I'm sure it did for everyone else too. "Well, I ain't been shot in the head yet, so I'm just gonna go with black. But the first time I get shot in the NODs plate, I guess I'll paint it."

"You should paint yours hot pink is what you oughtta do," Belgarde suggested. "And wrap one of those fluorescent V.S.17 panels around your neck, like a scarf."

Korengali Window Treatment

We were at Phoenix chillin' in our hooch. We'd just gotten back from patrol not too long ago, and so we were cleaning our weapons, smoking cigarettes and such. "Hey Mino, let me get that 203 bore brush from ya," Roberts said as he hopped down from his bunk bed. He crossed the tiny Hajj room, grabbed the bore brush from Mino, and sat down on the adjacent cot with his rifle. After he ran it through the 203 a couple times, he gave it back. "Get a couple of those Q-tips from ya, Shadix?"

"Sure, man." (For cleaning guns, Q-tips are the best thing ever invented.)

But as soon as Roberts stood to cross the room again, a shot came straight through our window (the one that faces Table Rock) and damned near sent Roberts to be with Allah. "Holy shit!" he jumped back. Everyone was wide-eyed. "Did you see that?! I almost got sniped in my own hooch! Really?!"

"I don't think this room is entirely safe," I said.

"Yeah we should look into some curtains or something," suggested Sergeant Miller.

The Wayward Sergeant Swoyer

There was a Team Leader in 2nd Squad named Sergeant Swoyer...

Well, actually, if you'll permit a brief flashback to November 2007: Vicenza, Italy. Home of the 173rd Airborne Brigade. Our Platoon Sergeant before Sergeant Hunt was Sergeant First Class Beeson. I was new to the unit so I'd only known him a couple of months, but long enough to know not fuck with him. He was a former Drill Sergeant, had two gold stars on his jump wings (from Panama and Iraq), and a good guy, but a serious Soldier. He was being promoted to First Sergeant of Chosen Company, and he was giving us his farewell address while we were standing at parade rest in Platoon formation. One of the very last things he said to us was, "We got some weak Team Leaders in this Platoon, and if I was going to stick around, I intended to fix it." I later asked Chico or Thomas or somebody who Sergeant Beeson was talking about and they said, "Williams and Swoyer."

Besides being on Sergeant Beeson's "To Do List," Sergeant Gallardo (the then Alpha Team Leader of 2nd Squad) despised Sergeant Swoyer. Gallardo was always ragging on him saying things like, "Why don't you take charge? What are your guys doing? Dude, how did you make E-5?" when something was wrong with one of Swoyer's joes or Swoyer displayed a blatant lack of N.C.O. knowledge, and just generally vocalizing the fact that Swoyer was not half the Soldier that Gallardo was. (But then again, who is? Gallardo was a bad mofo.)

I say all this simply to illustrate that Sergeant Swoyer was not in any danger of making it into the Non-Commissioned Officer Hall Of Fame anytime soon. Not that there was anything really wrong with the guy; he was just laidback, did the best he could, and wasn't into being hardcore.

Back to our deployment: So Sergeant Swoyer went on his mid-tour leave. Everybody does it. What most people don't do, is check into Walter Reed Hospital on their last day of leave, claiming to have a severe case of P.T.S.D. I'm not saying he didn't have P.T.S.D. I'm not saying anyone who ever served in that valley doesn't have P.T.S.D. But we had the balls to come back from vacation. We didn't just leave our Platoon hanging.

We found out about Swoyer's untimely admission to the Army's premier medical center via MySpace (which was the social network of choice at the time). He was on MySpace live from Walter Reed Hospital. As you can imagine, word spread like recently ingested Afghani goat through an American's bowels. "I can't believe he did that," one of our N.C.O.s said to another N.C.O. "How could he do that? Fuckin', Chico and Barnard and Thomas idolize that guy."

The Company, refusing to believe it was true, and probably not wanting to accept one of its own would pull such a stunt, seemed to kind of save a place for him for a month or so. But I'm pretty sure once a guy checks himself into a stateside mental facility, he doesn't come back to combat. Finally one day, we got a call on the radio to gather all Swoyer's things and put 'em on a Humvee. Which I was led to believe was the first leg in a trans-continental journey Swoyer's shit would embark upon. Next, I imagined, would be a Chinook helicopter, probably followed by a C-130 or other such cargo plane, perhaps onto Germany, then New York maybe, and eventually with acceptable losses, they'd find their way to Walter Reed.

Sergeant Hunt grabbed me and a couple others to get Swoyer's stuff, stage it up top, and load it all in one of Destined's Humvees as they drove back from patrol. Since he'd been gone so long, and since our hooches were so tight on space, 2nd Squad had his belongings already packed up, and they were sitting in the corner of the Skeet Shack (which was used for what you think it was, and storage for things you didn't mind getting sticky). Sergeant Hunt said to me, "Hey Shadix, get everything now. I don't wanna get a call a month from now saying we didn't send everything. All his valuables, all his personal items, all his military equipment, everything."

"Roger, Sern't," I said. "I would never do anything but make absolutely one hundred percent sure all this shit gets to the wayward Sergeant Swoyer."

Sergeant Hunt grinned.

Check Please!

Like I mentioned before, every Platoon in Battle Company had a small (15 to 20-man) Platoon of Afghan National Army attached to them. They lived with us on the firebases and would accompany us on patrols. The whole endgame in Afghanistan was to get the A.N.A. on their feet and trained up so they could defend their own country and we could go the fuck home and watch football on Sundays. Problem was, that would involve them becoming real Soldiers instead of the clown car that they were.

Every Platoon of A.N.A had a team of two E.T.T.s (Embedded Tactical Trainers) which normally consisted of a United States Marine and a Navy Corpsman (medic). Their sole job was to babysit, I mean train and mentor, the A.N.A. into soldierly perfection. Though we liked having a Marine to fuck with and an extra medic around, it was very difficult to not get frustrated with A.N.A.

I couldn't tell ya how their recruiting process takes place, but according to one of our 'Terps (interpreters), the A.N.A. were mostly thugs, lowlifes and criminals. Basically, the worst their society had to offer. They weren't here for service to country. They had no pride. They had no esprit de corps. They had no sense of professionalism. They didn't even jump out of airplanes, yall. This was just a paycheck to them. And it wasn't worth dyin' for.

The A.N.A. all wore the U.S. Army's old woodland camouflage pattern (which was much better than our current camo). They rocked A.K.47s, P.K.M.s (a light Russian machine gun comparable to our SAWs), and 1 or 2 guys would carry R.P.G.s, so they were pretty well armed. When we patrolled, they would usually take up the rear (which is the safest place to be). When we took contact on patrol, it was a very mixed bag. Some of them would return fire, some of them would run, some of them would hide behind cover and not pull the trigger. While they weren't too reliable out on patrol, they were pretty useful when Phoenix took contact. For what it was worth, when behind fortifications, the A.N.A. will lay out some lead.

I will say some Platoons we worked with were better than others, which leads me to our next problem. They ("they" being the unknown and all-wise decision makers, or, "deciders," as President Bush would say) kept rotating these guys out what felt like every 3 or 4 weeks. So right about the time they started to figure out what they were doing, here comes a fresh batch of clueless lip-twiddlers. The Korengal being what it was, common sense would dictate the A.N.A. would send us one of their best Platoons. Decidedly not the case. We'd often get a Platoon fresh out of basic.

We had a Brigadier (1-Star) General come down to visit Phoenix once. He asked us a lot of questions and then asked if we had anything for him. Sergeant Eddie commented, "Sir, I was in Afghanistan 2 years ago, and I gotta say, I just don't see any real improvement in the A.N.A. I half-expected them to be better this deployment," which was a pretty ballsy thing to say to a General. To which the General replied, "Uh yes, we are working on that. And once blah blah blah and blah blah blah blah, I think that you'll see blah blah blah. Agreed?"

One of the best examples of how worthless they were is this: One day the head A.N.A. dude told our P.L. that they weren't going on patrol until they had helmets. They said it was unfair that we had helmets and they didn't. So our P.L. sent the request up to higher. Weeks went by with the A.N.A. doing nothing but sitting on the firebase. Finally, we got them their helmets. So we were like, "Okay, here's your helmets, now let's go on patrol." Oh-so-reluctantly, the A.N.A. show up where we were staged to leave, and not a damned one of them had their helmet on. I never even saw the helmets again.

But really, they didn't even need an excuse to not go on patrol. It was not uncommon for them to just flat-out quit. And I mean the whole Platoon. They would simultaneously pack up all their shit, march back to the KOP, and we'd never see that Platoon again. It might be a month before their replacements showed. Was the Korengal hard? Was it dangerous? Yes. But here we are, fighting for their country, and they're the ones that are giving up?! It really made you despise them.

Campbell

Specialist Michael Campbell was probably not your average guy from Kentucky. He possessed a bachelor's degree and all of his teeth and I never once witnessed him wearing a 'coon skin cap nor flying the rebel flag.

He valued education and he was pretty smart. Smart enough to think he was more intelligent than his leaders, which led to a definite and well-catalogued problem with authority. Whereas, in the Army we're taught to follow orders without question, Campbell's S.O.P. was to at once question the order before executing it, or in some cases, not executing it, which normally ended badly for him. But that didn't stop him from questioning the next order.

He also couldn't run worth a shit, which in an Airborne unit automatically classifies you for turd status. But, you could strap a hundred pound ruck on him and he could hump all day, proving that you didn't have to run a twelve-minute 2-mile to perform well in combat.

He was a likeable guy, but kind of an odd fit in the Army. I think he stayed in the Army specifically to annoy it and anyone who was put in charge of him. He was what you might call a "Leadership Challenge."

Sergeant Major Vimoto's Cameo Appearance

Our Brigade Sergeant Major, Command Sergeant Major Vimoto, had come down to Phoenix for a little inspection. We were told to just hangout in our rooms, as I guess he wanted to see our living quarters (such as they were) for himself. He entered our hooch with Sergeant Hunt and we yelled, "At ease!" and stood at said position. Sergeant Major Vimoto told us to relax, but Army etiquette is to never relax in the company of a Sergeant Major. He was Samoan and therefore a big, stocky dude.

Part of your job as a Sergeant Major is to bust people's balls. But I guess Sergeant Major Vimoto wasn't in much of a ball-busting mood. This was more of a, yall're-doin'-great-things kinda visit. His voice was low and calm and he kept looking out the window. Down south. Where his son was killed. You had to feel for the guy.

Sergeant Hunt told him that I'd gone directly from getting off the bird from leave, onto a Con-Op. Which impressed Sergeant Major Vimoto enough to give me a coin. Challenge coins are an old Army tradition that dates back to World War II. Originally, in France, if you were attending a top-secret meeting, you had to show your coin as proof that you weren't a Nazi spy. That eventually evolved into coins being given out by people who have a lot of rank, to members of their unit for accomplishing something meritorious. I didn't consider what I did to be anything; I was just doin' my job. But hell I'd take a coin for it. That was actually the coolest coin I ever got in the Army. And not just 'cause it looked pimp, but because of who gave it to me.

Paraphrased, Sergeant Major Vimoto told us he knew this was a tough place to be but to keep up the good fight, then we yelled, "At ease!" once more as he left our hooch en route to Weapons Squad's.

Over the river and through the woods, to Hajj's house we go

The patrols to Donga weren't my idea of a good time. To get there, we walked down through Babyol, forded the river, then took this trail that skirted the bottom of the mountains for about half an hour, then you began a very sharp ascent up to the village proper. It was like a 500-meter staircase. Maybe more. I believe the locals were a little shocked to see us over there, but this had all the makings of a routine, so I guess we'd all better come to terms with it.

Patrols to Donga eventually led to patrols to Marastana. Marastana was a village on the next spur south, and boy was it ever bearing down on you that you were in serious fuckin' Indian territory. I mean hell, the next spur south was Honcho Hill and the spur south of that we didn't even have a name for 'cause nobody in their right goddamned mind would venture that far.

No one wanted to go to Donga or Marastana for the plain and simple reason that once you crossed that river you were in a tactically precarious situation. In this fight, the terrain always favored the Taliban, but now it felt like we were showing them our cards and betting the house at the same time. The river crossing completely exposed you to the enemy. Then, that trail that skirted the bottom of the mountains on the other side of the river was nothing but low ground, along which there were all these draws we had to cross that were wide open to ambush. Finally, once you began your ascent into the village there was zero cover and anyone setup on the adjoining spur could wipe out half the patrol at least. You were also so far from home.

Unlike Ali Abad, no way was our mounted Platoon from Destined Company driving down to retrieve our casualties, or God forbid, K.I.A.s. Which meant, we were either gonna have to carry them out (and dude, it was hard enough to carry myself out, much less throwing somebody plus all their gear over my shoulder), or wait for a medevac (and who knows when or if that would even show up). So the whole time you were over there, you had this creepy, sinking feeling in your stomach. You just knew this was not a good place to be.

Bottom Guard: Alright by day, not so much at night

    Having a guard position in your room that's manned 24-hours a day has a lot of drawbacks. Namely, there's always a goddamned guard in your room. It can be alright depending on who's got guard. You know, you get to hangout with someone, bullshit with 'em for a couple hours. You can discuss the finer points of mountain guerilla warfare, ponder what could possibly be happening in the N.F.L., or contemplate how in the world the locals coexist with the sand flea, and that perhaps the village elders have made some kind of pact with the fleas to only dine on American flesh.
    One perpetual topic was the latest inanities of Captain Kearney, and what he had brewing in that peapot next. Once in a while, the conversation would veer a little deeper, and his Soldiers would sort of psycho-analyze their C.O., debating on whether or not he was actually insane, and, if he gave a shit, even a little shit, even a deer dropping, about his guys. If he had any value for life whatsoever. Or whether he was just so hellbent on making a name for himself, nothing else mattered.
    But the point is, it was cool to bullshit with Barnard, or Chico, Fimbres and everyone else. Because mostly, once you got back to the Firebase, you just hungout in your respective Squad's hooch. But I'm talking about the day now. At night was another story. For a light sleeper such as myself, having somebody switch out every two hours was not an ideal situation. There was the inevitable rustling and exchange that accompanies every guard replacing another. Worse still, a night guard's favorite pastime is masturbation. And most guys wouldn't hold back just because he was in a room with six other sleeping men. He'd tug away and splooge all over our dirt floor.
    However, the all-time worst guard to have in your hooch at night, had to be V. The guy seemed to be training for a future career

in competitive eating. Not only was he about the one guy in the Korengal who hadn't dropped 20 pounds, he seemed to be gaining weight. Any time he was on guard, there was this constant crinkle of potato chip bags, the opening of yet another M.R.E., or Otis Spunkmeyer muffins and cookies, amplified by the sound of V. chewing and swallowing. He apparently had guard confused with chow time, and if he ever stopped eating to scan for the enemy, I never heard it.

A Week In The Life—Play By Play

Monday (a.k.a. H.A. Monday, a.k.a. Mefloquine Monday)

0200 Two hours of guard. Deeply considered my own mortality and prayed someone would send me some summer sausage—and maybe some crackers—like Toasteds—onion Toasteds.
0408 Turned my pants inside out, killed a couple of sand fleas then got an hour and a half of sleep.
0600 Patrol to Ali Abad (led by my Squad). Setup up my SAW in the graveyard. Pondered my own mortality, and the whereabouts of my summer sausage and onion Toasteds.
0900 P.L.'s negotiations with village elder end, on both their behalves with silent notes of cultural supremacism and teething intentions, as per usual.
0902 Troops In Contact (also as per usual).
0920 Firefight ended.
0921 Battle 6 insisted we hold-squat to draw more contact. Nothing happened. Except the whole patrol concluded Captain Kearney's an even bigger asshole than we believed yesterday—which is a substantial if not impossible development.
1100 Ex-fill back to Phoenix. Cleaned my weapon, ate two protein bars, slept about twenty minutes—and I'm talkin' drool-on-the-pillow sleep.
1200 Guard again.
1200 Another patrol (led by 2nd Squad) S.P.ed for Table Rock.
1244 Patrol took contact, I lit up 1705 with the 240.
1400 Relieved from guard by Bunnell who did not look like Afghanistan was agreeing with him—but then again, I don't think Bunnell agreed with Bunnell.
1430 Patrol returned.

1500 Third patrol of the day (again led by my Squad). Carried Taliban refreshments, I mean Humanitarian Aid (beans and rice) down to Babyol. Pulled security at the mosque while the P.L. bullshitted with the elder / known High-Value Target.

1600 Walked back up the 60° hill wishing we'd go to war with someplace flat. Ate a couple packs of tuna for dinner wishing we'd go to war with a country that had a Taco Bell.

1630 Doc Lee reminded everyone it's Mefloquine Monday (anti-malarial pill that gives a lot of guys bad dreams and possibly unborn children with extra appendages).

1722 Firebase attacked at dusk from Table Rock, Donga, and 1705.

1722 Everyone threw all their shit on and ran outside to take up gun positions and defend Phoenix.

1830 Phoenix defended. Cleaned my SAW.

1850 Turned my pants inside out, killed 3 sand fleas, started to watch a movie on my iPod, but fell asleep instead. Woke up multiple times drenched in sweat in our hot-as-hell hooch scratching at sand fleas.

2000 Platoon mandated Force-Pro session (meaning, fill sandbags and Hescos).

2200 Two more hours of guard again.

Tuesday (a.k.a. TIC Tuesday)

2400 Back to bed.

0600 Woke up, turned my pants inside out to kill sand fleas. Got 2 of them, 2 got away. Ate a protein bar, smoked a butt, began cooking up some poo stew.

0800 2nd Squad led patrol to Table Rock.

0844 Troops In Contact.

0844 Ran up the hill, jumped in the gun pit and started rocking the .50 cal.

0907 Went through 600 rounds, firefight ended, smoked a cigarette, began picking up brass.

0920 Returned to burning shit.

1000 Relieved from poo stew duties by Belgarde bearing good news: I got the guard.

1000 Guard again, smoked 1 butt every 30 minutes, worked on a letter to my wife, who doesn't get as many letters as she should.

1140 Relieved from guard early by Barnard to prepare for patrol.
1200 Patrol to Ali Abad again, led by 1st Squad, sang "Umbrella" by Rhianna, said my pre-patrol prayer before I walked out the rear gate.
1241 Setup in the same place in the same cemetery, sighed, wondered what the fuck we were trying to accomplish.
1259 Overcome with a hostile numbness.
1334 P.L.'s *shurra* with the village elder complete.
1337 Picked up, began running the Ali Abad 500. Didn't make it to the school house before the shit went down. Had a close one. Rounds only trailing me by a couple feet.
1343 We actually got air support. An A-10 came in and strafed the mountainsides.
1435 Returned to Phoenix.
1436 Took my sweat-soaked gear off, threw it down, immediately swarmed by about 93 billion flies.
1437 Cleaned my SAW, ate lunch (4 Army-provided Otis Spunkmeyer blueberry muffins), returned to more mellow task of burning poo.
1600 Guard again as 2nd Squad S.P.ed on a patrol to northern Babyol.
1641 Troops In Contact, both the patrol & the firebase taking copious amounts of lead.
1707 Firefight finished for now.
1756 Patrol made it back intact again.
1820 Firebase attacked at dusk.
1900 Mandatory Force Pro: everyone filled sandbags & Hescos.
2200 Racked out.

Wednesday

0400 I got the guard.
0600 Turned my pants inside out; killed 2 sand fleas, a third got away, fell asleep wondering when, if ever, sand fleas sleep.
0700 Went on patrol to Table Rock, got shot at.
0950 Patrol returned to Phoenix.
1000 Cleaned my SAW, ate.
1030 Maintenance Day for the heavy weapons. Cleaned the .50 cal.

1300 2nd Squad led patrol to clear the southern draws. No firefight.
1330 Finished burning shit while reading *Comanche Moon*.
1600 My Squad went on patrol to Donga. Firefight kicked off, second of the day.
1920 Walked in the wire hungry as hell. Made spicy tuna and rice for dinner. Running low on tuna and paprika. Belgarde still insisted paprika is a garnish and not a bona fide spice. Argument ensued.
1950 Cleaned my SAW, played a little Monster Hunter on my P.S.P., failed to kill the Tigrex again, fell asleep.
2200 Pulled 2 hours of guard listening to *The Otori Trilogy* audiobook.

Thursday

0000 Got 3 hours of sleep.
0300 Woke up for patrol.
0315 Smoked 2 Pines waiting for this patrol to S.P.
0330 Began slogging our way up Table Rock in the dark, intermittently wondering why the hell anyone would volunteer to join the Army.
0541 Patrol returned to Phoenix unscathed.
0542 Fell right the fuck asleep.
0800 Guard again.
1000 Wondered where the hell my relief was. Called down on the I-com to ask Headquarters that very question.
1017 Thomas finally decides to show up for his guard shift.
1023 Mino tried to convince me *Two And A Half Men* is a good show. I refused to watch (the ultimate insult to any movie or tv series: when a deployed Soldier would rather fill sandbags than see some stupid show).
1200 2nd Squad led patrol to northern Babyol (lucky bastards).
1400 Guard.
1428 Patrol returned.
1600 My guard shift ended just as the resupply trucks pulled up to the wire. Everyone formed a human chain and downloaded about 89 billion pounds of water, food and bullets. In addition, we got a number of care packages from anysoldier.com (best thing that ever happened to deployed soldiers).

1617 Twenty Soldiers standing in a line proved too juicy a target for the Taliban.
1636 Firefight complete. Downloading supplies resumed.
1728 Jingle trucks drove away finally empty.
1733 Raided the kitchen, confiscating a good half dozen each of Cokes and citrus-flavored Rip-Its (sodas went quickly).
1738 Sat on my cot brain dead, thinking this deployment will never end. Opened packages sent from my loving family and wife, who sent me food so I didn't have to eat M.R.E.s for 15 months straight.
1745 Tried to watch the worst $1 Hajj copy of *Transformers* imaginable. You could barely even make out what was happening.
1800 2nd Squad S.P.ed on a patrol to wherever-the-fuck.
1815 Movie deemed unwatchable. Fell asleep too lazy to turn pants inside out to kill sand fleas.
2000 Two hours of guard again, scratching at innumerable fresh sand flea bites while drinking a citrus Rip-It (courtesy of the resupply truck) and listening to more of *The Otori Trilogy* audiobook.
2200 Turned my pants inside out, killed every last sand flea, fell promptly asleep.

Friday

0200 Pulled 2 hours of guard, went back to sleep.
0600 Woke up, killed sand fleas, brushed my teeth, had a Coke and a smoke.
0630 Decided I might as well cook up some poo stew (since the shit barrel was already full again). Listened to David Grey on my iPod, as peaceful a morning as there ever was in the Korengal.
0800 Patrol to Ali Abad. P.L.'s meeting with village elder concluded with everything as unresolved as ever, they shake hands both knowing they are terrific enemies.
0930 Ran the Ali Abad 500, didn't take any contact.
1000 Two hours of guard again as soon as I walked in the wire. Finished that letter to my wife while doing said duty.
1200 Slept for a few hours.
1500 Patrolled to Donga, got in a firefight.
1800 Returned to Phoenix, and immediately went on guard again,

cleaned my SAW on guard, as everyone else was filling sandbags and Hescos.

2000 Got 6 uninterrupted hours of sleep (unless you count waking up and scratching at sand fleas).

Saturday

0200 Guard. Came to the conclusion I'd exceeded my recommended daily allowance for combat monotony, which was funny, 'cause it was only 2 in the mornin'.

0400 Sweated myself to sleep.

0700 Patrol to clear the Northern Draws. Took a couple potshots but no real firefight.

1000 R.T.B. (Return To Base).

1000 Chico hollered I got the guard as soon as I walk in the wire. FML. Sat on that crooked-ass log for another 2 hours staring blankly at Table Rock wondering whether or not I even cared if I lived through this godforsaken day.

1212 Relieved late by Roberts.

1215 Card game outside our hooch, took off my shit, sat on my bunk, yawned, passed out.

1500 Easy patrol through Babyol. Little village girl yelling, "Go, go, go!" in English. Got in a short firefight.

1637 R.T.B.

1700 Guard again. Prayer call in the background. But the good thing about this shift is the BUB was playing. Prophet said they got I-com chatter that the "wheat mill was broken." Wheat mill was probably code for a Dishka (Russian equivalent to our .50 cal), so that was good.

1733 As per Taliban's routine, Firebase attacked at dusk. Rocked the 240. Went through hundreds and hundreds of rounds.

1900 Slept. By this point though, I'd developed a really annoying habit. In my sleep, I guess I'd be dreaming of firefights, and I'd jump up awake, uncertain as to whether it was just a dream, or if in fact we were under attack. So I'd have to look around and see if everyone was throwing their shit on, or just chillin'. My Squad found this really funny. I did not.

2100 S.P.ed on a counter-I.E.D. patrol to the KOP. Once there, got to call my wife and parents, and also order a couple of much-needed items on the Internet.
2322 R.T.B. Slept.

Sunday

0200 Guard. Sat there looking through my generation 3 night vision wondering if Hajj was out there squinting through his beady little eyes at me. Listened to what I hoped was just dogs and monkeys scurrying about.
0400 Bedtime.
0615 Got woke up for patrol.
0630 S.P.ed for Donga again. Donga is a smoker of a walk.
0755 P.L. drank chai with Donga village elder. Butt-sniff and growling contest ensued.
0820 Ex-fill to Phoenix. No contact.
1007 R.T.B., ate, started burning shit once again. Drank hot water in the shade, listening to my iPod, thinking to myself we've all achieved soldierly perfection.
1200 Guard. Watched the choppers that were constantly flying in and out of the valley delivering supplies & personnel.
1400 Patrol to Table Rock with complimentary TIC.
1640 R.T.B.
1739 Obligatory firefight-at-dusk routine.
1806 Turned pants inside out, killed sand fleas, slept like the dead.
2200 Love those guard shifts.

Monday

0000 The madness started all over again.

The Road to Loot & Loved Ones

Korengal Valley, Afghanistan

Beleaguered but never without their sense of sarcasm, the Paratroopers gathered at 1945 local time in the dark, at the top of Firebase Phoenix. Embedded with the U.S. Army's 173rd Airborne, we were about to embark on a Counter I.E.D. patrol to the Korengal Outpost, or, the KOP, as it was called. In a tactical sense, that means you're patrolling the road, preventing the enemy from burying explosives in said route. But to the equipment-laden men of Battle Company, 3rd Platoon, who predominantly survived on a steady diet of nothing but water, bullets and bad cigarettes, this was more of a recreation run to use the phones and Internet their company base afforded them, and of which Firebase Phoenix was devoid.

"I'm running critically low on cigars," said Platoon medic Doc Lee. "This is no time to go black on stogies," the Humboldt County native declared. "Deployment is a good time to make bad life choices."

"All I wanna do is see some football scores," Texas resident Tim Hoff told us. "And maybe call my family. I wonder if A&M beat Texas..."

Many Soldiers donned empty assault packs (backpacks), with every intention of pillaging the KOP of its inequities. Most of the men had lost 20 or 30 pounds since the deployment began. Specialist Matt Roberts of Pennsylvania admitted, "I'm gonna raid the chow tent. I know those fuckers are sitting on all kinds of fat kid food. And who really needs fat kid food? This guy."

"I think they have too many sets of dumbbells up there. Probably gonna have to relieve them of a set or two," Sergeant Marcus Miller said.

Other Paratroopers had more practical things in mind. "Hey man, I just wanna talk to my wife, ya know?" said Sergeant Adam Rozenwald, also of Pennsylvania. "In a lot of ways, I think deployments are harder on the family than on the Soldier. Because they're back at home, with really no idea of what's happening to you, except what their vivid imaginations can conjure up. It feels pretty selfish to worry somebody to death like that."

"You know what else is selfish? The KOP having too many dumbbells," said Sergeant Miller.

The Platoon Leader, Lieutenant Steve Gillespie of Uranus, gave his patrol brief and then there was the inevitable struggle of the point man to unlatch the razor wire from the picket that served as Firebase Phoenix's front gate. Afterwards, it was a simple matter of walking in a staggered column (one man on the left side of the road, the next on the right about 15 meters behind the first, and so on), down the winding, third-world dirt road, with nothing but the green glow of night vision to go by, which offered no depth perception whatsoever. Every now and then a Soldier would fall prey to the "moondust," a fine powdery dirt which had a knack for concealing large rocks, potholes, and anything else that could cause one to trip.

It was only about a half hour walk, and not overly strenuous, even for this reporter. The point man, Sergeant Jason Slomiak, would put his infrared laser on the "flood" setting and use it to look into the draws as we advanced, even though the Taliban were not known for being nocturnal. "I have no idea why they never try to ambush one of these C.I.E.D. patrols," he later told us. "Shit would be so easy for them. It hasn't ever happened, but that doesn't keep you from going batshit crazy worrying about it."

Mino

Private First Class Richard Lindley, or Mino, joined the Army straight out of high school. I mean, who wouldn't wanna trade the tropical islands of Hawaii to be with a bunch of sweaty guys with guns in austere environments? Anyway. Mino was kind of goofy. Goofy in a good way. He was definitely different and hilarious. He would say the most random but (in a way) encapsulating things, delivered with flawless timing. His helmet was inevitably on crooked—cocked to one side or the other. And he never lost that weird Hawaiian accent. These things just added to his character.

Back in the rear, Mino was under the tutelage of 3rd Squad. Namely, Staff Sergeant Shelton and Sergeant McDonough (two of the best and therefore the most difficult leaders a guy could have). They continually addressed him as a "mouth-breather," which normally has negative connotations in the Army. But then they'd add, "He's a mouth-breather, but he's good." And hey, if you can win those two guys over, you gotta be doin' something right.

Mino was a loyal (in the best sense of the word), lovable, offbeat, good-hearted kid. And a guileless, genuine friend. (Qualities which plagued him when it came to women.) He was a good Paratrooper besides. And though you could argue, oh this guy's a badass or this guy's been to sniper school or this guy's Ranger tabbed—when it came down to living in confined quarters, constant patrols and details—there aren't too many guys you'd rather be deployed with than Mino. You couldn't help but love the guy and be happy he was there.

One September Night

The day had been relatively uneventful. Dusk had come and gone without the traditional firefight the Taliban are so fond of kicking off almost every time the sun sets in the Korengal Valley. Everyone in 1st Squad all laid in their bunks or cots, as comfortable as circumstances permitted, watching movies, listening to music, playing video games on their P.S.P.s, a couple already asleep.

"Hey can I charge my iPod on your computer?" Sergeant Miller asked Roberts. He walked across the room and began searching for the USB port in the dark. When all of the sudden, "BOOM! BOOM! Pa-pa-pow-pow-pow!" Phoenix was under heavy attack. We were taking an unprecedented volume of fire. Explosions and rounds were rocking our hooch, and every hooch on the firebase. So much so, you could feel the concussions sucking the air out of your eardrums. "Ratta-tat-tat-tat! KA-BOOOOM!"

"Everyone, get down!" Sergeant Miller yelled. We all hit the floor, laying as flat as possible. R.P.G.s were blowing up everywhere. The explosions were shaking the hooch, and dust rained down out of the ceiling. We weren't just taking fire from the east side of the valley, those fuckers were on the west side too. We were getting it from every direction. As we laid prostrate, the severity of the situation sank quickly in, and we all began scrambling to get our gear; none of us even had so much as our boots on. We had been caught totally unprepared for the onslaught we were now receiving. Our hearts raced as we rushed boots, body armor, and helmets on. Most of us had failed to mount our night vision goggles, the way every good Soldier is supposed to do before dusk. The entire process felt like it took forever. Sergeant Miller was the first out the hooch door, weapon in hand.

Finally the whole Squad was gathered, crouched down on the

covered porch. The whole world seemed to be exploding. The word daunting comes to mind. I'd honestly never seen so much concentrated gunfire and explosions, ever. It was to date the most intense bombardment we'd received. We looked up the walkway leading to Headquarters and up top where all the heavy weapons were, and we could see all the rounds impacting the only route we had to get out and up to good fighting positions. It was one of those moments (and we had many), where you knew what you had to do, and what you had to do involved risking your life with some really bad odds. In this case, it meant running through that wall of bullets and almost certain death.

Sergeant Miller screamed something then ran up the steep incline. He made it. And was now somewhere in the A.N.A. compound returning fire. My heart was pounding. I took a deep breath, and charged up the hill.

Machinegun fire ripped the night sky alight.

Night Attack Aftermath

In the morning light, our firebase looked like someone had started a fire in a munitions dump. We already had our share of pockmarks from our daily duels with the Taliban, so to go outside and actually notice new damage was pretty remarkable. It looked like a cadaver turned inside out. Pieces of I-don't-even-know-what were everywhere. Bullet holes dissected everything. Phoenix would've made someone a nice colander. Miraculously, none of us even got hit. By all rights we should've had 3 dead and a half dozen wounded. We were inexplicably alive and well.

"Too bad winter's comin'," Mino thought aloud. "We've got a lotta new ventilation in our hooch. Should be cooler at night. Oh well, we do have another summer here."

"This would be a good place to film a war movie," Skaines said.

"You're an idiot," said Sergeant Miller.

The E.T.T. hooch was probably hit hardest. Marine Corporal Parrish and Navy Corpsman Doc Cannon, who comprised our E.T.T., almost glowed with pride as they gave us a tour of what was left of their crib. They even had bullet holes in their weapons.

"We should allocate some Platoon funds towards a force field," suggested Campbell. "Or maybe some of those armored suits like they use in *Starship Troopers*. The book, not the movie," he added. "The movie has nothing to do with the book."

Sergeant Hunt came down to our hooch to check on us and assess the damage. "You guys alright in here?"

"Hooah, Sern't," everyone said.

"Okay listen, I know it's a pain in the ass, but we're gonna have to start implementing stand-to at 1700 every night." (Stand-to means everybody puts on their gear, goes outside and waits for a fight.) "We got really lucky last night. But we can't let them catch us like that again."

Doc Lee began gathering up a lot of the detritus, and nailed it to the tree outside our hooch. "I dub thee, The Shrapnel Tree," he proclaimed with a great sense of satisfaction.

On our next counter-I.E.D. patrol to the KOP just a couple days later, Sergeant Slo was talking to Taylor, one of the Mortarmen. "Did you see that shit?" Slo asked.

"Yeah! Looked like the goddamned 4th of July! That was fucking awesome!"

"Well it wasn't awesome if you were there, motherfucker."

Phones & Internet at First

When we first got to the Korengal, the phones and Internet at the KOP were crap. There were 2 phones and 2 computers for the entire Company. And I'd say at any given time you probably had 60 or so guys on the KOP. Thus, the wait just to get on a phone or computer was lengthy to say the least.

The phones had a 5 to 10 second delay on them so you were always talking over your loved ones, and the connection was terrible to begin with. A regular phone conversation went a little somethin' like this.

"Hello?"
"Hello?"
"Are you there?"
"Hello?"
"Hey baby, how are you? I just got a little downtime and..."
"Where are you at? It's so good to hear your voice. I was just thinking about..."
"Oh we're at the KOP on re-fit, I've got..."
"...you. I miss you. How is it going over..."
"...about a week here, so I should be able to call you every..."
"...there? Are you okay? Do you..."
"...day. Well I mean, hopefully. Anyway, what're you..."
"...need anything? What?"
"What? No, everything's fine. We're doin'..."
"What?"
"...good. How're you doin?'"
"Huh? I couldn't hear you."
"I said I'm good," and then like a bunch of mortars would start goin' off. "Hello? Are you there?"
"Hello? Yeah I, what's that noise? I hear..."

"Oh that's just a..."

"like explosions."

"training thing, babe. So what're you doing today?"

And then the phone would go dead. Awesome. It was so good to be able to reconnect with the ones you love, ya know.

The Internet was just as deplorable. The pages loaded at the speed of ludicrous. Often it'd take you half an hour just to order one thing. Then when you'd get to the checkout page and enter your credit card information and click proceed, you'd get an Internet Explorer error page. And with 6 or 10 other guys tapping their feet, clearing their throats and looking very impatient, you'd just say fuck it and leave all pissed off.

But we were in a perpetual state of improving things. Sometimes it seemed like slow going, but then one day you'd look around and say, "Wow. We've done a lot of work." I remember in a speech our Battalion Commander, Lieutenant Colonel Ostlund, once gave us, he said something to the extent of how, 10th Mountain essentially just handed us a bunch of razor wire. Which we all found funny, but I don't have any doubt that those dudes busted their asses. Thing is, when you're starting from scratch and people are constantly trying to kill you, creature comforts are a pretty low priority.

By early winter we'd have a new M.W.R. (Morale Welfare and Recreation center, but we mostly just called it the M-Dub) to replace the shanty tent the old M-Dub was in. The new M-Dub was the old TOC, which meant it was made of plywood, had an actual door to keep the flies out, and more importantly, climate control. They flew some computer geek out to hook up 6 almost crystal clear phone lines so you could actually have a real conversation, and 6 fairly fast Internet lines plus 3 you could hook your own computer up to. It was a godsend.

Sergeants Shelton & Blaskowski and Why We Don't Need Reporters In The Valley

Most of us were a complete joke compared to Staff Sergeant Shelton. You couldn't help but feel inadequate as a Soldier in his presence. The man could just look at you in silence and make you feel unworthy to wear the uniform. He was Ranger tabbed of course and God I can't even remember what all schools he'd been to. He was 3rd Squad's Squad Leader, and while I never envied the constant smokings they received back in Italy, I was always jealous of how Sergeant Shelton was constantly teaching them things. He demanded excellence. And he'd have no part of incompetence or excuses or anyone who was any less than 100% devoted to learning his craft. For all intents and purposes, the man was a badass.

On September 27, 2007, 1st Platoon's Platoon Sergeant, Sergeant First Class Blaskowski, was at the KOP waiting for a bird to take him home for mid-tour leave. Then some reporters showed up wanting to take a look at Firebase Vegas. I'm sure he would've rather not done it, but Sergeant Blaskowski volunteered to escort them back to Vegas. As he was showing them around, a firefight broke out, and Sergeant Blaskowski was shot and killed.

We got word of it down at Phoenix while we were all outside smokin' and jokin'. Everyone got real quiet. The fact that the guy was going on mid-tour leave and shouldn't've even been at Vegas just made it even more tragic.

Sergeant Miller broke the silence, "Bye-bye, Sergeant Shelton." Meaning, Company would probably take him from us to be 1st Platoon's new Platoon Daddy. Which they did.

Anatomy of a Platoon

An Infantry Platoon is composed of four Squads. Of those Squads, three of them are called Line Squads. Now ideally, a Line Squad has 9 soldiers. (Ours never had more than 7. See *Economy Of Force*.) In this ideal Squad you have the Squad Leader (a Staff Sergeant), and 2 fireteams. A fireteam consists of the Team Leader (a buck Sergeant (E-5) who cares the basic M-4; a shortened version of the Vietnam-era M-16), the Grenadier (a Private or Specialist who carries an M-4 but with a grenade launcher on the bottom of it), the SAW gunner (in the 173rd the senior Specialist has the dubious chore of lugging the "light" machine gun), and the mythical Rifleman (who would in theory, were a unit at full combat strength, just carry an M-4; this position is typically held by the lowest ranking and / or most incompetent man). So under optimal conditions, your Line Squads would account for 27 soldiers though the reality of it is 21 or fewer.

Weapons Squad is a whole other animal. Their sole purpose in existence is to carry a machine gun dubbed the M240 Bravo. As opposed to all the weapons Line Squads carry, which fire the meager 5.56 mm round (.223 to all you civilians), the M240 Bravo sports a 7.62 mm (.308) projectile. (I'll get into five-five-six bashing at some later point.) Like the Line, Weapons Squad has two teams, each with their own machine gun. And like the Line, they never had four guys per team the way Army doctrine states. So you'd in actuality have a Team Leader, a Gunner, and an Assistant Gunner who would also have to fill the role of Ammo Bearer (which if he had a good Team Leader, hopefully the T.L. would carry some of the rounds as well, because the primary purpose of the team is to carry enough ammo for the 240 which weighs significantly more than the five-five-six rounds.) These two teams of three with their Squad Leader (the senior-most Staff Sergeant in the Platoon) made for an additional seven.

There was also your Headquarters element. Two medics per Platoon and two F.O.s. Also, you had to pick someone from the Platoon to serve as the R.T.O., or as I commonly think of them, the Radio Geek. Then there was the true leadership. The Platoon Sergeant (the highest ranking N.C.O. in the Platoon—a Sergeant First Class). And last and least, the P.L., or Platoon Leader (some cherry Lieutenant who had about as much clue as to what he was doing as a brand new Private, but who quizzically was in charge of everyone else who was vastly more experienced / blessed with common sense.) In Afghanistan, we also normally had 2 E.T.T.s to take care of the A.N.A. (Afghan National Army).

Thus, if no one was on leave or injured, a Platoon had about 35 members. Minus the Squad that was on the KOP manning the O.P. meant 28, and with guys on leave you could probably muster 24 on your firebase under the best of conditions. Now when you think about Brigade dictating you had to have 20 Americans to go out on patrol, that didn't leave too much manpower on the ole firebase.

To Christen Or Not To Christen

We were S.P.ing on another counter-I.E.D. patrol to the KOP that night. I humped my happy butt up the hill, sat down winded as always, and lit up a cigarette. All the guys were discussing the mad push to rename our firebases that was taking place.

"I can see them renaming Atlanta after Doc Restrepo," said Eddie. "I mean, that was their guy. And the place is brand new, ya know. But why the hell do we have to call Phoenix Firebase Vimoto now?"

Sergeant Miller said, "It's because Major Beck wants to kiss up to Sern't Major Vimoto, that's why." Major Beck was our Battalion X.O.

"Yeah, but Phoenix just sounds cooler than Vimoto," Eddie said.

"Plus it's just hard to change since we've been calling it Phoenix for so long," Paulson added. "Why isn't 1st Platoon renaming Vegas after Sergeant Blaskowski?"

"I got chewed out on the radio last night for saying 'Battle Base, this is Phoenix.' Captain Kearney got on the radio and was all like, it's not Phoenix anymore! It's Vimoto dammit!" Briggs said. "He told me next person that calls it Phoenix on the radio is gonna burn shit at the KOP for a week."

"Don't threaten us with a good time," Roberts laughed. "No patrols, hot food, showers, Internet and phones. Hell I'll burn shit for the rest of the deployment."

"Yeah. Nothing against Sergeant Major Vimoto, or Private Vimoto, but Phoenix is just such a great metaphor for this place," Sergeant Rose added.

No one really said it; there was never any formal agreement made, but we collectively made a tacit pact that when we were on the radio, we'd refer to our home away from home as Vimoto since we had no other choice. But otherwise we continued to call it Firebase Phoenix for the rest of the deployment.

I took a drag of my cigarette and exhaled, "All I know is, if I die, and whoever decides to name some shitty-ass Firebase or O.P. after me, I'm gonna come back from the dead and haunt the hell outta alla yall."

Ambush in Ali Abad

October 2, 2007

    There was this pathway called the Donga Trail that ran high up on the Talazar (this enormous mountain to our east on the other side of the river). As high up as this trail was, we couldn't really see it from Phoenix, and we speculated that the enemy was using it as a movement corridor to get weapons and ammunition to the Taliban in the south. So the idea was, under the cover of darkness, we'd hike as high as we could up the Donga spur, so high the enemy wouldn't suspect we were there (as we'd never been there before), set in where we had decent cover and good eyes on the trail, and just watch it for 24 hours.

    Best case scenario, we'd catch a mule train of party favors bound for the enemy. Or, we'd just sit up there all day and all night and nothing would happen. Or, what was more likely, the Taliban would discover our position, and we'd have to fight our way back to Phoenix, which was much too far away for comfort. This was why, instead of the normal 20-man patrol, we had 25, which would leave Phoenix with minimal manning: just a fireteam to pull guard, Sern't Hunt, and the 2 E.T.T.s and 15 A.N.A. (as we had zero confidence in the A.N.A. being able to sit still for 24 hours).

    Two and a half hours before first light, we gathered for this very unpopular patrol. The enemy knew the terrain like nobody's business, and everyone's gut told them that no matter how motionless and disciplined we were, the Taliban would discover our whereabouts. I mean, hell we had to go through the village of Donga, so there was no way we wouldn't be heard. Everyone expected this to turn into a hellstorm by noon—mid afternoon at the latest. And if we took any wounded... we were in for a really long day.

    Still we assembled, smoked cigarettes in the dark, made fun of our predicament. "So," Belgarde began, "ya know what I wanna do today? I wanna climb almost to the top of the goddamn Talazar and hangout for about 24 hours. I'm hopin' they have a movie theater up there."

I nodded, "And, a taco stand. We don't ever have tacos around here. Where the hell are all the tacos?"

"You're not getting any tacos," said Belgarde.

"If I don't get any tacos, I'm probably gonna have to kill you," I told him. "I might even have to kill your mom."

He shook his head, "My mom'd take you out so fast it wouldn't even be funny. That bitch is lethal."

"Fuck your mom."

"Fuck your face."

Some guys sat in silence. As was my custom, I sang some hip hop song, which to me took the tension away, and which to others annoyed the living hell out of them. It went on like that till the P.L. started his patrol brief (signaling serious business) and finally the order of movement. "Three-One followed by Headquarters, Weapons and Three-Three Alpha." Then out the back gate, by the green glow of night vision, we descended towards the riverbed.

The trail running through Donga was no-joke steep. Hell, you got winded enough just getting to Donga. But once you were actually at the base of the village, it went straight up. However, knowing we had to make it as far as we possibly could before daybreak, we pushed hard. The SAW gunners and the gunteam were suckin'. It was 600 meters just to the top of the spur. From there it didn't get much better. We still had to move up probably another half a klick, and the sky was growing lighter.

Finally, the patrol reached an area that Lieutenant Gillespie found suitable, where we set in. Some of us scrambled down the sheer faces of the sides of the spur, found an alright spot and, after much labor, finally sat down. And just as we started to get comfortable, we were told to pickup and move higher. We set in again. Then were told to move again. And this went on at least twice more. Each time, moving further and further up, till we were probably 300 meters from the top of the Talazar. And the Talazar is a giant mountain.

In order to get a good perimeter on a spur going, half the patrol was set up on the north side of the spur, which was the direction the supposed mule train would come from. The other half of the patrol was dug in to the south side of the spur, which, in all likelihood, was the direction the bullets from the Taliban attack would come from. The guys on the north side thought things could be worse, while the guys on the south side thought this was some mo' bullshit.

"I have a question," I said. "Does anybody really think they're moving weapons during daylight hours? I mean, if I was movin' weapons I'd be doin' it at night."

"Yeah, so?" Sergeant Miller asked.

"Well the point is, if they're probably doin' this shit at night, why don't we in-fill just after dark, and ex-fill right before dusk? What're we sittin' up here all goddamned day for?"

"Well, to get ambushed of course," he replied.

"Makes total sense," I said and nodded.

"It's like a field trip. You don't like field trips, Shadix?"

"Yeah, well I ain't never been shot at on no field trip before."

"Well that's why you joined the Army, right? Go new places, do new things?"

The morning was, so far, uneventful. A couple kids and some old men south bound on the trail, goats in tow, was all we had seen. And the locals hadn't spotted our patrol. The day was early to be sure, and if an attack came, it would most likely come in the afternoon or just before dark. Still, everyone was feeling a little more confident that, just maybe, no one knew where we were.

I mean we were silly high up on that spur. There was no practical reason for anyone to be up there. We did smoke, or dip, but otherwise we hardly moved. To be honest, joe didn't give a fuck about a mule train. Sure, if one came along we'd be happy to put firing pin to primer. But all joe really cared about was making it back home alive. Bring all the mule trains of ammo into the valley you want; it'd still be safer to fight it out at Phoenix than to sit up there exposed on that spur so far away from the firebase.

I had no clue what was about to happen, but some bullshit was goin' down. Apparently, O.P. Restrepo had spotted some A.C.M. (Anti-Coalition Militia (a.k.a. Taliban)) on the northeast side of Ali Abad. These guys were carrying a P.K.M., and had decided to set it down and leave. Now, why Restrepo didn't light the dudes up, I have no idea. Our R.O.E. (Rules Of Engagement) state if you P.I.D. (Positively Identify) someone with a weapon, you can open fire.

So here was this P.K.M. in Ali Abad. That doesn't seem like a big deal to me. A P.K.M. is an old Russian light machine gun, highly favored by the Taliban. I don't doubt that there was a P.K.M. in Ali Abad. I don't doubt if you combed through every house, in any village in this valley, you'd find twenty of the goddamned things. The point being, it was a common weapon so what's the big deal? Well, to Kaptain Korengal, everything was a big goddamned deal. Battle-6 called down to Phoenix, and ordered a patrol be sent down to Ali Abad to retrieve the gun.

I know for a fact Sern't Hunt didn't like the idea. This was the most obvious ambush ever conceived in the history of combat. "We're gonna leave our gun in plain sight of Restrepo for no good reason?" Yeah right. And with 25 of us up on the Donga spur, and Second Squad manning the O.P. at the KOP, all Sern't Hunt had at his disposal was the 2 E.T.T. guys, the A.N.A., and half of 3rd Squad. He decided to leave 3rd Squad's fireteam back at the firebase to man the weapons, and S.P.ed with the Corporal Parish, Doc Cannon, and about 15 Afghan Army dudes.

Captain Kearney also spun up our mounted Platoon from Destined Company. They mobilized 4 Humvees and started hauling balls down to Ali Abad. About half an hour passed.

I wasn't aware any of this was going on. An Infantryman—particularly a joe—knows little but what's happening right in front of him. Meanwhile, the ever-changing battlefield unfolds. Life-threatening decisions are made by unseen people, and the deeds that must be done are performed by those like us who work with horse blinders on, and know next to nothing outside our tiny realm of unexplained orders, immeasurable toil and persistent danger. Omniscience is not in an Infantryman's job description.

So when the gunfire erupted from the southwest, I assumed we'd been compromised and the shooting was meant for us. *Fuck!* My heart sped up and I scanned the mountainside as hard as I could with my monocular, my right hand ready to charge the SAW and engage. I was one of the lucky guys on the northern side of the spur. It was unlikely I'd take fire or need to shoot back. Still, Sergeant Miller preached 360° security so much, he'd ingrained it in to me. Even if the fight's coming from the other direction, someone needed to play weak-side. But the thing was, the southern side wasn't receiving any direct fire either.

We were reluctant to shoot; everyone knew damned well if we did, every Hajj in the valley would know right where we were. Then without warning, I heard a SAW open up behind me. Apparently Paulson had P.I.D.ed someone with a weapon in Ali Abad. I grinded my teeth—we were fucked. But what I didn't know was what had transpired down in everyone's favorite village, Ali Abad, from which, came a cacophony of small arms fire and R.P.G.s.

Sergeant Miller hurried down to my location and hollered, "Shadix! Get ready to pickup!"

I was like, "What?! Where we goin'?!"

"Just get the fuck ready!" was all he said. I could hear a lot of frantic jabbering on his radio but I couldn't make any of it out. "What's goin' on, Sern't?!"

"Somebody's dead," he said. Anytime you hear those words, your mind starts reeling.

"From our Platoon?" I asked. He nodded. Since most of us were up on the Talazar, there were only so many people it could be: someone from Three-Three, the E.T.T., or Sern't Hunt.

"Let's move!" Sern't Miller yelled. I slung my SAW wondering what in the fuck we were about to do, but knowing without a doubt it was not gonna be something good.

We were maybe 300 meters from the top of the Talazar. And we were about to run, to Ali Abad. I'd say it was 500 meters to Donga, another 500 to the river bed, then probably 500 more meters from there to the actual village... almost a mile. With full combat loads. We all started sprinting down the spur. Even heading down hill, it didn't take long to get winded.

We were ready to get lit up at any time. Expecting it. There were a lot of long, coverless stretches. We could hear the heavy weapons at Phoenix blasting away. There was still more fire taking place in Ali Abad. When we got down to Donga, my Squad set in behind a couple of houses to provide overwatch, while the rest of the patrol proceeded down to the river. We weren't there long, but I was thankful for the opportunity to catch my breath.

No one had shot at us yet, but the sounds of gunfire filled the air. I asked Sergeant Miller again who was dead, but he wouldn't tell me.

He was like that, and it frustrated us to no end. Information to him wasn't something to be disseminated to the troops—it was some sort of secret. Something the rest of us weren't privy to. Which really sucks when you know someone's dead. 'Cause all you can think about is, *Who?* "Alright let's go!" he yelled.

We winded our way down through the village and came to the corn terraces on the east side of the river (which had already been harvested and were now bare, leaving us completely exposed). It took us a little time to find our way down. Finally, V. popped out of nowhere, and was like, "Hey come down this way." (Some of the corn terraces are 10 feet tall, so it's kinda important to find the shorter ones.) At last we came to the riverbed. The dreaded riverbed, where we all knew, if we were gonna take fire, this'd be the perfect place. Then all of a sudden, two Apaches came flying straight down the river, guns ablaze.

"Move!" yelled Sergeant Miller. "We gotta get across that river while those Apaches are still covering us!" We sprinted across the river in record time. The Apaches' guns were goin' crazy and intermittently letting loose their Hellfire rockets on 1705.

Once on the other side, things didn't get any easier for us. We were already smoked and now we had to haulass uphill. There was a narrow irrigation waterway that ran through the terraces, which would save us the time consuming endeavor of having to climb up each individual terrace, but even this was not what you could consider to be an easy way up. We all knew we had to get up to Ali Abad as fast as possible—judging by the immense gun battle goin' on up there, they needed our help.

Exhausted as we were, we went as fast as we could up the irrigation way. Slo began to fall out, and every step I took turned my legs to jello. At some point along our ascent, the majority of the gunfire stopped. We finally reached the schoolhouse and ran our butts into Ali Abad. I beat feet till I got to my favorite setup spot—a small rock-lined burial mound to the right of the pump house, facing 1705. Whatever had happened, it looked like we'd missed it.

What did transpire and what we'd find out later, was this: Destined had hooked-up with Sern't Hunt, Corporal Parish, Doc Cannon and the A.N.A. when they got to Ali Abad. The majority of the A.N.A. refused to go over to where the P.K.M. was. So, the willing A.N.A., Corporal Parish, Doc Cannon and some guys from

Destined (Torres, Farwell, Beechnaw, Doc McCray and their P.L.) had gone down to get the P.K.M. All of them with but one thing on their mind: this is a textbook ambush. It's not even textbook, because it's so damned obvious, nobody would ever fall for it. Except for maybe Captain Kearney who called the shots back in his air-conditioned office. I mean if he wanted the goddamned machine gun so bad, why didn't he come out himself and get it?

Well, guess what? It was an ambush. Our guys walked over there, and just got lit up. They simultaneously took fire from just up the hill above the Ali Abad graveyard, 1705, Dar Bart, and a house to the southeast in Lui Kalay. Doc Cannon was killed, Corporal Parish got shot in the side and in the face just below his eye. According to what I was told, the A.N.A. all huddled together behind a 2-foot rock wall and didn't fire a shot, and Destined's P.L. was hiding as well and also didn't fire his weapon. In fact, his guys were so pissed at him following this firefight, he didn't want to sleep in their hooch anymore for fear his own Soldiers would kill him as he slept. (He was subsequently fired and relieved.) The Destined guys had hell getting Doc Cannon into the Humvee. Doc Cannon was a big boy from Lubbock, Texas. And he was all muscle too. I guarantee he weighed no less than 220 without his gear on. And I know those aid bags weigh 50 pounds. Still, Torres, Farwell, Beechnaw and Doc McCray managed to drag his body back to the Humvees and after a lot of struggle, got him into the truck. With Corporal Parish in critical condition, the Humvees had to break contact and get back to the KOP as quickly as possible for medevac.

Meanwhile, by the time we reached Ali Abad, we were the only ones there, save the Apaches who had ceased firing at that point. A 500-pound bomb had been dropped on the house in the adjacent village of Lui Kalay. It came down from the radio that there were possible enemy headed down the staircase to the riverbed. Three-Three Alpha drew the lucky straw that got to go check that out. As he walked by I was like, "Paulson! What the fuck, dude? Yall're goin' down there with just three guys?!"

He just gave me this look like, *No shit and I wish it wasn't me.*

I had this bad feeling about them goin' down there, but they came back in about 10 minutes unscathed.

Our patrol held fast for at least another hour, hour and a half. I just had this really shitty, sickening feeling the whole time. I felt so horrible for Doc Cannon and prayed to God Corporal Parish would live. But the whole thing was really unsettling. I felt completely powerless. We were powerless to alter our jackass C.O.'s retarded decision, and from where we were (up on the Talazar), we were powerless to get to where we needed to be in time to save Doc Cannon. I concede the other guys in 3rd Platoon knew Corporal Parish and Doc Cannon a lot better than I did; me having been on leave for the first month that they were attached to us. But they were still part of our Platoon.

Corporal Parish survived but never returned to the valley. I think he might've lost his eye (that's just what I heard). Doc Cannon was unmistakably dead. No matter the circumstances, having failed them was a blow to all of 3rd Platoon. That we could exert such effort and still fail to save a friend's life was downright unjust. This was supposed to be the part of the movie where the Good Guys came in and saved their friends with no time to spare.

But this was no movie.

Sergeant Hunt's Favorite Deployment Pastime

Anytime Phoenix took contact, which was practically every day, Sergeant Hunt could be seen running up and down the firebase, shooting every A.T.4 he could find. An A.T.4 is what the layperson would consider to be a bazooka. It's a tubular, one-shot weapon that fires an 84mm rocket. It was actually designed for Infantrymen to be able to take out tanks. (The A.T. is for anti-tank.) But, since Hajj didn't have no tanks, we just shot the shit out of the mountains with them. It wasn't a reusable weapon. You shot it once and then threw the tube away. Phoenix was littered with these things, and there was absolutely nothing wrong with anyone who felt like it, picking one up in a firefight, and launching it towards our foes. We didn't really think they were all that effective, but they sure were fun to shoot.

The key to firing an A.T.4 (or its cousin, the SMAW-D), is to make sure you have a very large, clear area behind you, as the back-blast on these weapons is notable. Once early on in the deployment, Sergeant Slo decided he'd fire an A.T.4 in the narrow corridor that ran down towards Weapons Squad's hooch. It rung Slo's bell pretty good and I don't know that he ever shot off another A.T.4 after that.

Sergeant Hunt on the other hand, had no such qualms. The A.T.4 was his weapon of choice. Seeing one's Platoon Sergeant running with frantic purpose from one firing position to another and watching the enormous back-blast while rockets shoot out into the air and explode across the valley, bringing a gigantic shit-eating grin to Sergeant Hunt's face, was very much a source of inspiration to us all.

Lightning Never Strikes Twice... Does it?

The destitution that was our living conditions when we first arrived in the Korengal had finally been duly noted by higher. It was thus that a rep from K.B.R. arrived at the KOP in order to ascertain the exact degree of our depravity, and what said global engineering, construction and wartime profiteering services could charge our beloved country for. However, this particular man's first duty, as the-tip-of-the-civilian-contractor's-spear, was to evaluate the overall security of the KOP so that his brethren could swarm in and build a lot of stuff for us at the going exorbitant rate.

You, the American taxpayer might feel different, but to 120 sand flea-infested grunts who hadn't had a proper shower in a month, living in canvas tents with third-world telephones and Internet and nothing but patrols and firefights to keep them occupied, this seemed like money well-spent.

So our brand new buddy from K.B.R. got off the bird, and they put him in our (3rd Platoon's) tent, since none of us were there, and 'cause it was later in the day and so he may as well just start tomorrow and all.

Well the thing was, there's this little phenomenon which took place at dusk in the Korengal Valley. It was called, "Attack of the Taliban." Not real sure where this particular band of rebels was firing from, but it had to be up high somewhere in the vicinity of O.P. One.

They shot volley after volley down on the KOP. One particular barrage, went right through the tent we put our K.B.R. rep in, and a round pierced his leg. They had to medevac him out. I don't know what K.B.R.'s final assessment of security at the KOP was, but it suffices to say that K.B.R. did not attempt a follow-up during our deployment. The only evidence of K.B.R. ever being in the valley was the giant bloodstain on our tent's plywood floor.

If we happened to be doing a Con-Op that S.P.ed from the KOP, that would require at least two-thirds of the Platoon to be there. Our tent wasn't that large, so every square inch of space would be occupied by somebody. Sergeants slept on the bunks, and joes got the floor. So someone had to sleep on the bloodstain.

This led to an unyielding debate for us: was it bad juju to sleep where the guy got shot, or was that the best place to sleep (reason being, what are the odds of a bullet hitting the exact same spot twice).

So, who's sleeping on the bloodstain?

The Unsung

If I had to name (and I do) three groups on our little deployment that did not get enough credit whatsoever, it would be these: the cooks, Destined Company, and the Mortars. For the Mortarmen's part, they were the only support we could without a doubt count on while out on patrol.

We always knew that when we took contact, the mortars would be up and bangin' in just a couple or three minutes. And while you could debate to death how many fools they actually waxed, the mortar fire unquestionably helped end TICs and thus saved some of our lives.

Air support was always a crap shoot. Sometimes you'd get it, most of the time you wouldn't. But our mortars would never fail us. Nor would they get any credit. I never once thought I should've walked up to one of them and said, "Hey man, I really appreciate everything yall do for us. A lotta times yall save our asses." So, I guess I'm doin' it now.

Another couple of individuals I'd like to recognize is our cooks. Yeah, we were only on the KOP every so often, but when we were, having a hot meal to eat was the definitive shit. When you been eating nothing but the same ole crap for months at a time, just having something different, hot and tasty was a godsend. But not only that, our cooks were real characters. Namely, Bui and Lackley. Those guys were morale personified. You could always depend on them to bring you up a little bit. They were good people. And though they weren't Infantry, both of them would volunteer to go out on mounted patrols and get behind a .50 cal, just to go out and do it, ya know? Just to be part of the pack.

We had a Platoon from Destined Company attached to us whose sole mission it was to conduct all of our mounted operations (mounted meaning, in a Humvee). They had the unenviable job of driving those ragged-out trucks up and down the KOP road and in our (3rd Platoon's) case, sometimes they would convoy down after our patrol began, in order to cover us as we ex-filled. They knew that what they were doing was simply giving the enemy more targets to shoot at. That way, other than us, the Taliban had four trucks to try to eliminate. They did this for us day after day, and never once did I hear any of them complain that doing so was bullshit. They were like hardcore, well-armed angels, trying to look over us, and they deserve a lot of props.

Soldiers On The Front Getting Finger Fucked

Kunar Province, Afghanistan

    Paratroopers in the 173rd Airborne Brigade Combat Team report that the Army is screwing them out of a finger. The entire debacle came to light when a member of Battle Company's 2nd Platoon lost a hand in an R.P.G. attack. Sources close to the wounded Soldier say he was given $200,000 in compensation for his missing meathook. However, around this same time it was also revealed that the Army reportedly pays 50 grand per finger.

    "I ain't no goddamned M.I.T. grad or nothing," proclaimed one anonymous grunt, "but I'm pretty sure most of us got five fingers on each hand. And that five fingers times fifty thousand is $250,000. So why do we only get 200 for a whole hand? And one of those fingers is an opposable digit for cryin'-out-fuckin'-loud."

    In a war with no prostitutes, a thumb is a G.I.'s lover and best friend. Imagining the consequences of being deployed without their thumb, most Soldiers spat, talked shit, or smoked in solace. All concurred they'd rather have their thumbs than 50 large, and that no way should a pinkie finger be worth as much as a thumb.

    Sergeant Tyrell Edwards was quoted as saying, "It's egregious. What's the Army doin'? Buyin' in bulk?"

    Army representatives at Walter Reed Hospital refused to comment on the compensation scale.

    When asked exactly which finger they thought they were getting screwed out of, the deployed Soldiers unanimously agreed, it was the middle one.

My Debut in the Italian Vanity Fair

It wasn't what you would call good news. Our mission was to patrol up through northern Babyol and linkup with a couple of Italian reporters, who were being escorted down there by some element from the KOP. There was a certain dichotomy to having reporters in the valley: 1) I think most of us felt it was good for this insane place to get some publicity, since it was apparent no one even knew there was still a war in Afghanistan, let alone one as savage as the one we were fighting. But, 2) we'd been exposed to reporters enough to know their very presence, coupled with the megalomaniacal mind of Captain Kearney, meant he was going to place us in one dangerous situation after another, until those reporters got their story and then some. He was all about showing off how hardcore the valley was, and was very willing to place us in jeopardy to prove it.

But these reporters were from Vanity Fair. Vanity Fair for godssake. The Italian Vanity Fair at that. What do a buncha fashion enthusiasts care for readin' about the rougher side of life? Does that make them feel like they've somehow done their civic duty, reading about the war? I could see somebody flipping through the magazine, and here in between the Dolce & Gabbana and Louis Vuitton ads, is this piece about a group of filthy American Soldiers, slugging it out in some obscure corner of the world. The liberal Italian populace is just gonna label us a pack of Baby Killers no matter how the article's written. If they even read it at all. They'd probably scan the pictures then pass it right by and go on to the "How To Keep Your Age-Defying Skin Even More Age-Defiant" piece.

Before we S.P.ed on the patrol, the P.L. told us we were not, under any circumstances to talk to the reporters. About anything. The Army does love it some censorship. And as Soldiers, we were subject to the Uniform Code of Military Justice if we said something the Army deemed *bad*. But for now, you could do a lot worse patrol-wise, than walking through northern Babyol. That's a pretty easy, short, and safe patrol. And it counted as one of our patrols for the day too.

We linked up with the guys from the KOP who'd brought the reporters down; one of them was a female, the photographer was a male. They had their mandated tactical vests and their bright blue combat helmets on (only God knows why they make them wear those bright blue helmets). I'm sure they received a little extra attention from the Taliban. If somebody handed me a bright blue helmet, I'd promptly break their nose with it.

We policed up our news hounds and marched on back to good ole Firebase Phoenix. Once inside the wire, it was pretty common practice for a lot of guys to just plop down on the ground and catch their breath. (Even though it was an easy patrol like I said, going anywhere in this country winded you. But plus too, on this particular occasion, I think the guys wanted to get a look at this female. Didn't get to see a whole lotta women not wearing a *burkha* in these parts.)

The P.L. started showing the news crew the finer points of Firebase Phoenix. The shitter, the kitchen, the burnpit (we burned our garbage), where the water was—like he was having open house. And I'm sure the girl meant to be more discreet when she turned to her counterpart and said in English, "These guys stink," but everybody and their dead dog heard it. Hell yeah we stink, woman. We only get to shower once a month, and we're in a constant state of sweat patrolling up and down these goddamned mountains, which somebody with a penchant for inclines, created.

Besides being told I wasn't the kinda guy you wanna be downwind from, I was also informed that I had the guard. So I went to our hooch to drop my top and grab some goodies to keep me occupied for the next 2 hours. Just before dusk wasn't a bad time to have guard. The BUB was about to start, and that would kill the first 30 minutes. Provided the Taliban weren't up to their firefight-at-dawn shenanigans, it would probably be pretty mellow, then I could go back to my cot and get some serious sleep on.

So I humped up that godawful hill on which our Phoenix was perched, and out of breath I found Campbell in the guard tower, only he was not alone. That crazy news chick was in the tower with him. Screw me.

"You about ready to come outta there?" I asked him.

"Sure thing," he said. Then he gave me a look. I guess it was the, hey-there's-a-girl-in-the-guard-tower look. I kinda rolled my eyes and shook my head. Whattaya gonna do?

So Campbell climbed down the ladder and I went up. She said hello in English and I said hi as I set my SAW up in the glassless window and began checking the 240, made sure the extra ammo cans were setup the way I liked, plugged the Claymore clackers in (still amazed someone preferred them disconnected), gauged the battery in the radio, looked whether we had ample extra batteries and then did a radio check on the I-Com.

I'd made up my mind I wasn't gonna say shit. Pleasantries, okay. Anything of a tactical nature, absolutely not. I'd already been ordered not to speak to her, but here she was in my goddamned guard tower. Which I had to admit, was a pretty smart move on her part. 'Cause here you have a guy, who hasn't been in the presence of a woman in months, and who had nothing to do for the next 2 hours. I was a captive—with all the time in the world to talk. I'm not sure exactly how she had developed this ploy, but it was a good one.

Almost immediately, the drilling began. Subtle though it was. What was my name, where was I from, the basic stuff. Followed by questions of more substance. I kept it simple at first, skirted around all the interrogation I could, but she wore me down. And well, frankly, I'm one of those opinionated types to begin with.

She asked if I thought we were doing any good here. I told her that I didn't really know. I wasn't sure if anyone really knew. Are we out here, holding the enemy at the border, keeping them at bay, and thus protecting the rest of the country? As in, if we weren't here, there would be nothing stopping them from wreaking mayhem all the way to Kabul? Or, if we weren't here, would there just not be any reason for these people to fight and thus, peace?

Like I said, no one knew the answer. And if we pulled out of here, and the former proved to be true, it would be an absolute bloodbath re-taking this valley. It was bad enough on a day-to-day basis as it was. And we'd fought hard to hold this ground. Giving it up would be like all that we had sacrificed was for nothing. I couldn't feel good about that.

She continually asked what I thought about Captain Kearney,

and I continued to decline to comment. The sun was setting so I began to mount my NODs. She (I can't for the life of me remember her name) was curious about them, so I dismounted them from my helmet so she could look through them. They are pretty cool, especially if you've never had the privilege to use a pair. For an Army that boasted about how high-tech it was, this was one of the few advancements that the average Infantryman had access to. They gave us a distinct advantage over our enemies. But you also got sick of wearing the goddamned things, as they weighed on your helmet.

Then I guess she decided to get deep on me. She asked why I'd enlisted in the Army. It was a good and relevant question. Why would you want to expose yourself to all this hardship and madness? I asked her, "You're a reporter, right? So you might be able to relate to this: Haven't you ever wanted to be part of something that was bigger than yourself? Haven't you ever wanted to know, what it would be like, to make a real sacrifice? And to be part of something—something great—something you'll never forget? Even though it sucks right now, I think that once this is over, it's something we'll all be really proud of. And we're not murderers. We're out here trying to help these people. I understand they don't appreciate it, don't even want us here. But we really are trying to do good. And also, it's a little cliché, but, there is the camaraderie aspect of it too. You really come to love these guys you work with. There's a, like, a real bond that develops, after having sweated, and fought, and suffered so much together. A lotta times it doesn't feel like it, but in the end, I really do believe this will be a rewarding experience."

She asked me, for about the forty-seventh time, how I felt about Battle 6. I sighed and carefully submitted, "I think he's ambitious," I paused, "And that's not always good for his men." She slowly nodded, full knowing she'd gotten from me what she'd been after all along.

When the article finally came out, I'd been poorly misquoted about nineteen times. I never got in any trouble for it, but I never talked to another reporter either.

Plight of the SAW Gunner

 Being a SAW gunner ain't the easiest job in the Army. A SAW is by no means light, and all the ammo that goes with it is a helluva lot heavier than the weapon itself. The SAW, with its M145 scope (which I most definitely prefer), comes in around 16 pounds. A hundred rounds of five-five-six link weighs about 7 pounds. I carried no less than 600 everywhere I went, for a minimum total of 42 pounds—in just bullets. Add to that your body armor, helmet, camelbak... I weighed myself on the scales once at the KOP, and my gear alone was 85 pounds. After the appropriate emaciation that comes with your average Afghanistan deployment (not having any real food to eat while burning more calories than P-90X ever thought possible) I was weighing in at 150 (I deployed at 172 pounds). So my gear weighed over half as much as I did.

 Conversely, I'd say a Team Leader only carries about 60 pounds. I mean, an M-4 with a loaded 30 round mag is about 7 pounds. Maybe he's carrying 8 or 9 additional mags, but besides that, all he's got is water, body armor and a helmet. It's not like we had enough MBITRs (radios) to go around for even the point man to have communication with the P.L. or the KOP. Anyway, one of those isn't more than 3 pounds. So as you can clearly see, what we have here is a very uneven distribution of weight. As in, it's all on the goddamn SAW gunner.

 I spent 10 out of 15 months with the SAW. The other 5 I was playing Team Leader. Sern't Miller offered several times to move me to grenadier, to give me a break. But I always refused.

 To me, there's something great about having to work harder than everyone else—to have to suck more. And it's not just that. The SAW accounts for 80% of a Squad's firepower. It is the most important weapon in the Squad. And I liked being that guy. I was the guy that laid out the lead. As bad as that thing sucks to carry, it's fucking awesome in a firefight. Shooting a machine gun in combat is awesome shit. And too, I didn't really trust anyone else to do it.

It got to be a pride thing. That's *MY* machine gun. And nobody's a better SAW gunner than me. I can hump this thing, up and down these goddamned mountains, and through these low-life villages, I can choose the perfect spot to set up in every time, and when Hajj feels like getting his *jihad* on, I'll be the first one to pull the trigger, and give those fuckers what for. And when I get back to the firebase, I'll take her apart, clean every last piece till every Sergeant says I got the cleanest SAW in the Platoon, and I'll have her ready to go for the next round. To me, being a SAW gunner in Afghanistan? Well hell, it's gotta be the best job in the entire United States Army.

Rock Avalanche

The most ambitious Con-Op Battle Company undertook during OEF VIII, was called Rock Avalanche. 2nd Battalion (ours) was nicknamed "The Rock," for an assault our forefathers made in World War II on a Philippine island called Corregidor. On this island was a large rock plateau that gave new definition to the term "heavily fortified." The 173rd Airborne nicknamed it "The Rock," and after they conquered it, they took the nickname for the Battalion. So anyway, practically every Con-Op we did had to utilize the word "Rock" somewhere.

As far as Rock Avalanche was concerned, the idea was this: we couldn't walk any further south than Ali Abad. So the enemy had safehavens further south. Primarily in a village called Yaka Cheena. In this village the Taliban could walk around toting weapons and plan attacks uncontested by American forces. It was like their Command & Control center, and that's where their bigwigs were. Captain Kearney, being the industrious C.O. that he was, wanted to air assault into Yaka Cheena, thus achieving surprise, and "take the fight to the enemy." (If only we had a day off for every time I heard Captain Kearney say, "Take the fight to the enemy.") A pretty ballsy plan really. But no one ever accused him of being timid, or, not being able to find new and dangerous things for his men to do.

Part One: Assault on Yaka Cheena

So 1st and 2nd Platoon somehow drew the lucky straws to go on this mission, while us (3rd Platoon) and Destined were just gonna cover down on all the firebases. But Yaka Cheena wasn't the half of it. This was like a double feature Con-Op. After Yaka Cheena was properly ransacked and burning to the ground, 1st and 2nd Platoon were then gonna air assault onto this ginormous mountain called the Abas Ghar, and walk up and down searching for these alleged "cave complexes" in which the Taliban stored weapons. It sounded like a hoot, and I was real sorry 3rd Platoon wasn't chosen to go on this goatfuck.

I did manage to get separated from my Squad again though. Weapons Squad along with the P.L., Doc Lee, and a few others, were headed up to Restrepo and decided they needed an extra SAW gunner to plus them up and give 'em a little more firepower. Since 1st Squad was technically on refit on the O.P., they asked Sergeant Miller for a guy, and guess who he chose? I didn't say a word. Just packed up my shit and headed out, but I knew being separated from your Squad was never a good thing. Something was gonna go wrong and I was gonna end up on this Con-Op, I just knew it.

We humped up to Restrepo that day and relieved the rest of 2nd Platoon. All we had to do was pull guard and we had plenty of guys so it was pretty easy. The firebase had only been there a couple of months, thus there wasn't much to it. The perimeter was semi-solid, but certainly not what you would call impregnable. There weren't any hooches or anything up there yet. You just slept on a cot under the stars, which was kinda nice that time of the year, and would undoubtedly be not so nice in another month.

That night, Rock Avalanche kicked off. With your NODs on, you could see the infrared lights flashing from the Chinooks carrying our guys down south, escorted by some Apaches. As expected, no sooner did our guys touchdown, than the proverbial shit hit the fan. From Restrepo we heard sporadic gunfire, missiles, bombs, and people shouting or whispering on the radio with frantic bravado, all night long. There was a lot of action going on: fighters moving all over the mountains and through the towns, and chases, and Apaches gunning people down. It sounded especially intense.

I was thankful to be where I was. To me there wasn't any shame in it; 'cause I knew goddamned well, I'd seen plenty of action already and would see plenty before this deployment was over. And if we weren't on this Con-Op, we'd damned sure be on the next one. And another Platoon would be doing this covering-down-on-the-firebase gig, and they'd be sitting here being thankful they weren't on the current Con-Op.

In the morning, after the dust had settled, there were a lotta dead civilians. The reports I heard coming over the radio said thirty-something. But then, I also heard official reports that it was just five. To me, "civilian" in the Korengal Valley, is a pretty subjective term anyway. A lot of "civilians" are just combatants who aren't armed at their time of death. But it didn't change the fact that dead Hajj infuriated the Taliban. Well, now I guess it was time for another goddamned *shurra* with the village elders.

It probably went something like this:

Captain Kearney, "What are all these weapons doing here?"

Village Elder, "I don't know. I never seen that shit before in my life."

Captain Kearney, "Well what about all those fighters we saw last night?"

Village Elder, "They were just passing through. I think they were Pakistani. What are you going to do about all these dead people of mine?"

Captain Kearney, "Why you wanna jump off topic like that? I'm talking about the Taliban. The Taliban are bad."

Village Elder, "You're bad."

Our guys stayed there the rest of the day and flew out later that night for Part 2 of Rock Avalanche, with every Hajj and their Taliban-loving goat screaming, "We want *jihad*! We want *jihad*!"

Part Two: Cave Search on the Abas Ghar with Entire Valley Enraged

Forty-eight hours in, with smoke still rising to the south from Yaka Cheena, 1st and 2nd Platoon began their search of a mountain so large and heavily forested, it could conceal a pork-free McDonald's that you'd never find without an 8-digit grid. (In land navigation, an 8-digit grid will get you within 10 meters of the point you plotted.) The Abas Ghar ("*ghar*" being Pashtun for mountain) sat on the eastern side of what was known as the Shuriak. There was no American presence in the Shuriak whatsoever. The goddamned Taliban could've been training Yetis over there for all we knew. This being a Battalion-level Con-Op, our sister company, Chosen, was gonna clear some of these villages in the Shuriak, and Battle Company, in addition to searching for these weapons caches, was gonna make sure none of these hoodlums escaped over the Abas Ghar.

The concept thus changed to that of Small Kill Teams, or S.K.T.s. That's the militarily correct way to say that you have too much area to cover with too few Soldiers, but you wanna execute the mission anyway, so you're gonna break the guys that you have into small elements that are readily overrun by the enemy. But "Small Kill Teams" sounds so much more badass than "Small Teams That Can Be Easily Killed."

It started off real quiet. As in, there hadn't been a shot fired by either side since Yaka Cheena. There was, however, a lot of chatter from the Taliban on their radios. This was a little eerie, since everyone knew how pissed off Hajj was.

I can't say for sure what happened, 'cause I wasn't there. In combat, an Infantryman hears things—some of them from valid sources and some of it just speculation—and then there're some facts, and you just gotta kinda put the pieces together yourself.

The gist of it was this: the Scouts (led by Staff Sergeant Rougle) and a gun team (led by Staff Sergeant Rice) were up on the high ground covering some very tactically important terrain, when a large element of enemy managed to scale a cliff the Americans didn't have eyes-on, and then proceeded to overrun the position. Sergeant Rougle was shot multiple times, including one round to the head. He was pretty much the biggest badass in the entire Company. And he was dead.

Vandenberge, this mammoth of a guy—some farm boy from the Midwest, like large enough to be an offensive lineman who I once on a training rotation in Germany saw lift a loaded 500-pound weapons cage up by himself—was shot in the arm and bleeding out profusely. Sergeant Rice had been shot in the gut. The rest of the guys had tried to defend the position but ultimately realized it was impossible and fell back, while other elements of 2nd Platoon, namely Specialists Cortez and Pemble-Belkin, rushed forward to reinforce them. But the enemy had already fled.

The loss of Sergeant Rougle could not be overstated. He was unanimously considered the best Soldier Battle Company had. Not only was he highly respected and liked by everyone, but his death really brought home the seriousness and lethality of the enemy we were fighting. If they could kill Sergeant Rougle, they could get any of us.

To make matters far worse, the Taliban had run off with Rougle's suppressed M-4 (an M-4 with a silencer on it), the gun team's 240 (a machine gun) along with 2 assault packs full of ammo for it, Rice's M-14 (a very lethal, scoped sniper rifle), and 2 sets of NODs (night vision).

Part Three: Landigal

25 October, 2007

We didn't have a whole helluva lotta choices at that point. You can't just let the Taliban waltz off with American weapons. The major issue was, everybody who'd been on that Con-Op for the past few days was smoked. Asking them to hump their exhausted butts after those weapons was deemed too much. While on guard, I heard a couple of officers talking to each other on the radio about their Platoons, "They won't say it, and I know they want to go recover those weapons, but I know my guys are just smoked." Captain Kearney decided he needed fresh legs out there.

But where would they get these fresh folks from? Well, I knew it; I knew I was gonna get sucked into this Con-Op somehow. So what happened was, some of the 2nd Platoon guys that came down off the Talazar relieved what few men we had at Phoenix, and us at Restrepo. And they did look dead-tired when they got there. We made the sharp descent down the mountain, and were at Phoenix in about 15 minutes, where we re-geared ourselves to be out for 3 days, and plans were set in motion.

The Taliban that overran the American position were believed to be in the village of Landigal, which sat kinda high up between the Talazar spur and the Gatigal spur. It was a village we'd never been in to, simply because of the distance for one; and two, it wasn't a village we thought we could make it out of. That was a rubicon we dared not cross. Well, until now anyway.

Just before dark, about half of 1st Platoon joined us at Phoenix. Similarly, we had about half of our Platoon too. The plan was to in-fill after dark, climb all the way up Honcho Hill till we had good eyes-on Landigal, set up fighting positions, then at first light, the A.N.A. along with the E.T.T. and some of 2nd Platoon were gonna search every house in the village till the weapons were found. At which point we'd return home. Sounds simple enough alright. But of course, these things never go the way they're supposed to.

Sergeant Navas told me that Hotz was gonna be my Team Leader, which suited me fine. Hotz was a redneck from Texas (my home state) who'd been on the previous deployment to Afghanistan. Though he was still just a Specialist, he was way overdue to make Sergeant. He was pretty laidback, practical and knew what he was doing.

Since I was technically attached to Weapons Squad, I was given 100 rounds of seven-six-two for the 240, in addition to 800 rounds of five-five-six link for my SAW, 6 liters of water, a woobie (which is Poncho Liner, or blanket), 5 packs of Pines, a couple M.R.E.s and a snack-sized Ziploc of gummy worms. My kit was well over a hundred pounds. This is what I hated about Con-Ops: Let's carry way more weight than we're used to, walk much farther than usual, and do something entirely more dangerous.

As dark descended, we stepped-off. We did not take the easiest route up Honcho Hill. And that mountain is deceptively steeper than it looked. I bet that thing has a grade of no less than 45° and in a lotta places, more like 60°. Added to which it's composed of some really loose shale. Often taking one step forward, meant sliding back two or three, and much of it you were trying to scramble up on all fours.

That SAW was swinging like a pendulum from my neck. The whole ordeal was absolutely miserable. The worst thing was, for the first time the whole deployment, I was sucking more than anybody else. Sergeant Hunt finally had to come down and ask me what I was carrying, then ordered me to give him the 100 rounds of seven-six-two after I refused several times. I still struggled like I've never struggled before.

By the time I made it to the top of that bitch, I had to sit right the fuck down for a few minutes. I was on the verge of falling-out, and the last thing I wanted to do was fall-out on a patrol. Partially because of pride, and partially because if Sergeant Miller found out I fell-out of a patrol, he'd undoubtedly make me quit smoking.

That, obviously could not happen.

So I finally got to my feet, but the thing was, yeah we got to the top of Honcho Hill, but not high enough on the spur to overwatch Landigal. So we proceeded up (though at a much more agreeable grade). I was drinking water like a madman, but my right leg was still cramping. I'd never really had a leg cramp before and it was downright painful. I thought if we had to go too much farther, I was indeed gonna fall-out. We were told to set in. Which is something that takes a little bit of effort. Then we were told to pick up and move higher. Then we set in again. Then we were told to pickup again and go even higher. That went on another three or four more times. But at long last we made it to a spot where we could shoot the living bejesus out of Landigal. Landigal was maybe a little bigger than the village of Marastana. Somewhere between a few dozen and 50 houses. So anyway we settled in, with 1st Platoon down below us a hundred or so meters to watch the other end of the village.

We then proceeded to freeze our nuts off all night. All we had were our woobies and even when you weren't on guard, you weren't sleeping so much as shivering. It seemed like a godsend when Bob finally showed his sunny face and started to warm the place. And we could finally smoke again (even though after last night's ascent I thought I might oughta quit—but really, Afghanistan's not a good place to stop smoking).

So at this point we were all ready to get this village pillaging on. Captain Kearney had used a lot of strong language to indicate our intent here. He essentially said, "We're gonna tear that village apart until the weapons are recovered." But here it was first light, and everyone was still waiting for the destruction to begin. And we waited, and we waited. Morning turned to lunch. I ate a couple of my Sour-Brite gummy worms.

The only good thing was that we hadn't been hit yet. There were a few houses about 600 meters to the south that we'd been watching all day, but we hadn't seen anything overly suspicious. But we knew that the entire valley was aware of our location, and that was a bad enough feeling as it was.

The question on everyone's mind was, *What the hell are we doing?* And everyone agreed that giving them more time to hide or run off with the weapons was retarded. Hotz said to me, "Well this makes sense. Bust our ass all night to get up here in a hurry, then sit around and do nothin' all day."

What we didn't know, and what we never knew (till it was way too late), was what was going on in the minds of those unseen jackasses we call Battalion and Brigade leadership. And apparently, the B.C. (Battalion Commander), ole Lieutenant Colonel "Wild Bill" Ostlund, had determined that, instead of ransacking Landigal, the best way to get these weapons back and get through to these violent mutants, was to smother them with generosity. Something like, "Let not this village's first experience with Americans be one of brute force and relentless pursuit. Rather, let us show unto them our kind, New Testament-like philanthropic side."

Which is to say, he wanted to deliver a shit-load of H.A. (Humanitarian Aid) to the village. Rice, beans, flour, winter coats, shoes, school supplies… The works. While we were sitting up on this spur, as deep into enemy territory as you'd ever wanted to not get, just waiting for the bullets to start flying, and knowing that it's coming.

We couldn't believe what was going on. Sergeant Rice was shot, Vandenburg too, Sergeant Rougle was dead, and we had a missing M-14 fucking sniper rifle, an M240 Bravo machine gun, a goddamned suppressed M-4 and a couple pairs of NODs. Pretty much three of our deadliest weapons, and one of our biggest advantages over the enemy: night vision. And we're giving out coats. What can I say? We like our enemies comfortable I guess.

This took all goddamned day. In order for it to happen, all this H.A. had to be accumulated, then loaded onto choppers, then flown-in, then distributed, and Colonel Ostlund decided he'd fly in himself and have a *shurra* with the village elders. And if there was one thing we all knew by this point, it was that *shurras* never accomplished shit. And this one would be no exception.

Ostlund met with the elders, drank his chai, and then flew away with the air support, achieving absolutely nothing, and leaving without having recovered a single bullet, much less the weapons we'd come for. What started out as a hard-charging, we're-gonna-get-those-weapons-back-or-level-Landigal mission, had turned into a pansy patrol. It was now about 4 p.m. local time. The sun would be setting soon.

"That's it?" Hotz said. "That's really it? And now we're just gonna leave?! Unfucking believable."

"Guess we didn't want those weapons back so bad after all," I said. "Well you know the good thing, Hotz? Now we can look forward to being shot at by an M-14, a 240, and a goddamned suppressed M-4. How do ya like that?"

"I'm more afraid of that M-14 than anything," he said, "With that Leupold on there? How can they not hit us?"

I agreed.

At sunset, everyone braced for what we believed to be an imminent attack. No way were the Taliban just gonna let us walk out of here without firing a single shot at us. But the sun went down and not a gunshot was heard. It was an creepy relief.

We sat put for about another hour, hour and a half. I had been told that the plan was we were gonna pickup first, move down past 1st Platoon and take the lead out of here (since it was really 3rd Platoon's A.O. and we knew the area better than they did). I don't know if I was just told wrong, or if plans changed, but either way 1st Platoon got point. An Apache that was supposed to support us, allegedly scanned our ex-fill route with their high-tech thermal imaging, then flew away.

We picked up and we weren't moving but for maybe two or three minutes before the shit went down. We heard P.K.M. fire, and bullets and R.P.G.s were flying all over the godforsaken place. Everyone dropped to the ground. We were seriously pinned. Rounds were snapping and cracking everywhere and I mean within inches. We all got as flat as we could on our bellies. I was even pulling my arms in to make myself as small as possible. It's amazing none of us got shot.

In retrospect, I feel horrible for being up there on our stomachs, while 1st Platoon was getting chewed up. If we were taking that much fire, I could only imagine the onslaught they were going through. But not knowing exactly where 1st Platoon was in relation to the enemy, we couldn't return fire to help them out.

However, everyone knew we had to do something. 1st Platoon called on the radio to send our Medics forward. And here's where the chaos came in. Lieutenant Gillespie, having been with us for an entire month, wanted to take the whole Platoon down the southern side of the spur, which seemed like a dumb idea to everyone, and Eddie got up in his face and said, "Sir! That's the wrong goddamned way!" They fought it out for way too long till the P.L. finally listened to Eddie. Meanwhile, Sergeant Hunt, undaunted, hauled-ass straight-line down the mountain with Doc Lee and Doc LeFave. (We'd brought both our medics with us 'cause everyone knew the likelihood of this turning into a shit storm.)

Lieutenant Gillespie however, refused to take the most direct route down, and it thus took us much longer than it should have to get down to 1st Platoon's position. Once we arrived, the fight was over, and all that was left for us to do was establish security around the C.C.P. (Casualty Collection Point), which had been setup by Sergeant Hunt and Sergeant Shelton (formerly from 3rd Platoon, but now 1st Platoon's Platoon Sergeant).

1st Platoon had walked right into a near, L-shaped ambush. (Near being about 20 meters.) Sergeant Brennan, who was walking point, had taken the brunt of the attack. I didn't see him, but heard he was shot in the face among other places. Hajj had then tried to drag him off. (Something similar had happened to Able Company a couple of months ago—they were dragging our dead and wounded off so they could take our equipment, particularly our NODs.)

Staff Sergeant Gallardo took a round to his helmet that flattened him onto his back. After dragging his Squad Leader to safety, the Bravo Team Leader, Specialist Giunta, had rushed forward to save Brennan, through all that hellfire, and capped one of the two guys that was dragging his friend away. He would be the first living Soldier to receive the Medal Of Honor since Vietnam. He had driven off the other members of the ambush, but not before one of them had shot Doc Mendoza in the leg as he charged forward to render aid.

One guy (I can't remember who it was) had a round go inside his helmet, right at the ear. The bullet whipped all the way around the helmet and exited the other side. Other guys had rounds pierce their rucksacks. Pretty much Sern't Gallardo's entire Squad had been shot up. Eckrode, the Alpha team SAW gunner had been shot four times. Miraculously, most of them were okay. It could've been way worse than it was.

However, Doc Mendoza was shot in the femoral artery. He didn't live long. That femoral artery is serious business. If you don't get a tourniquet on it, you've only got a couple of minutes till you bleed out.

We set up a 360° perimeter around the C.C.P. For all we knew, there were more of these guys out there and they were just waiting to come in here and roll us up. And there was nothing we could do but sit-put and wait for the medevacs to come retrieve our wounded. Which would take an eternity. The first bird arrived within 30 minutes. Since there were too many trees for the Black Hawk to land, the casualties had to be winched on board. That meant you had the damned bird hovering overhead and I swear to God it must've taken half an hour to get one guy onto the chopper. During that half hour, you were getting sandblasted by the rotor wash. I couldn't see more than a few feet in front of me. If anyone was gonna attack us, this would be an awesome time. We expected R.P.G.s to start flying at any moment. My orders were to shoot anything I saw coming towards me.

Finally, the first medevac was away and everything was calm again. We spit the dirt out of our mouths and attempted to wipe it out of our eyes with our filthy hands. I think it took 6 birds total. You'd wait about half an hour for one to show up, then every single one took about 30 minutes to winch the casualty up, then they'd fly away and you'd wait for the next one to show. So we were there, getting pummeled by rotor wash for about three miserable hours. I was really worried, 'cause I knew all that dirt in the air had worked its way into my SAW. That thing had to be beyond fouled, and I seriously doubted it would get off more than a couple of rounds before it jammed. If we got in another firefight now, we'd be really screwed.

But we got the last of our casualties out, and not a shot was fired. Now it was time for us to pick up again. As we headed out, I walked by the Taliban guy who had been trying to drag Brennan off. This guy had been fuckin' shot Lord knows how many times. I bet he had a hundred bullets in him. Every bone in his skull was crushed; it didn't look like he had a skull. His face was just lying there all flat and bloody and gruesome in the moonlight. It reminded me of a Halloween mask. That's what it looked like. I'll never forget it.

We (3rd Platoon) took point now, and we made it off the Honcho Hill spur, then literally slid down the side on our asses, trying not to cause rock slides for the guys beneath us. We reached the bottom without incident, though I continued to worry about whether or not my weapon would actually fire. We then walked down the river, someone (and I won't name names, only that it was someone with enough rank that they shouldn't've been losing their weapon) dropped their M-4 in the river, but finally found it again.

We then humped our exhausted butts up what was known as the "Stair Master" and made it into Ali Abad. Which was an enormous relief. It's a pretty extreme state of affairs when you consider Ali Abad to be safe. Part of 2nd Platoon was there and Destined had driven the trucks down to support our ex-fill. I remember seeing Sergeant Mac, and he said something empathetic to me and he's not a guy who's known for empathy. It made me feel pretty good anyway.

We walked the road from Ali Abad to Phoenix. It was akin to a hard-fought glory march. Like the finish line to an outrageous marathon. I just remember when I finally got back to Phoenix, when I finally got home and went down to my hooch, taking off all that gear felt so good it was absolute ecstasy. Since the rest of my Squad was still on the O.P. at the KOP, I had the whole hooch to myself. Sweet solitude. I then proceeded to use about 57 billion baby wipes to clean my face, neck, arms and hands. I had dirt in places that did not take dirt. I blew brown boogers for 3 baby wipes straight. I had more crap in my ears and eyes than I ever thought possible. I wish I'd taken a picture first. When I was finished, I seriously wanted to clean my SAW, and knew that was the right thing to do, but I was just so damned tired. I opened the receiver and with my headlamp saw just how fouled it was.

I'd never seen it so dirty. I closed it and instead took out a Gatorade that I had stashed, reached behind my bunk for the water bottle filled with vodka, and made myself probably the best drink the world has ever known. Put the earbuds to my iPod in, listened to music, and sipped away at my drink. I didn't know how beat I was till I laid down. My body was shot. That wood-planked rack felt like some sort of super mattress made for a king.

I felt so horrible for Brennan and Doc Mendoza. What a shitty way to go. What a waste. It just didn't seem like it should've happened. And what did we accomplish? We didn't get the weapons back. All we got was 2 more dead dudes. I felt bad for their families. Bad for Brennan and Mendoza that they'd never take another breath. That they didn't live to see it out of this shit hole. But then, at the same time, I felt so fuckin' relieved that it wasn't me. I was so happy I was I alive, and I felt bad for feelin' that way. I guess this is what they call survivor's guilt. I thought about it for as long as it took me to finish the vodka and Gatorade, then I promptly passed the hell out. No one woke me for guard all night. I thought I was in a really twisted version of heaven.

Epilogue

Though we were expecting massive retaliation in the days and weeks that followed Rock Avalanche, scarcely a shot rang out. Winter was fast approaching, but something more than that stayed the Taliban's trigger fingers. The operation had taken a heavy toll on Americans and insurgents alike. I honestly don't see how either side could quantify the events as a success. But that we could air assault into Yaka Cheena anytime we damned well pleased, had to make them seriously consider their own security.

The death of Rougle (even though I doubt the Taliban knew how important he was to us), the ambush on the Abas Ghar, and the capturing of the weapons, especially with us not recapturing them, I would think would be huge victories to them. If it was, they sure weren't celebrating out loud. And lastly, the ambush on Honcho Hill. Maybe the sight of a lone Paratrooper charging through a hail of enemy gunfire to save his friend made an impression on the Taliban. But the longer the cease fire endured, the more it became apparent that our enemies were in a far worse state of shock than we were. Ultimately, it was Rock Avalanche that forced Hajj to fear and respect Battle Company. They understood. We meant business.

III. WINTER

Voice In The Field

(Transcription from a series of videos I made.)

Everyone was gathered prior to patrol, donned with armor and weapons, smoking cigarettes and making last minute preparations.

I pointed the digital camera towards me, "I'm Specialist Darren Shadix of the 173rd Airborne. Today we're conducting a routine patrol to northern Babyol, a relatively safe area. Our purpose is to retrieve two reporters, and bring them back to Phoenix with us. Meet, P.F.C. Matthew Roberts."

"Hi!" he smiled and waved a long time as he sat on the makeshift wooden bench.

"Roberts, how do you feel about reporters in the Korengal Valley?"

He laughed, "They're awesome."

"Is it true that, among the troops, there's a general consensus that, with the last reporters in the valley, the C.O. was trying to show off. Making you do things that were, unnecessarily dangerous?"

"The reporters don't have to be here for him to do that."

"That's a good point. But wasn't the frequency of these stupid ideas a little greater?"

Squinting, "Yeah a little bit, a little more," Roberts nodded.

"Good deal."

"Wow," Sergeant Hunt said in the background, "Shadix even has stuff written down."

"I've been pullin' a lotta guard, Sern't," I explained. "This is P.F.C. Cody Belgarde. Referred to affectionately as *Cheeks*, though this reporter doesn't believe a man should ever call another man *Cheeks*. Belgarde, I see you're carrying the M249 SAW. Tell me about carrying the SAW."

To Quell The Korengal

He looked down at the machine gun, "I don't know a lot about it. I was in JAF, eatin cheese sticks. So..."

"Yes. Do you care to comment on recent reports you went to the safe haven, Jalalabad Air Field for E.M.T. training, and were gone a suspiciously long 6 weeks."

"I wasn't actually at the E.M.T. course," Belgarde explained. "They needed a manager for Pizza Hut. So I took over, the managerial position at Pizza Hut. They needed a high-speed Private."

"Well that would explain the falsified K.B.R. credentials we found in your assault pack."

"And the added 25 pounds I brought back," he smiled.

"Belgarde, what kinda turd are you?"

"The good kind."

"Where's Lindley?"

He came walking out of the hooch, "What's up?"

"Specialist Richard Lindley."

"Mino," he cut me off.

"Mino. This area is expecting a massive attack in the next 24 to 48 hours. How do you sleep at night?"

"I take lots of sleeping pills. And I whack off constantly on guard. It tires me. That's how I get through the day here."

"We have several sources that say you can't cook rice properly without the use of a rice cooker."

He opened a bottle of water, "Yes, that is true because in Hawaii we grow up with rice cookers."

"As our resident Hawaiian, how do you hope to ever take home a Hula girl, if you can't even cook an edible pot of rice?"

"I can. I just need a rice cooker."

"How's your recipe for poi?"

"Actually, I don't know how to make poi."

"You're screwed," I told him. "Where's Hotz at? This is Specialist Brian Hotz, acting Squad Leader for Weapons. Hotz, including yourself, you have three guys in what's ideally supposed to be a 9-man squad. Do you find current troop levels in the Korengal Valley adequate?"

"Negative," he said as he worked on his radio, "We're gettin' screwed."

"Hotz, what's up with your wife not sending us Cowboys games?"

"Apparently, she's too lazy to make her way up to the store to buy the D.V.D. player that would record a television show, or, the Dallas Cowboys football games, onto a D.V.D."

"Isn't it true that I even offered to pay for the D.V.D. player if she'd record those games?"

He broke out his Gerber multi-tool and started prying on his radio, "Once again, money is not the situation. It's her laziness, and her ability to procrastinate."

I turned the camera towards myself, saying, "Laziness and ability to procrastinate. A heartfelt message from the homeland. For the 173rd Airborne, I'm Specialist Darren Shadix, every Soldier's voice in the field."

Trash Man and The Precision-Guided Mortar

As part of our ever-so-successful hearts and minds campaign, and in an effort to make them financially dependent upon us, we tried to employ as many natives as we could. We paid top dollar of course. I was told the average Korengali made between 1 and 2 dollars a day, and we paid between 5 and 10 depending on the job. Now, one would think we'd have a whole line of qualified applicants just "dying" to work for us. But I suppose the threat of the Taliban cutting your head off for consorting with the infidels was enough to make most Afghans seek employment elsewhere.

The majority of the "locals" that did work for us were not from the Korengal. They came from Asadabad and Jalalabad and other assorted places. One exception was Trash Man. Trash Man lived in Babyol, just right down the way. I don't know why we never learned his name, but we just called him by his title. He would come to our hooches and take our trash. A chore we easily could've done ourselves but whatever. He was a very old man, very pleasant, always smiling (minus a lot of teeth). When he came to our hooch, Sergeant Slo would always yell, "Trash Man!" and the old man would always laugh and give us two thumbs up. He was a pretty cool old dude.

Well, one day he began his 5-minute walk from his house to Phoenix when there was an explosion. He was severely injured. As in, it pretty much blew his legs off. We got him to the KOP and called for medevac, but he died en route. Battle Company's head medic, Doc Sanchez, said it was one of the nastiest wounds he'd ever seen.

At the time, we didn't know what to make of it. How did they manage to blow Trash Man up like that? It was really odd. The going theory was, in retaliation for working with Americans, the Taliban had launched a mortar with pinpoint accuracy, specifically to kill Trash Man. Even though we knew how wildly inaccurate the Taliban are when it comes to mortars, we just didn't think much of it. But we should have.

In Which The Trails Turn Against Us

It was what you might call a split patrol: the Main Element (consisting of 1st Squad's Alpha Team and Sergeant Miller, along with Headquarters and about 10 to 12 A.N.A. fuck-sticks) moved across the river and into Donga, while the Overwatch Element (composed of 1st Squad's Bravo Team, Weapons Squad, the Platoon Sergeant, and 2 new E.T.T.s) went into Ali Abad to cover the Main Element. It's not something we did regularly, but for whatever reason someone decided this was what was up on this particular day.

We humped up through Donga, the P.L. tried to find somebody to talk to (preferably the village elder), but there wasn't anyone around (which is a bad sign). With nothing left to accomplish, we turned to ex-fill. We made it down to the large grove of trees at the base of the mountain and setup to cover the Overwatch as they ex-filled from Ali Abad. It didn't make a helluva lotta sense to me, 'cause from that position, we could only hit Dar Bart, 1705, and the northern side of Marastana. If the Taliban were on the southern side, they could light our guys up and there wouldn't be shit we could do to support 'em. But I just did what I was told, and honestly I didn't mind taking a break before we forded the river.

Sergeant Miller yelled to us that the Overwatch was moving out. Everyone was diligently scanning. I had 1705 in my sights, watching for any kinda movement / funny business. Maybe 2 minutes had gone by when all of the sudden, BOOM! An explosion shook the valley floor. A gigantic plume of dust began to rise behind the schoolhouse. "What the fuck was that?!" was everyone's general reaction.

"Jesus." I started thinking. "Bravo must've been in the lead," I said to Slo. "That's Eddie and Belgarde and Mino." We sat in dismay, but continued to scan hard, waiting to see if this was gonna be accompanied by small arms.

On the other side of the valley, Belgarde rushed into the dirt cloud to try and find Eddie, figuring he was probably dead. From Belgarde's point of view, the bomb detonated right underneath Eddie, threw him up in the air, and he was then consumed by the dust. He found his Team Leader on his back, wincing in pain. But miraculously, there wasn't much blood. Belgarde having been to E.M.T. (Emergency Medical Technician) training a few months ago, was a good guy for the job. He did everything you're supposed to do, made sure he was breathing, asked if he hurt anywhere, and searched Eddie with his hands for blood. But aside from having his bell being rung with a sledgehammer, and some cuts and scrapes, he was alright. Eddie had been carrying an A.T.4 (a bazooka) over his shoulder, and it miraculously had shielded him from most of the shrapnel that otherwise would've cut him to pieces.

"Are my balls still there?" Eddie asked Belgarde. I don't know if Belgarde went so far as to feel Eddie up or not, but he assured him his testicles were not the latest Taliban trophy.

Sergeant Hunt rushed to the scene as well. Battle 6 was demanding an update, but as of yet, no one knew what the hell had happened. We'd never experienced anything like it. I.E.D.s were common on the KOP road, of course. But an I.E.D. on a goddamned foot trail? It was unheard of. Captain Kearney was getting irate. He started yelling over the net about how we had become complacent. Complacent? In order to ex-fill from Ali Abad, you have to run. Because there's absolutely no cover for about 500 meters. And how the hell you gonna scan every patch of ground while you're running with 60 to 85 pounds of gear on? What was even more, Captain Kearney never even asked if Eddie was alright or showed any concern about whether his guy was even alive. He just went on a rant about complacency, followed by the "look-for-the-triggerman" routine. (Anytime an I.E.D. goes off like that, there had to be someone within line-of-sight of the bomb, to detonate it.)

Back at the base of Donga, "Keep that rear security goin', watch for an ambush," Sergeant Miller shouted. But the valley had gone completely quiet. There were a couple of women working in the fields below Babyol. Then we saw this old man with his long white beard, walking stick and manjams making his way along the banks of the river below us. Not a very likely suspect, as he wasn't what you'd call a "fighting-age male," but Slo told me to pick up, and him and I moved down to the river to intercept the old man. "*Deltarasha!*" Slo said to him. (Pashtun for "come.") I think the guy was predominantly deaf, but he finally understood. I kept the SAW on him while Slo checked him for any kind of detonation device. The guy was clean, as well as confused, slightly belligerent, and a victim of the language barrier, so we let him go.

We walked back up to our former location. We stayed out a couple more hours at least. But we never found the triggerman. Destined came down with the Humvees and took Sergeant Eddie back to the KOP for evaluation. Eddie was R.T.D. (Returned To Duty) the next day. Jokes about Eddie being blown up by complacency would proliferate for months.

"Oh goddamn, Eddie, you complacent motherfucker, oh you got blown up by the complacency."

"You better not get complacent, dude. Hajj'll bury a bomb right under your foot if you're not careful."

"Okay, let's go out on patrol, and not get complacent, I mean blown up."

"Battle Base, Phoenix. Got eyes-on complacency, bracing for explosion, over."

No one could ever accuse Captain Kearney of not providing enough material for our C.O. bashings. The man was a sarcasm-lovers wetdream. But seriously, now, on top of everything else we had to worry about, you had to wonder whether the next step you took would blow you 5 feet into the air and into invalidism.

First trip to Marastana "memorable"

November 29, 2007

The Marastana spur sat south of Donga, on the east (bad) side of the river. I don't believe that 10th Mountain ever went there. If I'm recollecting right, I wanna say the village's actual name was Lanyol. But since 10th Mountain called it Marastana, so did we, I guess for continuity's sake. Well, once we started venturing into Donga, I suppose patrols to Marastana were inevitable.

My Squad drew the lucky card and was chosen to lead the first patrol to said hive of villainy. The route we took matched exactly that of going to Donga (down through Babyol, ford the river, skirt the bottom of the mountains through all those blind and wide-open draws, only instead of cutting up to Donga, you just kept heading south on that little trail into more blind and wide-open draws, till you made it to Marastana, and then you went up).

We reached the village without incident. However, about the time we got to the base of Donga, we noticed there was a guy on the roof of a house in Ali Abad, who was doing nothing but watching us. Not good.

I'd say they were surprised to see us in Marastana, except for the fact that there weren't any males around. Also not good. We finally found this one guy, along with probably the ugliest, inbred looking woman I've ever seen in my life. This girl needed someone to slap a *burkha* on her, and quick. The old man must not've gotten the message for all males to evacuate the village. Lieutenant Gillespie started questioning him ("Where's everybody at and where's your village elder?") and finally this numb skull takes us up to this one house (and I mean way up).

Every village we went into smelled like equal parts piss, livestock and garbage. Marastana was no different. The infrastructure of the Korengal being what it was—which was nonexistent—people threw buckets of human waste right outside their front door or wherever they fancied. Good luck getting away from the ubiquitous goat in Afghanistan. If there's a good smelling goat, I never met one. And I never seen a trash truck, dumpster or landfill in said country. Trash was just strewn about everywhere. So that explains those smells.

Anyway. You might've heard me say this on more than one occasion, but this was taking entirely too long. In the Korengal, from the second you stepped outside the wire, a clock was ticking. We all understood the precarious situation we were in, and just wanted to get the hell out of it. I had cover behind the corner of this house, and had my SAW setup on 1705 and Dar Bart. The guy on the roof in Ali Abad was still there, still watching our every move. Everyone's spidey-senses were going off like a firehouse alarm. Shit was just too quiet.

As per usual, a SAW gunner is busy pulling security, and so a lot of stuff is meanwhile happening that you have no clue about. But something went down to make the P.L. think this village idiot was shady and was hiding somethin', or, there was just something suspect laying out in the open; I don't know which. But Lieutenant Gillespie sent the A.N.A. in to search this guy's house. (We were not allowed to search houses. Only our Afghan Army counterparts could do that.) Normally when the A.N.A. went in to search a house, they didn't find shit which made you question how hard they actually looked. Well not on this day.

This old fucker had a P.K.M., three R.P.G. heads, and a giant roll of det. cord (detonation cord used to build I.E.D.s). But that wasn't all he had. In June 2005, a 4-man Navy SEAL team was reported to have been wiped out near here, along with the 16 guys who came in a Chinook to rescue them. (The Taliban shot the bird down.) The only guy that survived was Navy SEAL Marcus Luttrell.

Inside this dude's house, was an American assault pack, nine M-14 mags, one M-4 mag, several American smoke grenades, an American flight suit, and Luttrell's helmet complete with the Lone Star of Texas on it (just as he describes in his book, *Lone Survivor*).

Well, that's unusual. Quite a score, but it involved us staying there longer, which I was very much against. But you had to question oldboy. One would think that you'd detain him and take his ass back to the KOP, but that's not what we did. For whatever reason, we confiscated everything and just let the guy go.

Our new dilemma was how to get back home. The guy on the roof in Ali Abad was still watching us. He was waiting to remote detonate an I.E.D. and we all knew it. But the thing was, by our Rules Of Engagement, we couldn't just shoot the guy for watching us. Well, since we were already so high up on the Marastana spur, the P.L. made the call that we'd descend into the Donga-Marastana draw to avoid as much as possible, taking the same route home, but we'd still have to pickup on the Donga trail. Before we did though, we passed the rock spine that jutted out of the Marastana spur (a place from which we'd taken God knows how much fire). It was tactically a very sound place, offered tons of cover and limitless fields of fire. There was enough room up there for a dozen guys. You had to nod your head and admire it.

We went down the draw and up the other side, and for some reason, up into the lower part of the village of Donga. This didn't make a whole lot of sense to me. We have a potential I.E.D. triggerman. Okay, this was our first patrol to Marastana, so no way would they have put an I.E.D. between Donga and Marastana. They were obviously waiting for us to go to Donga. Now we were in Donga. The I.E.D. had to be between Donga and the river, and somewhere that this guy had eyes on it. Meaning closer to Donga than to the river. And now we were about to ex-fil on the same trail we came in on.

Smart, right?

But hey I just do what I'm told. And when I was ordered to pickup and run down that trail, that's what I did. Sern't Slo ran down the rock staircase first, I was next, then came Roberts followed by Sern't Miller, then Eddie, then Belgarde, then BOOM!

There is no Battle Drill for React To Dismounted I.E.D., but if there were I think it would be something like, "Push out, establish 360° security, prepare for ambush and secondary I.E.D., send in element with Medic to I.E.D. site to assess casualties, get accountability."

But this being (to the best of my knowledge) only the second trail I.E.D. in military history, surprise and chaos just got the better of us. We got our shit together, just not as fast as we should've.

Since Alpha Team was all accounted for, we took cover and started looking for badguys to shoot. The I.E.D. had detonated under Lindley, and Belgarde kept shouting, "Mino! Mino!" So Bravo went back to look for him and did find Mino all in one piece. He was mostly deaf and completely disoriented, but otherwise alive. Miraculous.

Well our new S.O.P. for trail I.E.D.s seemed to be, you send in the P.L. and the F.O., they measure the bomb crater, take pictures, and stand around for about 2 hours. Which sucks. But what was interesting was the construction of this I.E.D.

The Taliban had found one of our Willy-P rounds. Willy-P is armyslang for white phosphorus, which is an incendiary munition. And a damned effective one for the enemy we were fighting, where you're not even sure where the hell he is. Anyway, when the Willy-P round detonates, it spreads this really nasty white chemical crap all over the place, which burns the shit out of everything. And keeps burning. If it gets on you, what we're told to do is immediately dump your camelbak onto the ground to make mud, and pack the wound with mud, 'cause the white phosphorus needs oxygen to work.

So the Taliban had found one of our Willy-P rounds we had shot that didn't go off. (But the white phosphorus inside I'm sure was still good.) They'd taken that round and attached an explosive and a detonation device to it, then buried it in our trail for us. However, the charge they used wasn't powerful enough to pierce the mortar casing, thank God. If it had, that one Willy-P round probably would've been enough to take out almost the whole patrol. Scary. We'd all be crispy critters right now. As it was, we just had a hearing-impaired grenadier who didn't know which way home was. Headshake. You talk about lucky.

Replacements

    Between September and January, we finally got some newguys. But only 1 per Squad. To be fair, it must've been tough comin' into a valley so fierce, among guys who'd been fighting there 6 months, and training together for a year or more before that. But to be honest, we didn't give a flying fuck. All we saw were a buncha candyass cherries who hadn't earned our respect, and weren't even worthy of the uniforms they were wearing. They were tactically inferior, and they weren't scared enough of the Korengal. They didn't even know what D.T.V. meant. Still, they were guard shifts in my mind. And that meant more sleep. It was kind of a resentful relief.

    The first was Bass and he came in right before Rock Avalanche. He seemed to have the most potential out of the group. He was a RIP dropout (RIP being the Ranger Indoctrination Program, meaning he had tried out to be in the Rangers, but didn't make it), and those guys are usually pretty squared away and in a lot better shape than most dudes. They wanna be good Soldiers and have that kind of mentality and better military bearing—more disciplined.

    Bass ended up in Weapons Squad but initially he was given to 3rd Squad. God knows Sern't Rose gave him a hard enough time. Rose came in as a replacement in O.E.F. VI (the 173rd's previous deployment), and was assigned to Sergeant Shelton's Squad. Tales of him Iron-Miking around the firebase holding a sandbag straight-armed over his head for hours at a time tend to leave an impression. And I'm pretty sure it's safe to say Sergeant Rose left an impression on Private Bass.

    I believe the next to arrive was Newberry. I think he was a Specialist already. He was thin, very young with acne that did not approve of our substandard living conditions. My Squad was re-fitting at the KOP when he showed up, and Sergeant Miller (after an ample smoking I'm sure), sent him out to O.P. Three to orient him to the valley and help us pull guard. This was late November-ish. He walked in the O.P. and received our coldest shoulders. But his existence did mean 2 more hours we'd have off in between guard shifts. And after the 6 months we'd just had, that was welcome, even if Newberry wasn't.

We mostly inundated him with the silent treatment at first. Just told him the basics of what to watch out for, so while he was on guard we could rest in relative ease. But after a few days, you had to see what this pimpley-faced kid's story was. Apparently, he was in some chill Ops job or something, in J-Bad or Blessing or somewhere real cush. Livin' in A.C., taking showers on the daily, Internet access, phones, hot chow, all that.

And this stupid fucker actually volunteered to come out here. We vehemently told him what a dumbass he was. He kinda shrugged it off. I thought it through: I mean, the kid enlisted to be Infantry. Which is what I did. It wasn't his fault somebody stuck him in some lame-ass office job. If that had happened to me, I would've volunteered to come take part in this amenity-free shooting gallery too. 'Cause you gotta understand, the kinda guy who enlists to be Infantry in a time of war wants to fight. And if he don't get it, and he's true, he'll do everything it takes to get in that fray. I would.

I'd go so far as to say I respected this line of reasoning, except no combat Infantryman respects a cherry. Fuckin' cherries.

Anyway, Newberry was going to 2nd Squad, so he was Sergeant Bullock's problem as far as I was concerned.

Then there was Spangler. I don't think anyone was too impressed with Spangler. He apparently came from a long line of military officers, but decided to go enlisted and seemed to be having second thoughts about it. His military bearing was far from what it should've been for a guy coming into a pack of battle-hardened sadists such as ourselves. Weapons Squad was hurting for the most guys, and since Spangler was a little larger than the other replacements, he was headed for one of the gun teams.

About the same time, we got Monroe. He was kinda quiet at first, which I think is probably the best attribute a cherry could have. Just keep your mouth shut, watch and learn. They placed him in 3rd Squad. He almost fell out of his first patrol, which wasn't uncommon.

There was very little way anyone, and I mean anyone, could step off a bird and into that valley and keep up with the rest of us on day one. Afterwards, Sern't Rose loaded him down with all his kit plus an assault pack full of I don't know what, and made him walk up and down the firebase about 12 dozen times. (For there were few steeper climbs than the one that went through Phoenix.)

On New Year's Eve, my Squad was again back at the O.P. on refit. It was my day to be on the KOP proper, and this was right after we had this group of Army engineers come in and build what's called a "beehut" (that being a plywood building) in place of the big olive green tents we used to have. And so in comes this very large and loud Bostonian, incapable of pronouncing the letter "R" unless it was the first letter in a word.

The guy was just a cherry like the rest of them, and a RIP dropout like Bass, but it was obvious he was there to learn. If he could get over his own arrogance anyway, which he brought plenty of. He was also an accomplished wrestler of sorts and into the whole M.M.A. thing. I always got the feeling that when he was told to do something, he was constantly considering whooping someone's ass instead. But in the Army, a Private is a Private, and it doesn't matter if you can beat up your Team Leader or not. You still have to obey orders.

Slo just kinda dropped him off in the tent, and proceeded to go get drunk with Robi. (Between those 2, they always had a bottle of something.) The Bostonian, McLauchlan, talked entirely too much. He was going to my Squad so I gave him a scant description of the valley and what we did, then I mostly just ignored him while I played *Monster Hunter* on my P.S.P. This was supposed to be my break and I really didn't appreciate having to spend it babysitting. Plus, this was like the twenty-ninth time I'd tried to kill this goddamned Rathalos and it was kicking my ass. I had to slay this thing before we went back to Phoenix or the whole fuckin' world was gonna end as far as I was concerned.

This all sounds stupid, don't it? Here we were, trapped in the most violent valley in country, short-handed as hell, and we're like all being picky about who they sent us. (As a little caveat, with time, these replacements became pretty squared-away and part of the family. We just didn't think much of 'em at first.)

Thanksgiving Korengali-Style

After an early lunch for themselves, Destined drove down to Phoenix with Captain Kearney, First Sergeant Caldwell and a trunk full of mermites. (Mermites are not nubile young mermaids with a penchant for satisfying Soldiers, as one might assume, but rather they are big green thermal containers that keep food hot.) They were setup and Captain Kearney and First Sergeant, along with Lieutenant Gillespie, began dishing out turkey and dressing. There was also infidel ham, mashed potatoes, gravy, vegetables, pies, soda—we had a veritable American cornucopia on our hands, right smack dab in the middle of Muslim central. It was Army turkey to be sure. But oh my god it was good. We even had a Happy Thanksgiving banner that we hung on the wall with these cheezy little turkeys on it.

I'm guessing Bui and Lackley were probably up at some awful hour cooking it all. And Destined was even pulling guard for us up top so we all could eat together. I went up and thanked 'em later.

After Battle 6 and 7 left, and in lieu of not having any football to watch, apparently it was time to haze the replacements. Newberry, Spangler, Monroe and Bass, our cherries, had to eat a whole cherry pie apiece, then chug a bottle of Worcestershire sauce till they puked their guts out. I didn't get off on that kinda thing the way some guys did. I thought it was juvenile and unnecessary but I watched anyway, since clearly I wouldn't be watching Dallas play. It was a little slice of entertainment if you will.

Don't know that anyone reflected on it, but we did have a lot to be thankful for that year. Yeah, Vimoto, Restrepo, Blaskowski, Cannon, Rougle, Brennan, and Mendoza were dead. From our Platoon alone, Parish, Loza and Johnson were wounded, but by all rights it could've been much worse. At least on that day, things didn't seem so bad. Not so bad at all.

That's Not Mine!

Any time your Squad came down on the patrol for northern Babyol, it was a great relief. Nothing ever happened in northern Babyol, it was such an easy walk, and you'd probably be back in your hooch in just a little over 2 hours. It was the shammest patrol we had. You almost felt guilty for going on it.

I can only guess at the populations of these villages. Babyol was by far the largest in the Korengal, and if I had to take a stab at it, I'd say, including northern Babyol, there were maybe 1,500 people there or maybe just 1,000; I really don't know (whereas Donga and Marastana comprised populations of just a two or three hundred each, and 500 tops for Ali Abad with another 100-150 in Dar Bart).

We cruised through the trash-strewn village and down through the corn terraces. I mean, you were always on guard of course—we all knew anything could happen at any time, anywhere—but the probability in Babyol was really low. So we were walking past this raghead's house, and someone spotted somethin' that wasn't right. I don't know what it was, but the P.L. went over and started questioning this guy. And he didn't like the answers he was gettin'. So he made the call for the A.N.A. to search oldboy's house.

Meanwhile, we (Sergeant Miller and Alpha Team) got ordered to push up to some high ground and establish an overwatch. So we found a suitable spot, and we waited. The valley was completely calm. Not the kinda calm where it's like, oh-shit-it's-too-fuckin'-calm-right-now-somethin's-about-to-go-down. This was just plain ole ordinary calm. So we were doing some scanning, doin' some smokin', doin' some jokin', and an hour goes by. Then another hour.

"What in the hell, man?" asked Roberts. Obviously something was happening that we weren't wise to.

I started singing "Umbrella" by Rhianna, and Roberts

accompanied me. Then we did some "Cry Me A River" by J.T., and kinda continued with a hip hop theme. It did something to pass the time, but this was seriously taking forever. We'd S.P.ed around 1500 local time, and it was almost 1900 now.

What we finally found out was, the A.N.A. had gone through this guy's place, and tucked away in the barn, was a giant Russian anti-tank mine! So of course some intense questioning was underway.

"Where did you get this? Do you have more? Who are you working for? Where are they?" etc. And this guy wasn't talking. His story was like, "How'd that get there?! That's not mine!"

Since they weren't getting anywhere, Captain Kearney ordered us to bring the guy to the KOP. Well, I should say, the rest of the patrol took him to the KOP, while we remained in our overwatch position. We watched them walk this perp by us. They had him carrying the mine, which weighed in excess of 50 pounds.

And we were thinking, *Alright. Now that is a badguy. They are gonna take this dude in and lock him up.* So they get him to the KOP and hand him over to the T.H.T. (Don't ask me what T.H.T. stands for, but they're like military intelligence types who're allegedly trained in interrogation.)

Hours pass. "Oh my god, I'm so fucking hungry," Sergeant Slo said.

Roberts shook his head, "I bet those fuckers on the KOP are eatin' hot chow right now."

"We stay out here any longer and we'll be mounting NODs," Sergeant Miller agreed as the sun was setting behind the mountains. We were starting to run low on water too.

Eventually, the rest of our patrol returned. We'd been out for 9 hours. The next morning I asked about what had happened to our anti-tank mine guy. The T.H.T. at the KOP had questioned him for an hour or two, then set him free. That bastard was home in time for dinner and slept in his own bed. I couldn't understand it.

A few days later we were at the KOP on one of our counter-I.E.D. patrols. I walked in the M.W.R. and all the Destined guys came up to us, really appreciative of us having taken that mine out of the field of play. Murphree came up and gave me a big hug. He was like, "Thanks, man. Really."

I shook my head, "Yeah. But if they've got one, they've got more."

At Odds

The trail I.E.D.s continued. The way things went for the next couple of months was, you walked out the wire knowing something was gonna go boom. It was nerve wracking. The next step you took could very well blow you into oblivion. You treaded lightly, and scanned the trail for any perceivable funny business. But you had more than just the trail to worry about. There were still bullets flying. So you had to continue to scan the mountains as well. Running out of Ali Abad seemed even dumber than it had before, and yet we still did it.

There was a 2nd Squad-led patrol to Marastana that got blown up right in between the Donga-Marastana spur. They escaped largely unscathed, but it was accompanied by shots from a high-powered sniper rifle, which nearly blew Sergeant Bullock's head off. Missed literally by inches. Some suspected the rifle was just a Dragunov, but I had a feeling it was Sergeant Rice's M-14 that the Taliban captured on Rock Avalanche.

It was not a pleasing turn of events—bombs and a sniper rifle. Awesome. It felt like we were playing Russian Roulette. And no way could our luck hold up. But we kept patrolling, the trail I.E.D.s kept detonating, and somehow some way, we'd manage to make it back to Phoenix with cuts and scrapes and future T.B.I. (Traumatic Brain Injury) candidates. Our only saving grace was that the Taliban weren't very good at building I.E.D.s. That, and The Man Upstairs was watchin' over us really close. Regardless, it gave you this awful feeling in your gut that never went away. 'Cause you knew— someone was gonna die. And probably pretty soon. And it might be you.

C.I.B. Ceremony

Though by this time we had earned our C.I.B.s about 70 times over, First Sergeant Caldwell decided we were due for a C.I.B. ceremony. It took a little doing—getting all the joes to the KOP from our respective firebases—but we made it happen.

The Combat Infantryman's Badge was established by the War Department in 1943 to boost morale and prestige of—in my biased opinion—the greatest facet of any of the armed services. The three basic requirements for receiving a C.I.B. are, you have to be an Infantryman satisfactorily performing Infantry duties, you must be assigned to an Infantry unit during such time as the unit is engaged in active ground combat, and you have actively participated in such ground combat. Meaning, pull the goddamn trigger.

See, every new recruit passing through the School Of Infantry in Fort Benning, Georgia, does little but dream about getting two things. One, a combat patch, which is worn on your right shoulder. It's your unit's patch (the unit you've been to combat with, that is), and wearing it signifies you've been in a combat zone with that unit for 60 days (for some units it's 30 days, or, it differs). It's one of the first things you notice about a guy in the Army. If you don't have a combat patch in this day and age, you ain't getting' no respect. And the second thing recruits have in their starry eyes, is the C.I.B. In the Infantry, you ain't nothin' till you got that combat patch and that C.I.B. And you're motivated with every blue fiber in your being to get both.

So everyone gathered down at the L.Z. in the dark and made a Company formation by Platoon (something we hadn't done since we left Italy). Palettes and pieces of loose wood were stacked up in front of each Platoon. Which they lit on fire. 2nd Platoon couldn't hardly get theirs to burn, but Sergeant Hunt had gone the extra mile to pour gun powder on ours, so it sizzled to say the least. Once lit, the bonfires blazed like a big burning middle finger in the center of the Korengal. It was like sayin', "Yeah bitches. We've fucked you up so bad we can light giant fires in the dark and stand in formation."

First Sergeant called us up one at a time; we ran up there, and he pinned us with our C.I.B.s. The bonfires were blazing, literally burning the eyebrows off the first rank, and after the official ceremony was over, Squad Leaders and Team Leaders and Sergeant Miller in particular, took turns punching the pins into our chests until we bled and bled some more. Not that any of us cared. We had our C.I.B.s. We had our combat patches. We were officially bona fide Infantrymen.

I'm sure it was First Sergeant Caldwell's idea. And I'm sure that he did it to boost morale. I'm also sure it fuckin' worked. We all felt a sense of pride we'd never known before.

To Quell The Korengal

Canned Air

In a war technically without alcohol, but still with all the stresses of combat, I think it's natural that guys will look for a little release. One thing about Soldiers is, they have an uncanny ability to improvise—bending whatever resources they have at their disposal into whatever it is that is actually needed. I remember one time during deployment, First Sergeant Caldwell was addressing us at the KOP and he said of Battle Company, "No one will do more with less." But I don't really think this is what he had in mind.

Company had on hand a good supply of canned air for cleaning computers. The stuff was also somewhat handy for weapons maintenance. Anyway, they dispersed the canned air down to the Platoons on a regular basis, then each Squad would get a can or two. In a way it was legit. Our living conditions were as filthy as it gets, and every Platoon had these government computers on which normal Army business had to be conducted. (Writing counselings, awards, putting in leave forms, and plus all the who-knows-what-the-hell that the P.L. and Platoon Sergeant have to send up to Company regularly.)

But, inevitably, there you were in your hooch, having just gotten back from a patrol you nearly got killed on, or maybe you just got off guard or were especially bored, and there's some canned air sitting there. What to do?

For those of you that have never tried it, it's pretty hilarious stuff. You just stick the nozzle in your mouth, push the button, and inhale. Then you wait a few seconds and the world goes whacky. Your head sounds like, "Womp womp womp womp! Wank wank wank wank!" And you begin laughing uncontrollably. It doesn't last more than a minute, but it's a fun minute.

Everyone did it, but Sergeant Slo had a real problem with this practice. "Man, quit using all my canned air!" Slo was under some crazy misconception that canned air was supposed to be used to save electronics or something. He was constantly hosing his personal computer down with the stuff, to the horror of us all. "You guys are wasting it," he'd proclaim.

I was taken aback, "We're wasting it?! I'm not sure you understand or appreciate the true purpose of canned air."

And Sern't Miller would pull rank just to aggravate Slo, saying, "Yeah, for the good of the Squad, stop spraying that shit on your computer. This can is all that's holding us together."

"It's vital to Squad sanity," I added.

"Yeah, vital to Squad sanity goddammit. Now lemme get that canned air."

The epidemic of canned air eventually reached unacceptable proportions when one of the Mortarmen at the KOP was found unconscious in his rack, canned air in one hand, and a frag (grenade) on which he'd written "For Battle 6" (Captain Kearney's call sign) in the other. On the BUB that night, First Sergeant got on real pissed declaring that, from this point forward, only Officers were allowed to be issued or possess, canned air.

Epilogue

Slo actually might've been onto something. Two weeks after we got back from deployment, my Mac keeled over on me. When I disassembled it to take the hard drive out, about two pounds of dirt was buried behind the keyboard. But if I had it to do all over again, I still woulda huffed all that canned air.

The Game Of Risk

We started the deployment with two guys constantly on guard, but eventually we nixed the bottom guard position so that we only had one guy pulling guard up top at the gun positions. Then, it was determined that one guy on guard at night to defend the entire firebase was not enough. The solution to this was to have a Sergeant Of the Guard, or S.O.G. Obviously this was an N.C.O. duty, and the idea was to have the S.O.G. kind of rove around the firebase and thus detect any nocturnal Taliban infiltrators. The practice however, did not usually go so well as the N.C.O. who was on S.O.G. was much more likely to just be hanging out in his hooch playing video games, or simply sitting in a chair down at the base of Phoenix waiting out his two hours. A lot of times the damned S.O.G. would just fall right back asleep, which sucked since he was supposed to wake-up your relief which meant you'd be on guard an extra 20 minutes or so.

But one N.C.O. who pulled proper S.O.G. was Sergeant Rose. Rozenwald was a college-educated redhead from Pennsylvania, who had left his job as a coach (high school I think), to fight The War On Terror. While on S.O.G., he would walk around and from time to time he'd come up in the guard tower, not so much to check up on you as to just kinda keep you company and bullshit a little bit. He was without a doubt one of the cooler dudes you'd ever meet. He just had a way with people. He was very smart, calm, especially articulate and had a helluva a knack for putting any situation into perspective. I really admired the guy.

So anyway there was a general consensus that, there just weren't enough of us in the valley to accomplish what command wanted us to do. A lot of times it seemed like 120 dudes to fight in a valley so vicious was nowhere near enough. When in all reality, to quell that valley, you would need no less than a Platoon-manned O.P. on top of every spur, from here all the way to Pakistan.

And this one night, Sergeant Rose said to me after climbing up into our little tower, "If I'm playing Risk, and my opponent moves all his armies to say, Russia, do I move more of my armies to help fight them, or do I leave just one army to face the Mongolian Hordes? Ya know? And this is a game for children ages 12 and up."

Like Cranking on a Jack-In-The-Box

In lieu of every other patrol we sent out ending in a giant explosion, Captain Kearney came down to Phoenix for a pep rally. We weren't in much of a mood for speeches, and we already knew what he was gonna say anyway. He began with something to the extent of, "Hey guys, I just wanted to come down here, and sort of, touch base, to see what you guys are thinking... So are there any thoughts, anything anyone wants to say, about what's been going on here with the I.E.D.s?"

And there was nothin' but silence. This was something that I felt very strongly about, that I knew everyone in the Platoon felt strongly about, and how could you not? I mean now more than ever, we all felt the clock was ticking and it was just a matter of time before the Taliban got better at building bombs, and we just couldn't keep getting as lucky as we had been.

People were gonna die. But not just any people. Guys from our Platoon were gonna die. Guys that we'd fought with, guys that we'd been on 4-day passes with to Florence, guys we'd spent every day with for the past seven months, guys we trusted our lives to. You just couldn't escape this thing for very long. And by very long I mean, a week? Two, tops? So Belgarde broke the silence and said, "I'm not gonna lie, Sir. I don't wanna leave the wire. It just doesn't make sense to go walkin' on a trail we know has an I.E.D. in it."

Captain Kearney tightened his eyebrows, and if he could've, I think he would've struck The Thinker pose, "Let me just play Devil's Advocate for a minute," he said. "What if we stopped going on patrol? All that would do is give the enemy a chance to get closer and closer, and before you know it, they'd be crawling up, and attacking you from right outside the wire."

I didn't say it (I was just a Specialist at the time and as it was I spoke out of rank more than just about anyone in the Company), but what I was thinking was, *Fuckin' let 'em attack the firebase. 'Cause I like my chances fighting those bastards behind fortifications with a whole Platoon, unlimited ammo and heavy weapons, better than the thought of going out every day, essentially walking two trails, one of which undoubtedly had a goddamned bomb on it.*

But you could just tell Captain Kearney wasn't gonna change his mind no matter what anybody had to say about it. We were gonna go out, every day, and pray to God the bomb wasn't on the trail we were taking. And if your Squad got lucky, and didn't get blown up, then chances were, your buddies in another Squad, would find it the next patrol.

Operation Beanie Baby

16 December, 2007

Destined had driven down and dropped off these boxes for us. Inside of these boxes were goddamned Beanie Babies. I kid you not. There we were, front and center, in the most dangerous area of operations in the entire theater, staring at Beanie Babies. "What the hell are we supposed to do with these?" Roberts asked.

Lieutenant Gillespie began, "Okay, guys. Um, so, the story is, uh, there's this Colonel, and he has a daughter, and uh, she's got terminal cancer. And this little girl's dying wish, is, um, for us to take these Beanie Babies, to the children in Ali Abad."

"What the fuck?!" was everyone's general reaction.

I guess you would classify this as Humanitarian Aid. And we did these H.A. runs all the time. Every Monday, we'd take beans, rice and flour down to Babyol. But it didn't stop there. We were always carrying shoes, jackets, and school supplies to Ali Abad too. If we hadn't already pulled all of our patrols for the day, people wouldn't've been half as upset. But with all these trail I.E.D.s we'd been encountering of late, this was just us risking our necks again, for no real reason.

"Wait, wait, wait, wait, wait," said Sergeant Slo shaking his head incredulously, a cigarette out the corner of his mouth. "This girl, specifically said, for us, to take those, to Ali Abad?! How the hell does she even know where Ali Abad is?! How has she even heard of it?! There's no way. There's no fucking way."

"Look guys," Lieutenant Gillespie said, "we were told to do it, so we're gonna do it."

"Hopefully we don't get blown up on the way down there," said Fimbres as he looked at the sky.

"Hey," Wilson said, "I'm just here to get other people promoted."

Sergeant Eddie turned to me, "I hope that little bitch dies a slow and painful death."

The next order of business was for everybody to stuff their cargo pockets till Beanie Babies were brimming out of them. I didn't wanna refuse orders, but I couldn't abide by this. There was a large pink pig. I picked it up and wedged it in between the carrying handle on my SAW. *I'll take this pig*, I thought, *but I ain't takin' nothin' else.* I looked at Fimbres who just shook his head and rolled his eyes.

We S.P.ed a little past 1500 local time. After some debate about where the I.E.D. might be, someone made the call to walk the road into the village. There was no real way of knowing, but we'd done the Donga trail earlier that day and didn't get blown up. So intuition told us, it was probably on the school trail. Anyway, we made it into Ali Abad without anyone goin' boom.

We setup in the cemetery as usual, with the gun team to my west. I unslung the SAW, extended the buttstock, charged the bolt and sat it down on a grave behind a shallow rock wall. I took the pig, placed him on the same rock wall, pointed south. "Pull security, Pig," I said. "This is no place to be screwing around."

I was all by my lonesome, with the rest of my Squad down by the pump house. I pulled out my monocular and began to scan. (They issued us binos but those things take up too much room on your kit, whereas you can fit a monocular into a flashbang pouch that only takes up 1 strip of MOLLE.) I had excellent fields of fire on 1705, Dar Bart and Honcho Hill. Nothing was moving.

"What's that? Yes, this is stupid, Pig. I think so too. No, I don't think we'll die today. But that's the thing about this place, Pig. Ya never really know."

I focused in on 1705, scrutinizing every last tree and bush. Not a soul to be seen.

"What's that, Pig? You don't wanna live with dirty, filthy Hajj?" I pulled out my pack of Pines and lit one. "Well, I don't blame ya. Tell ya what, I'll see what I can do. Now keep scanning, Pig. No, I don't see anyone either. But trust me. They're there."

Cigarette in one hand, monocular in the other, I began looking house to house in Dar Bart and watching the surrounding mountainside for any funny business. But all was quiet on the southern frontier. I exhaled and shook my head, "It's too quiet, Pig.

Way too quiet. They probably saw us leaving the firebase and they're already in position." Regardless, we kept scanning.

After much ado, The P.L. sent Campbell around to collect everyone's Beanie Babies.

"Shadix, you got any Beanie Babies over here?"

"Just this pig," I said continuing to look through my monocular.

There was a weird silence. "Well, can I have it?"

"No."

"Uh, why not?"

I looked at him, "Campbell, this is a pig. And Muslims hate pigs. It's like sacrilege to them. If you try to hand them a pig, they could get insulted, the village elders would throw their hands up in fury, and the whole valley could erupt in anti-American protest. We could have a real *jihad* on our hands, Campbell. So by not giving you this pig, I could very well be preventing a serious international incident."

He shook his head, "Well, we wouldn't want that, would we?"

"No. We decidedly would not."

"Is that the only Beanie Baby you have?" I nodded and Campbell gave up and went on to the next guy, as Sergeant Eversman (our new E.T.T.) came by to see how I was doin'.

As the last of the Beanie Babies were dispensed in the village, the sun began to set behind the mountains. Everyone's hope at that point was for us to sit put and ex-fill under the cover of darkness. But I guess Captain Kearney didn't consider that very exciting. Sergeant Miller yelled, "Shadix, pick up, let's go." I collapsed the buttstock, tossed the sling over my head, swung the bipod forward, and put the pig back under the carrying handle. "Yes, Pig, this is bullshit." I asked Sergeant Miller if we were running the Ali Abad 500 and he said no, at which point I felt somewhat relieved, but somethin' just wasn't right here and everybody knew it.

We weren't movin' more than a couple minutes before the rounds came flying in. It wasn't a very vicious firefight. Pretty routine really. Just kind of a going-through-the-old-motions sorta gunfight. But nonetheless, it really irritated me. We came to your village to give your children toys. For the love of God, or Allah, or whoever-the-fuck.

Couldn't you just let this one go? Ya know? It was like a reaffirmation. That it didn't matter what kind of good we tried to do in this valley. These people genuinely hated us. And there was nothin' that was gonna change that. Not even some innocent pretense of some dying Colonel's daughter (fictitious or otherwise), wanting those destitute kids to have a little stuffed animal to play with. Didn't change a goddamned thing.

We made it to Phoenix with no casualties. I sat on my cot and looked at the pig. "Yeah," I said, "you can come back to America with me. What? No, sure we'll make it. Nothin' to worry about, Pig. Nothin' to worry about."

The Informant Fiasco

December 2007

    The patrol gathered a few hours before first light. It was one of those classic hurry-up-and-wait ordeals the Army so loves. The short of it was this: the oxymoronic military intelligence guys known as the T.H.T. at the KOP, had some sort of informant, who (allegedly) knew a specific house in which (allegedly) a Taliban commander spent his nights. This house was in the village of Donga—a renowned place for getting your ass handed to you. To top it all off, it was snowing, and had been snowing the majority of the night. Still, a patrol's a patrol, and it was time to check the goddamned box.

    However, the T.H.T. (which we all understood to stand for Tactically Hopeless Turds) were taking their sweet time getting to Firebase Phoenix so we could get this goatfuck underway. Fifteen minutes went by, cigarettes were smoked in the dark. Half an hour passed—more butts were burned. After forty-five minutes, asses began to freeze to the makeshift benches on which we waited. Finally, an hour. Some guys had already smoked five or six or even eight cigarettes and were on the very verge of contracting lung cancer. Still we waited. "Patience isn't so much a virtue, as it is a nuisance," someone said. "Where the fuck are these guys?"

    At last, about an hour till dawn, the long-anticipated T.H.T. arrived at Phoenix. Two of them actually, and one was a chick. We immediately noticed not only was a female in our presence, but she was wearing a fleece jacket no less. Of course it was cold, and a fleece was great for guard when you weren't moving, but five minutes after you stepped off on patrol, you were sure to sweat, and that's just wearing your top and a t-shirt. So a fleece? She was gonna melt. It was a clear indication that she'd never been on a patrol, at least in the winter.

In addition, the T.H.T. were rocking M-16s. Which looked about as professional to modern Infantrymen as having a hot-pink Hello Kitty strapped to your kit. And goggles. The girl was wearing goggles. Of course it was on everyone's packing list for deployment, but goggles were one of those items you stuffed in the bottom of your B-bag and left at the company FOB, never to be seen again. What was more, was the informant. They had him all dolled up in ill-fitting A.C.U.s, with a balaclava (ski mask) covering his face and a baseball cap on top of that, with really dark Oakley's on. They had thrown a fleece on him too. He looked like a character alright. But not the kind of character that possessed any credibility whatsoever. "Aw man, this is some mo' bullshit right here," said Sergeant Miller.

We still had about another hour or so of dark left when we stepped off. The initial plan was to go to the Babyol mosque and find a way down the corn terraces from there, as the slip-n-slide was pretty much impassible in this weather. (The slip-n-slide was a 7-foot deep irrigation way we normally took to the river because of the cover it offered, which on a good day, no mortal could get down without falling about twelve times due to the supernatural slipperyness of its banks.)

The problem was, the corn terraces were no less than six feet tall, and some of them upwards of ten. The other problem was, Sergeant Miller didn't care anything about accomplishing this mission. To the contrary, he was doing everything he could to ensure it failed. So when we got to the mosque, we pretended to look around to kill time, then Sergeant Miller informed the P.L. that there was no way down without somebody getting hurt. Which was maybe true, but, I would've done it.

I told him as much and he said fuck that. He yelled at me, "Shadix, I ain't trying to get to no Donga! We do get over there and this H.V.T is holed up in one of those houses, he ain't gonna just give himself up. And if he is an H.V.T., I seriously doubt he's alone. He'll have a security detail. In this weather, we're gonna be on our own, with no air assets, no medevac, and if somethin' goes down, we'll be suckin' dick for Skittles money."

But the P.L. then insisted we start making our way towards Ali Abad and find an alternative route to Donga. By the time we were a couple hundred meters from Ali Abad, there was enough light to see by, and then Lieutenant Gillespie had the bright idea that we could work our way down what could only be described as an incredibly steep irrigation cliff. Water ran down it in between the terraces.

You were grabbing onto tree trunks and rocks and anything else that looked rooted or planted enough to try and stay on your feet, but there were portions so steep you had to slide down on your ass, and those portions were invariably covered with running water so that, by the time you arrived at the river, you were already drenched from the waist down.

There was even this great part where you had to jump across the irrigation way. It was a pretty far jump and when you landed on the other side it was by your toes and you were trying not to fall backwards into the water, which would've sent you tumbling down a good twenty or thirty feet. Someone, I can't remember who, but someone didn't make it, and fucked themselves up pretty good. It might've been Fimbres.

Either way, it was decided the gun team would stay on the west side of the river for overwatch. The rest of us proceeded across the river. Our feet were already soaked so we just walked through the icy water. Once across, the P.L. told my fireteam to stay at the base of Donga to ensure no one escaped down the Donga trail or attempted to attack the main element from this avenue of approach, while the rest of the patrol proceeded up into the village in search of the house containing the noted badguy. Sergeant Miller opted to stay with us.

It all seemed asinine at this point, since the informant had said that the H.V.T. usually left the village at dawn, and it was no less than thirty minutes past that. On top of which, the informant refused to cross the river—said he was scared. So he too stayed on the west side of the river, as did the T.H.T. The chick had fallen into the river—and I mean all the way in—and didn't want to go any further. So our patrol was literally in pieces now, and proceeding without the informant to show them which house to go to.

We did have comms with the T.H.T., who relayed to the patrol via the gunteam where to go. The informant said the house the H.V.T. was in had green paint on the balcony portion—the railing, that is. Problem was, there must've been some sale at Hajj's Home Depot or something, 'cause half the 30 or 40 houses in Donga had painted their railings and windows green.

Thus, the patrol went up to the first house the informant insisted on. There was nothing there, at which point the informant said they were at the wrong green house, and it was actually the one up higher on the hill. Once the patrol got to the next house and no one was there, the informant decided it was at yet a different house a little lower down and to the north. Same story at that house. Then the informant changed his mind, No, no, no. Not that house, but up a little and to the south. But that was the wrong house too, and then he was adamant it was the first house.

This went on for hours. The weather wasn't getting any better and we weren't getting any warmer. Personally, I think I would've rather been with the portion of the patrol that was on the move, 'cause I was fucking freezing—shaking uncontrollably, teeth chattering. If I'd ever been any colder, I couldn't tell you when it was. Probably because my brain was encased in ice at that point.

It was obvious to all involved that this was just a proverbial wild goose chase. Except to the P.L., who insisted on pursuing the goose. Besides being on the very edge of hypothermia, we all knew damned well what Sergeant Miller said was true—no birds were gonna fly in this weather. If the shit went down, we'd have no medevac. We'd be totally screwed. We'd have to carry any casualties, back up that steep-ass slope, all the way to Phoenix, call Destined to come pick 'em up in the Humvees, and drive 'em back to the KOP. Where they still wouldn't get medevaced. If someone was seriously injured, could we even carry them from here all the way to the road, in time to save his life? No fuckin' way.

In due time, even the P.L. declared that this mission was going nowhere. We were wasting our time, again. Endangering our lives, again. For no good reason, again. The main element descended to our location, we forded the frigid river, again, linked up with the T.H.T., informant, and the gun team, and began to slog our way back up that bullshit irrigation route through the thickening storm. Guys slid, guys fell, and were pissed and freezing their asses off. The last time I could feel my toes was about four hours ago. Which probably didn't help with the ascent.

When we finally arrived at Phoenix, everyone just glared at the T.H.T. and informant as they went to their rooms to get warm. I stripped off all my sopping gear. Dry clothes and a warm sleeping bag never felt so good.

Sergeant Eddie

Sergeant Tyrell Edwards, or Eddie as everyone called him, was the only white guy named Tyrell I ever met. He was from Florida, and like a lotta paratroopers, had a thing for partying. In Italy, on the weekends, you could be sure to find him in one of Vicenza's many strip clubs. He was the kinda guy who would go out and party till 0430 on a weekday, and still make 0630 P.T. formation.

Eddie had been with Battle Company on their previous deployment, and had spent a lot of time in Weapons Squad since then. His joes generally loved him because he wasn't into being a hardass just for the sake of being a hardass. I remember once in Italy, Fimbres (then one of Eddie's joes) said that Eddie had told him, "Look if I smoke you," (make you do pushups till you're ready to puke) "it's not because I'm mad at ya. But if I don't, the other N.C.O.s will think I'm a weak leader."

That isn't to say Sergeant Eddie wasn't serious about soldiering. Eddie was always talking about wanting to work for a Squad Leader who could teach him things. So he wasn't thrilled about being in our Squad, because even though him and Sergeant Miller hung-out on the weekends in Italy, Eddie was aware that either Sergeant Miller didn't know much more than he did, or, if Sergeant Miller did know something outside of Eddie's skill set, he wasn't likely to teach it to anyone.

I was on guard one afternoon when Eddie strutted up the hill, waiting on Destined to come back from patrol so he could hitch a ride back to the KOP 'cause he was going on leave. I don't think I ever seen anyone so happy in my entire life. He was up there dancing and laughing, and his giant square jaw smiled ear to ear. Lord knows what kinda trouble he was about to get himself into, but you couldn't help but be happy for the guy. And at least he wouldn't be getting blown up for the next few weeks.

All I Want For Christmas

Christmas went a lot like Thanksgiving. Captain Kearney did make us pull a patrol. It was just a Babyol run, but still the idea of pulling a patrol on Christmas did not increase his numbers at the popularity poll. Afterwards, Destined drove the trucks down to Phoenix, packed with turkey, dressing and everything that went with it, which Captain Kearney and First Sergeant dished out to us. They even wore Santa Claus hats as they did so, and proceeded to smoke these gigantic cigars after the meal.

1st Squad got probably the best gift in the whole Korengal—refit on O.P. Three. Said Mino as we packed up our things that evening to go on the counter-I.E.D. patrol to relieve 2nd Squad, "If I can just make it to the O.P., I can, update the software on my computer and watch a movie."

I replied, "If we can just make it to the O.P. we'll probably live a week longer."

"Yeah," Mino thought, "I don't know why we put so much, emphasis on living."

On the night of the 25th, I pulled guard on O.P. Three from midnight to 0200 and when it was finished, tired as I was, I just didn't wanna go to sleep. I'd brought along some vodka, which my wife had sent over in a care package disguised in a bottle of hydrogen peroxide. I also had this movie on my iPod that I'd never seen called *The Family Stone*.

I wanna make it clear. Besides this little instance, I never abused alcohol during my deployment. And no one in my Platoon (save one or two) ever did either. As a Soldier assigned to the Korengal, you couldn't. When you were at Phoenix, you never knew when something was gonna happen. You could be pulled out of your bed and thrown onto some horrendous Q.R.F. mission at any time and we all knew and respected that. I never had enough alcohol to drink on a regular basis. So I saved it and I'd just have a lightly mixed drink before bed on a really bad day.

But there had to be a "give-time." There were opportunities when the probability of you having to go do something as perilous as it was spontaneous was low. For example, when you were on the O.P. And honestly, on this particular occasion, with all the trail I.E.D.s and the holidays and all, I just needed to get good old-fashioned drunk.

So after my guard shift, I knew I wouldn't have another for eight more hours. I grabbed my iPod, clicked on *The Family Stone* and started sippin' away. If you've never seen it, it's a well-written and sort of sappy movie about Christmas, and Rachel McAdams is really hot, and it was just the ticket for someone who was as alien to feeling as any of us were at that point in our lives. I enjoyed the hell out of it, and after it was over, I woke Mino up for some vodka straight.

We drank till it was gone. My tolerance for alcohol seemed to have lessened since deployment, and I ended up getting so obliterated the next thing I remember, I woke up on the west side of the spur just north of the O.P. with a buncha A.N.A. in my face laughing and talking Hajj.

At least I passed out on the most tactical side of the spur, I thought with the unusually warm December sun on my face as I began to puke all over the mountainside. Merry fuckin' Christmas, yall.

Merry Christmas, Battle Company!

Captain Kearney had come to Battle Company around December 2006. The Army norm is for a Captain to spend one year as a Company Commander. After that, they get a desk job and put the office into officer. The same was true of Lieutenants as well—1-year Platoon Leader time—but we weren't all that concerned about P.L.s.

What everyone in the Company wanted for Christmas was for Santa Claus to stuff Captain Kearney in his big brown sack and whisk him away. We'd been hearing rumors that Captain Kearney was gonna defer. Meaning he'd stick out the rest of the deployment with us, and then get reassigned somewhere else once we got back to Italy.

I was pulling guard on the O.P. when I heard Battle 6 get on the radio with Lieutenant Winn from 1st Platoon.

"Hey Brad," Captain Kearney said (officers always call each other by their first names), "I guess you've heard that Matt," (Lieutenant Piosa from 2nd Platoon), "is going to be the new P.L. for the Scouts, and I suppose you already know about my intention to defer."

Goddammit!

"And I was curious if you wouldn't mind staying around as my new X.O."

Oh, sonofabitch. I think somebody just shit in our stockings.

Return of the Anti-Tank Mine

It was December 27th, 2007. My Squad was still on refit manning O.P. Three. There had been a rash of I.E.D.s on the road lately. The stupid thing was, they kept putting the I.E.D.s in the same spot every time. They did it so much, we called it "the I.E.D. site." It was where the Table Rock spur met the road, just above Ali Abad. There was a big turn in the road there, and I guess the Taliban figured the trucks had to slow down for it.

Anyway, 2nd Platoon had pushed a patrol out to Lui Kalay (a village southwest of Ali Abad), and Destined had driven down there to cover their ex-fill. I can imagine Destined wasn't real crazy about driving over a place named "the I.E.D. site," but we all did what we were told, no matter how dumb we thought it was.

Destined always sent four Humvees out. If I recall the order of movement correctly, the first one was a .50 cal, the second was a Mark, the third was the TOW, and the fourth another .50 cal. The TOW truck fires a missile—a damned accurate one. It can even be adjusted in-flight to hit whatever you want it to. The Taliban of course, hated that shit because it was so lethal. There was a TOW Gunner in Able Company rumored to have nineteen kills. Which I guess makes him the Audie Murphy of the Kunar Province.

However, according to Destined Company's Specialist Jesse Murphree, the TOW truck was not the place to be. He said that it always received extreme favoritism when it came to Taliban gunfire. Which I'm sure it did. One of the most basic principles of warfare is you try to take out your enemy's most casualty-producing weapon first. What sucked for Murph was that he was the only guy Destined had who was qualified on the TOW. And though he offered to train someone up, no one was volunteering for his classes. Murphree was one of the most loveable guys you'd ever meet. True salt of the earth, always joking, didn't have a bad word to say about anybody, I mean if Murphree wanted to date your sister, you'd be alright with it. He was that kind of a guy. So Murph being Murph, he got behind the TOW every single patrol.

After 2nd Platoon had ex-filled from the village, Destined followed suit. Somehow the practice had come about, that right before they came to the I.E.D. site, the T.C. (the guy riding shotgun, who was the highest ranking man in the vehicle) would dismount and walk alongside the truck to try and spot the I.E.D. before the truck rolled over it. The first truck rolled past the I.E.D. site. Nothing happened. The second Humvee rolled past the I.E.D. site. And nothing happened. As Specialist Jonathan Farwell drove the TOW truck over the I.E.D. site, there came a resounding BOOM!

I was on guard at O.P. Three at the time and saw a giant plume of black smoke billowing from the I.E.D. site. The radio was alive with the frantic chatter of what-the-fuck-just-happened. As we'd find out later, what did happen was, the TOW truck was hit by a Russian anti-tank mine. And Humvees don't do so well against anti-tank mines. The explosion had rocked and shredded the truck, catching it on fire to boot. Farwell, the driver, was able to get out, but not without his A.C.U.s melting to his legs. Sergeant Alcantara, who had been walking beside the truck, was more or less okay. But the explosion had blown Murph out of the turret. And ripped his legs off on the way out. It threw him up into the air, and he had landed about a 150 meters down the mountain. They couldn't even find him for the longest time.

3rd Platoon was spun-up from Phoenix to help secure the site. Sergeant Al finally found Murphree and began applying tourniquets to what was left of his legs. Murph of course was in shock, but he was alive.

"Can I still come to your wedding?" he asked Sergeant Al.

"Of course you can, buddy."

The fact that it had been a Russian anti-tank mine, the same as what we had found in Babyol, infuriated us. And they'd just let that fucker go too.

Both Farwell and Murph were medevaced out of the valley, never to return. I suppose at some point there was a knock on the door of the Murphree residence, a Soldier in dress uniform telling his parents that their son had lost his legs. It was two days after Christmas.

Kill Me Please

    Once while I was on a training rotation in Grafenwoehr, Germany taking a piss in a port-a-john, I saw someone had written a quote: "Only the dead has seen the end of war." -Pluto. Now, the problem with that besides the fact that it lacked subject-verb agreement and it wasn't Mickey Mouse's dog, but rather Plato who said it, is I think it's good sometimes to make light of combat. But in utter honesty, some days I just wanted to die. It was not lost on us that we were being used as bait. Every day. There were times when humping the SAW and the 85 pounds that go with it up some godforsaken mountain with a 45° incline on another pointless patrol to a hostile village that didn't want our help in the first place, when we'd come to a large open area where the usual tactic is to sprint across it, and I'd just shake my head, say fuck it, and walk with my Team Leader screaming at me, and I'd just think, *Ya know, I wish somebody'd open up on me right now. Put me outta my misery already.*

    Just one good volley of machine gun fire, and this could all be over. No more humpin', no more patrols, no more guard, no more sand fleas, no more shit to burn, no more filth, no more sweat, no more cigarettes, no more sandbags to fill, no more jingle trucks to download. I could just get shot and it'd all go away.

    But for some strange reason there was still a little unrelenting part of you that actually wanted to live. And as sweet and easy as death sounded, you sucked it up and you starting running anyway. But always there's the omnipresent thought that dying would not be so bad. Not so bad at all.

In Recognition of Our Illustrious Leader

Right after New Year's Day, Captain Kearney was selected to receive the MacArthur Award. According to their website, the General MacArthur Leadership Award "recognizes company grade officers who demonstrate the ideals for which General MacArthur stood - duty, honor, country." I guess they pick twenty-eight of these bozos a year to be big shots, when in this Paratrooper's opinion, it was their joes and N.C.O.s that did all the work to get 'em where they were.

Regardless, we were all very happy for Captain Kearney for the simple reason that he had to leave the valley to receive his prestigious award. In his stead, Lieutenant Winn would be acting Company Commander. Lieutenant Winn was 1st Platoon's PL. But his time there was done so, if you recall, Captain Kearney made him our new Company X.O.

Everyone loved Lieutenant Winn being in charge. He didn't make us do half the dumb-fuckery Captain Kearney did. We still went out on patrols of course, but we didn't ford the river but once a week. If we did take contact, he didn't make us wait out there for another two hours in the freezing cold to see if we could draw more fire. When a really big storm blew in, he didn't order us go out stomping through six inches of snow the next day. (Walking in snow with all that gear on was exhausting work and dangerous besides. It's remarkable we never had a serious injury from someone just slipping and tumbling down the goddamned hill.) With Captain Kearney, a patrol was never cancelled. You went out no matter what. Even in weather when the medevacs wouldn't fly.

The thing was, it couldn't last. About the third week of January, our freshly decorated leader was back in the TOC puffing on cigars and polishing his new medal, feeling validated, if not obligated, in honor of the MacArthur Award, to game plan as many cockamamie new ways to make our lives as miserable as he possibly could.

An Occupational Hazard Turned Good Riddance

One day, there was a really loud explosion that came from a house on the cusp of 1st Platoon's A.O. For quite a while, there was nothing but speculation as to what it was. It certainly was not of American doing. But afterwards, there was a complete absence of I.E.D.s in the Korengal Valley—much to our relief. Building I.E.D.s is dangerous work. It's not uncommon for a bomb builder to go boom. Putting two and two together, it was generally decided that the Taliban's bomb-maker must've blown himself up.

What's in your draws?

Captain Kearney had a hunch that the Taliban stashed weapons caches in the draws on the east side of the valley. Since the fighting had fallen off for the winter, it was a lot more feasible to ford the river, search the draws and not come home dead. So we started dedicating probably a third of our patrols to going up and down the draws in between Donga and Marastana and all the draws north thereof.

Turned out Captain Kearney was right. We found several. They were usually hidden under a large rock or in a shallow cave. One cache consisted of ten R.P.G. heads and seven assorted mortar rounds. Another we came across was probably a couple hundred loose Dishka rounds (the equivalent of our .50 cal), some loaded A.K. mags, and several hundred really old British .303 rounds on stripper clips. These were good things to find and get out of enemy hands, but what sucked was, you had to carry it all home. Dishka rounds be heavy.

To Quell The Korengal

Soldiers Report O.P. Three, "Coldest Goddamned Place In The Korengal"

Soldiers in the 173rd Airborne Brigade Combat Team proclaim O.P. Three is the coldest American position in Afghanistan's abominable Korengal Valley. O.P. Three, which was built on a spur that effectively runs in the middle of the valley, is reported to thus channel all the wind in the Korengal. With lack of a proper thermometer or any other meteorological devices, it is impossible to quantify the precise windchill-susceptible temperatures experienced at O.P. Three. Although this determined wind is considered an ally in Afghanistan's sweltering summers, the men of Battle Company's 3rd Platoon wished their fair weather friend would take a season off.

The electricity-free O.P. is heated by a spartan pot-belly stove with a voracious appetite for fuel, requiring two Soldiers per day to make the long haul across the barren spur (rife with opportunities for any willing Taliban to take a shot at them), through the lackadaisical Afghan National Army compound where someone always shouts, "*Singay!*" past the KOP's semi-fortifications, and traverse the span of the L.Z. to the fuel point.

Finding the fueler (the only Soldier on the KOP allowed to oversee the pumping of fuel) could prove to be a chore in and of itself. For fuelers are known for their ability to abandon their post, for their reluctance to get along with others and for their generally bitchy dispositions. Sources Army-wide report the average fueler is a derelict anti-socialite devoid of any sense of duty or punctuality. However, once the culprit was apprehended and forced to perform the demanding and elaborate task of unpadlocking the pump, the Soldiers from the O.P. were then free to pump their own gas and begin slogging it back to O.P. Three.

However, despite their daily efforts to keep warm, the very composition of the O.P. renders their efforts almost pointless. O.P. Three appears to have been constructed by local workers, meaning that it consists of small rocks stacked upon more small rocks. While this design is well known for its ability to repel bullets and the like, the rocks do not stack without gaps in between them, allowing for the immense valley wind to blow straight through O.P. Three. Soldiers manning the O.P. noted that unless you are standing practically on top of the pot belly stove, you feel little to no warmth whatsoever.

This forces the Paratroopers to practice using their entire sleeping systems, composed of a light sleeping bag inside of a heavy sleeping bag inside of a Gore-Tex cover. The majority of men were noted to get into their full sleeping systems wearing every piece of warm clothing they could muster and going so far as to pull even their heads down into the bags to stay warm, only to be awoken in four hours for their next guard shift. One Trooper disclosed to this reporter that the best way to warm a sleeping bag was to get naked, but no one was willing to strip down to their birthday suit in such temperatures every four to six hours.

Naturally, the gunpit was where the wind and thus the temperatures were worst. Soldiers on guard did very little but don their body armor and helmet then wrap up in the nappiest blankets our armed forces could provide. When questioned whether he considered the blankets sanitary, Specialist Cody Belgarde said, "I wouldn't care if they were infested with small pox."

Night guard was worse still. The average member of 3rd Platoon regarded it as a 2-hour practice in frostbite repulsion. With only two or maybe three firefights a week to attend to in the winter, it was little wonder priorities had shifted from pumping Hajj full of .50 cal, to trying to maintain feeling in their toes. 1st Squad Alpha Team Leader, Sergeant Tyrell Edwards was quoted as saying, "It's egregious. But it still beats being at Phoenix pulling patrols."

Wintertime Antics

 Patrolling didn't stop for the winter. It didn't matter if it was 0° degrees with twelve inches of fresh snow on the ground. Whatever patrol you were scheduled for, you were going on. Carrying a combat load on dry terrain is tough enough, trudging through deep snow or trying to stay upright on the slippery patches of ice under that kind of weight made things immeasurably worse.

 Guard would have been especially unpleasant were it not for what was nicknamed the "poofy suits" which were issued to us as part of the Extreme Cold Weather Clothing System (E-CWiCS), as well as all the hand warmers that came in care packages from anysoldier.com. Still guard at night was something you never really looked forward to, unless experiments in hypothermia were a hobby of yours.

 However, you did have cold water finally, which was a pleasant change of pace from the hot water you'd been mercilessly sucking down all summer. And we finally had a refrigerator. It was called putting meat in a kickdown box outside. Problem was, while cats weren't as prevalent as dogs in Afghanistan, Phoenix managed to draw a good swarm of them, and the cats conducted 24-hour ops to get into the kickdown boxes.

 We had one Soldier who was apparently born with a cat-intolerant chromosome; either that or he just didn't like to eat meat that had little cat bites taken out of it. This unnamed vigilante went so far as to set up all sorts of homemade cat traps (sponsored by ACME, I believe), and upon catching a cat (which he caught many), he would kill them. The disturbing thing was, back in Vicenza, this was a gentle, good-hearted guy. Someone you could have a real conversation with, someone who was a good friend. A man of morals and admirable character. Definitely not someone you would need to report to the A.S.P.C.A. But dudes were seriously starting to wig. The isolation and stress, and the ever-present possibility of death began to manifest itself in strange ways.

Doc Lee must've been particularly bored, 'cause one night, Sergeant Miller bet Doc one hundred dollars he wouldn't snort a rail of Thai Chili powder (sent by my wife), which Doc Lee did, but not before saying, "That's huge," as he lined the chili powder up. Sergeant Miller reminded him, "You shook on it. Be a man." We handed him a sawed-off straw.

There was a flush of red to his face afterwards and Doc gasped and poured water up his nose and blew it into a pre-stationed trash bag by his side. Then Sergeant E. (one of the Marines attached to us to babysit the Afghan National Army), said, "Two hundred bucks; I'll give you two hundred to snort some wasabi," which was also provided by my wife. Doc and Sergeant E. even shook on it, but I asked Doc Lee sometime after the deployment if he ever got his two hundred bones and he said, "No." Which was too bad as it looked painful and required Doc to snort numerous bottle caps of water afterwards.

Doc Lee must not've had a P.S.P. (Play Station Portable) because that's how the rest of us semi-sane people passed the winter in Afghanistan. My personal game of choice was *Monster Hunter*. One could play *Monster Hunter* for months on end. We had more than one incident of guys getting busted playing P.S.P. on guard whilst back at the KOP. This led to First Sergeant Caldwell assembling us all for a berating. First Sergeant was notorious for malapropisms (using a wrong but similar-sounding word in place of the one he was searching for, especially when he was angry). "And goddammit!" he screamed in his Louisiana accent. "You on guard, you on guard! You on guard, you ain't got no helmet on, no I.B.A., you playin' the P.C.P.!" It was not an easily suppressed laugh. I guess First Sergeant wasn't much of a gamer.

If you weren't gainfully employed, the absolute and only place to be was in your bag. The Army sleeping bag (a.k.a. Military Sleeping System), despite (or most likely because of) its enormous weight, provides womb-like warmth. We had a pot belly stove, but there were three rooms in our little hooch-slash-house, so in the interest of anti-favoritism, you couldn't put it anywhere but in the hall, where it warmed no one. I ain't gonna lie, it helped a little bit, but the damned thing had to be fed and we only had enough fuel to run it about six hours a day.

Anyhow, one bit of good news for the winter was that the Taliban were fair-weather fighters. As lethal as they could be at times, they still weren't an organized Army, and as such, if they chose not to fight, I guess they didn't. One day we got I-Com chatter coming from a guy behind a Dishka saying, "It's too cold out here, I'm going home." And I think that was their mentality. Whereas our dumb-asses were going out regardless of the temperature or the presence of the enemy, it was like the Taliban had gone into half-hibernation. Firefights had fallen off from several a day in the summer, to maybe one every day or two after Rock Avalanche, to maybe just one or two a week during the winter. And, as a critic of firefights, even the one or two felt somewhat forced on the Taliban's behalf. It was as if they weren't putting enough effort into it. They were more of a, going-through-the-ole-motions kind of firefight.

Captain Kearney said with a sense of pride that we were "expanding the security bubble" with all of these patrols. Whatever that meant. Though it was true we were pushing farther south than ever (patrols to Marastana took place once or even twice a week (but not without us all silently cringing at the thought of it). Yeah, I guess if the adversary chooses not to fight, an officer could consider that security bubble expansion. So it seemed, but we knew they'd all be back in the spring. Which would be a bad time to be in Marastana.

To Quell The Korengal

The Witch Hunt

I don't wanna call anyone out here, but someone from another Platoon was caught with hash on them. We were in Afghanistan and hash was everywhere and it was cheap. Given how much stress we were under, guys just needed a release. But of course, this wasn't something First Sergeant and Captain Kearney could take lightly.

One by one, each Platoon, and I mean the entire Platoon, was called in to the KOP, while Destined covered down on their firebase. We were held like prisoners in one of the KOP's new hardstand buildings (they'd been doing a lot of construction, to the point I doubt 10th Mountain would even recognize the place). I'm not sure what criteria they used, but they selected six to ten guys from each Platoon to sit down with the C.O. and First Sergeant for an interview or interrogation or whatever you wanna call it.

Well, 1st Platoon and 2nd Platoon got off without a hitch, and returned to Vegas and Restrepo, respectively. I could imagine they just said the right and obvious things: "Nope, never seen any hash. Nope, nobody's doing it," and went back to fighting the war. But we had a rat in our midst. A rat by the name of Bullock.

Sergeant Bullock had come over from 2nd Platoon to replace Sergeant Loza after he got shot in the shoulder while building Restrepo. Bullock wasn't a particularly likable guy, and he sure as shit wasn't any Sergeant Loza. God only knows what he told Captain Kearney and First Sergeant, but it got the entire Platoon a free Chinook ride to Camp Blessing for 100% urinalysis.

Despite the fact that nobody pissed hot, Battle 6 fired Sergeant Hunt and decided to move Lieutenant Gillespie to 2nd Platoon, while we would get their P.L., Lieutenant Moad. We were indifferent about losing Lieutenant Gillespie, but we all loved Sergeant Hunt. And everyone knew this had more to do with Sergeant Hunt not being the yes-man that Captain Kearney wanted, than him being in charge of some insubordinate Platoon, which we weren't.

Sergeant Hunt gathered us all in our hooch at the KOP after we returned from Blessing. "Look guys, I feel really bad about the way things went down. I don't think any of this is right. But it is what it is. I just wanted to tell you all that it has really been a pleasure and an honor to serve with each and every one of you. All this talk about how this is an undisciplined Platoon is a bunch of garbage. Don't let anybody tell you differently. When we get back to Italy, free beer at my house. You guys stay safe. Keep your heads down. And remember, when in doubt, porcupine."

We were all part of Battle Company and there was no way to avoid it. But this chain of events made 3rd Platoon feel supremely isolated. Now it wasn't just the 173rd Airborne against the world, or the 2/503rd against the world, or even Battle Company against the world; it was 3rd Platoon against the world. We felt as though we had nobody but ourselves. That Company was against us, and that every echelon above them was even more detached from us than Battle was. It felt kinda shitty to be sure, but in a weird way it galvanized us. Thirty-some-odd Soldiers on one tiny, filthy firebase in the midst of a war untold, fighting for their lives on a daily basis. We were the fringe of the fringe.

Fuller Comes To Town

In January, as part of Battle Company's "Let's Repair 3rd Platoon" Campaign, Sergeant Slo was traded out with one of 1st Platoon's Team Leaders, named Sergeant Fuller. I had no idea who he was and was thus worried. "Is he some kinda asshole?" I asked.

I kinda felt like an outsider was comin' in, and this was all part of some treatment to fix an ailing Platoon that didn't have anything wrong with it to begin with. Plus, an asshole Team Leader in your Squad can make your life far more miserable than it already was, and I had a vested interest in my life not succumbing to any more misery.

As it turned out, all of this anxiety was for nothing. As much as I hated to see Slo go, Sergeant Sam Fuller was an outstanding, no-bullshit kinda guy, who was a lot of fun to have around. We had a humorously disputatious relationship from the very beginning, and in fact I don't believe Sergeant Fuller ever had a relationship of any kind that didn't encourage adversity.

The man lived to argue. But not in the sense of being a dick. He just knew that everything he believed was correct, and wanted to get into it with you about why your point of view was wrong. And when one of these conversations got going, he would talk really fast and really loud and all the while moving his head about.

"Oh yeah yeah yeah! Sure sure, and that's not right because this is going on, and you don't know what the hell you're saying because of that, and this is true and, in my experience, no that would never work, you just have no idea what you're talking about, so why don't you just go ahead and admit it."

The man spoke in a single continuous sentence and never paused for one breath on these tirades. Not that he wouldn't let you get a word in edge-wise. To the contrary, he wanted you to retort, because that just gave him more ammunition for the rest of his rant. Whether you were right or not (and half the time he convinced you his perspective was the only accurate one in the universe), ultimately, the only thing you could do was concede. 'Cause there was no way he was ever gonna shutup otherwise.

He'd been with the 82nd Airborne prior to coming to the 173rd, which would be good credentials to any other unit, but in The Rock, it's kind of a black mark. (The units don't like each other.) Regardless, he'd deployed before and to his credit, he was a smart Team Leader. He knew his shit and he looked after his guys. Sometimes with all the hell I gave him, I wonder if he knew I felt that way, but it was the truth.

He even got along with Sergeant Miller, and a few times called him out on things he thought was stupid. It was a nice thing to have someone around who could persuade Sergeant Miller's thick head to do something differently. To be clear though, no one in the Squad wanted to see Slo go (except Sergeant Miller), but we really believed we'd scored with this new T.L.

Atrium House Firefight

We rushed up the trail on the barren spur for there would be no cover till we reached the house. The Atrium House is what we called it and as we reached the entrance, without any pre-planning or so much as a word said, my Squad spread out in twos across the courtyard to clear what we believed to be an abandoned compound. The place was huge, the atrium was 50 x 50 meters or so, and it had more rooms in it than I think anyone had realized, but they were all Taliban-free. Sergeant Miller was in another room, co-located with Bravo Team. Sergeant Fuller chose a room for us (Alpha Team) that offered excellent fields of fire. It had two large south-facing windows and one window to the east. Sergeant Miller called our location in on the radio, and the E.T.T., A.N.A. and Headquarters proceeded to clear up the draw between Donga and Marastana in search of weapons caches.

We began to scan the Marastana spur as the enemy would be most likely to attack from there. We were still trying to catch our breath. Not that there was any place in this cursed valley that was easy to go up, but Donga always seemed particularly steep to me.

Doc Lowe had only been with us a month or two, but he was already a well-liked Texan (there were about a half dozen of us in 3rd Platoon from the Lone Star State). He plopped down against the wall and sweat dripped down his forehead. I looked back at him. These guys we were getting that hadn't been here for the summer didn't understand the valley. "Hey Doc, I'm not tryin' to tell you what to do or anything, but you're sittin' in full view of that window," I pointed. "You sure you wouldn't be more comfortable maybe over there?" I pointed to the southern wall. He nodded, heaved himself and the Medic's 2-ton aid bag up and moved.

Our element in the draw would be mostly exposed to any attack so I scanned up and down the Marastana spur through my optic, hoping I could catch them before they got a shot off. But in all likelihood, they'd simply walk up the southern side of Marastana, then set in real careful-like, and we'd never see a damned thing. But it was all I could do and I didn't wanna let my people down.

Meanwhile, Sergeant Fuller was coaching Lindley about what he wanted him to do when the shit started flying. Sergeant Fuller had this thing about using smoke grenades in the 203s to mark where we wanted fire from the heavies to go—which was pretty smart.

It was cold as crap and sunny outside. The sky was beleaguered blue. Our sweat started to cool under our filthy uniforms.

It didn't seem like they got very far up the draw before they found a weapons cache. I bet it wasn't fifteen minutes. But we'd left Phoenix over an hour ago, and when you think about, having to police up all the weapons and ammo, and divvy them out ('cause somebody has to carry them back)—that kinda thing takes more than a minute.

We were right at the threshold it takes for the Taliban to setup on us. And we'd been doing a number of these "search-the-draws-for-weapons" patrols lately, and I mean if somebody took my guns and ammo I'd be fuckin' pissed. I might even want a little blood. So anyway, sometimes you just get this eerie feeling. Like you know it's coming. You can't predict exactly where it'll come from, you're not sure the exact second, but there's a palpable tension you could almost reach out and punch.

And then there it was. The crackling of a P.K.M. ripped through the valley. Then more. More and more guns. The SAW already charged, I started working rounds up and down the Marastana spur. I had no fucking idea where these bastards were at. I never saw so much as a muzzle flash but obviously they were there. I presented as little of myself through the window as possible, squeezed off a 5-round burst, then went to the eastern window (only a few feet away) and did the same. Thinking Hajj might catch onto to this pattern, I decided it prudent to mix it up. So I'd shoot out the same window two times, then once out the other.

Meanwhile Sergeant Fuller was yelling at Lindley to fire a 203 on where he thought the enemy was. Once he landed the round in the right place he said, "Okay, now load a smoke round and put it in that same spot!" *PHOONK!* went the 203. Sergeant Fuller called into the KOP, Restrepo and Phoenix for them to lay their heavy weapon fire on the smoke round. The Marastana spur was taking a beating. Still the enemy fire never ceased.

Sergeant Barberet (our new Platoon Sergeant) was running for his life down in the draw, and popped some smoke of his own in order to conceal their position. (As I said, there ain't a lotta cover in a Korengali draw.)

I just got madder and madder. Nothing pisses me off more than someone shooting at me and my friends. I'd pop into the window, lay out some rounds, pop back behind the window seal, then do it again. Then shoot for a bit out of the eastern window, then go back to the east. I peppered the shit out of that spur, but I never saw a single soul. (Assuming Hajjs have souls.) I could hear nothing but the blaze of battle and it rushed through my veins sure as bullets through the barrel.

The firefight went on for twenty minutes or more. Then finally, the enemy withdrew. Despite a number of close calls on behalf of the guys in the draw, none of us was hurt. Well, at least I wouldn't have as much weight to carry back.

To Quell The Korengal

She's My Best Friend's Girl

Captain Kearney had come by our firebase to share the latest edition of combat similes. We all gathered outside our hooches at Phoenix, and he was explaining our current strategy to us like this: "Guys, it's like, you know how when you have a best friend, and maybe, your best friend has a really hot girlfriend? And let's say your best friend has to leave, he has to go somewhere out of town and he's gone for a long time. So what do you do? You know, you kind of, check up on his girlfriend, make sure she's doing okay. And you'll see her out, on the weekend or whatever, and at first you're just kind of playing this big brother role. But you keep being nice to her and that eventually evolves and you end up hooking up with her. And that's kind of what we're doing here now."

"The Taliban are mostly gone, so now's the time to get in good with these locals, so that when the Taliban do come back, hopefully these people will be more likely to give us information."

He went on like that for a while. The summary of it was hand out more H.A. (Humanitarian Aid) and push these projects we had going (such as the road, the pipe project, etc.), and eventually Hajj was gonna realize we weren't bad guys, and even potential bedmates, I guess (although the thought of sleeping with Hajj made most guys cringe).

So after that was over, we went back to our hooch. I laid down on my cot and Belgarde said to me, "Hey Shadix, remind me to never leave my girlfriend alone with Captain Kearney."

I said, "Belgarde, ya know, what we're doing here, is exactly like fucking your best friend's girlfriend."

"I don't know about where Captain Kearney's from," Belgarde continued, "but usually if you sleep with your best friend's girl, when you're best friend gets back and finds out, he's gonna wanna whoop your ass."

To Quell The Korengal

Roberts

Matt Roberts had joined Battle Company during one cold training rotation up in Germany. He had previously been assigned to Destined. I was happy to have him in my Squad. He was a fun guy and he seemed to know a lot more than I did about soldiering. Whereas at the time I could do nothing right by Sergeant Miller back then, Roberts could do no wrong.

He hailed from Pennsylvania, was kinda short, not the prettiest guy in the Platoon, and he had a really bad cauliflower ear from fighting too much. He was good in the field, and good in combat. In garrison? Not so much. He excelled at getting into off-duty incidents.

During deployment however, Roberts was a squared away guy. He often went to great lengths to take care of details around the firebase and elsewhere. One winter day while manning O.P. Three, Roberts came into the hooch sayin' we needed to make a fuel run. That time of year, O.P. Three was like living in a really windy freezer and our only means of heat other than our sleeping bags was this pot belly stove which didn't even warm you unless you were standing two feet from the goddamned thing.

Belgarde and I didn't see the point. It was just too much trouble. If you're not on guard, just stay in your bag, was our philosophy. So Roberts comes in saying he wanted help getting the fuel, and we just laid there. And then he left. Belgarde said to me, "You know the great thing about Roberts? If somethin's gotta be done, and you don't feel like doin' it, he'll get all pissed off and do it by himself." About an hour later, here comes Roberts lugging two 5-gallon fuel cans. And not at all happy with us.

Another thing he wasn't happy with was Sergeant Miller. We all had our differences with "Darkness." Hell I mean, you know there's something wrong with a guy, when you have to move two other

Soldiers (Sergeant Williams and Bunnell) to another Squad, just to keep Sergeant Miller from choking them both to death. Roberts had had enough of Sergeant Miller and his neurotic ways. Simultaneously, I guess Campbell was tired of playing R.T.O. So Campbell went to Weapons Squad, and Roberts volunteered to carry a radio around the rest of the deployment, just to get out from under Sergeant Miller.

New Plan of Action Raises Eyebrows, Concerns Over Command's Sanity

February 4th, 2008
Korengal Valley, Afghanistan

After just eight months in country and over half way through their 15-month deployment, command revealed to the Paratroopers in the 173rd Airborne's Battle Company their purpose for being in Afghanistan's perilous Korengal Valley. This revolutionary double feature strategy to win over the hearts and minds of the homicidal populace is as follows:

1. Road construction for social and economic growth.
2. Village cataloging to distribute Humanitarian Aid.

When questioned, Staff Sergeant Marcus Miller replied, "This is good. Now our lives finally have meaning. So all we gotta do is write down everybody's name, age, next of kin, and favorite way to kill an American, then pave a road the locals are intent on stopping, and we can go home. Too easy."

The idea is for the road construction project to "pave" the way for commerce to move in and out of the valley. To a population whose livelihood is so closely tied to the timber trade, this would seem an easy sell. But what some think the strategy fails to take into consideration is that the Korengalis' need to make an honest living is superseded by their inherent and uncontrollable desire to *jihad*.

One anonymous officer at Brigade told us, "The idea here is to show these people that there's something greater out there. We build this road, we can start a shuttle service. Start taking these people out of their little valley, show them Nangalam and Asadabad. Places that are seeing visible economic and cultural growth."

But these would-be field trips face one glaring obstacle. It is a well-known fact in the Korengal that insurgents take any and all measures necessary to halt construction of the road project. The Taliban regularly attacks the crews of Afghan workers building the road and often murders them in their sleep if they can find them.

A high-level source within the Army told this reporter, "Death threats to our Afghan *companeros* will not stop us. We'll simply go recruit some more road crews. With the salaries we're offering, we've got a virtually unlimited supply of desperate and impoverished Afghans who'll do anything for the good ole American dollar."

The second portion of this plan calls for recording the name of every man, woman, child and love-goat in the valley, under the pretense of determining exactly how much Humanitarian Aid is needed in the area.

"Addicting these people to welfare, I mean, Humanitarian Aid, is crucial to our success in this region," asserted one American official.

"So we're here to conduct a census?" Private Daniel Monroe asked. "But, we don't even have any census forms. And, before we enter a village, all the fighting-age males leave."

The implications of taking a census in an area with only one road, no addresses, and an estimated 500,000 assault weapons, are cause for much skepticism. Even if the populace were to cooperate, the terrain is imposing and many residences are isolated.

"Uh, hello, these people are trying to kill us," stated Private Scotty Bass.

Specialist Michael Campbell added, "Sure. We can get these illiterate and irrationally xenophobic people to fill out a census. No problem. I'm sure they won't mind at all."

"We're talking about people who still wipe their ass with their hand," said Specialist Kristopher Paulson. "And, they really hate us. Infidel isn't exactly a term of endearment, ya know?"

When asked his thoughts on how well this new approach will be received, Sergeant Tyrell Edwards was quoted as saying, "This is egregious."

"I don't know what's worse," said Private Cody Wilson. "How bad the plan is, or that it took 'em eight months to come up with it."

Provided We Patrol

For reasons unbeknownst to us at the time, Battalion had sent down a provider by the name of Major Milstead to accompany us on patrols. A provider, from what I was told, was like a super Medic—capable of surgery even. So this Major shows up, older guy, good demeanor, pretty hooah, and hell, couldn't be a bad thing to have an extra Medic around, right?

What struck me as remarkable was Major Milstead only went out with us on the really perilous patrols—Donga, Marastana, and clearing the draws in between. Those patrols across the river without question had the highest probability of us coming out resembling a long-neglected fishing net, the 9/11 conspiracy, the roof in O.P. Three, or anything else that has a lot of holes in it. But every time we went, without fail here's this Major walking with us.

I thought it was admirable. Talked to the guy several times, and said things like, "Wow, Sir, most guys don't really wanna go to Marastana in broad daylight." And he was always real humble and hooah about it. And I thought, *That's cool. Here's an officer who don't mind sticking his neck out.* That was fresh to me. (I do realize and admit my opinion of officers during deployment was probably a little too harsh.) He was in good shape too. Especially considering how old he was. Never fell out of a patrol.

Can't remember how exactly we found out, but one day Sergeant Miller was like, "Dude. You know why they're sending that provider out with us? It's 'cause Brigade or whoever mandated that if you have a provider with you, you can still go out on patrols even when the medevacs won't fly."

Sergeant Eddie looked at him, "Are you serious? That is fucked up. I don't care if he is a surgeon, him workin' on ya on the side of a mountain ain't the same as bein' medevaced to a hospital. If I take a bullet, I wanna go to a real hospital goddammit, wear one of those paper robes with my ass hangin' out, with nurses bringin' me ice cream and fluffin' my pillow, sponge bathin' my balls." He shook his head, "This shit's egregious."

What Leap Day Means to a 15-Month Deployment

Leap day means one more day in February. One more day in this goddamned valley. One more day I gotta wake up and say, "Fuck! I'm still in this stinking country." It's one more day away from my sweet wife. It's one more patrol up the mountains that gets in one more firefight. (Though thankfully without one more wounded. Unless you count the Afghan Army, which I don't.) One more pack of cigarettes I gotta smoke. Two or three more guard shifts that have to be pulled. Another day's worth of filth and b.o. on my body. One more day I gotta listen to, think about, and mock my command's inanities. It's also a day I ain't gettin' paid any extra for. It's like a fucking freebie. A freebie for the Army, and a big green donkey dick for me.

IV. SPRING

The Security Bubble's Great Inexistence

I guess it began one dumb day in November (2007). The Army had a thing for pulling a new term out of their ass, plugging it in for the first time during the nightly Company brief, and passing it off as if it had been a part of Army nomenclature since time immemorial. And so there it was: Security Bubble.

Among the officers, it was all the hype. You couldn't even have a conversation without saying Security Bubble. "Hey have you heard about the Security Bubble?"

"What's goin' on with the Security Bubble?"

"Yo, the Security Bubble's straight-up steady bangin'." Someone even contemplated the construction of a Security Bubble barometer. The thing already had its own MySpace page with 541 friends (not counting Tom). A bubble buffer was on backorder from Battalion. We considered switching our Company crest from dual battle axes to that of a single Security Bubble. We could be Battle Bubble Company.

And the big question on all the enlisted men's minds was, "What the hell's a Security Bubble?" Was it some sort of advanced body armor we were about to receive? Maybe a big transparent ball you get in before patrol, and you roll and rock around in it like a bulletproof hamster? But it was nothing so useful or concrete. And as all the enlisted men came quickly to understand this "Security Bubble" was but a figment of our command's detached imagination.

But there it was: the Security Bubble. And for the last five months, it was used as a pretext to send our patrols farther and farther into the dubious south. Into Taliban thresholds unthinkable to venture in during the summer. If in August someone had said to me, "We're going to Marastana tomorrow," I would've asked, "Us and what army?" And what was all this "we" business anyway? "We" is the most over-used pronoun in military history, and can almost always be construed as "you." Was the C.O. going to one of the most dangerous villages in the entire theater? You could bet the oak leaf clusters he'd get after this deployment that he wasn't. As everyone by now well knew, the best way to get promoted was to quit, claim you're crazy, or sit in a climate controlled office telling other people to do very deadly things.

Still, there was this Security Bubble. And apparently the only way to appease it was to ford the river and patrol south. It seemed obvious to us troops, the state created by the term Security Bubble was called winter. As in, all the fighters went to Pakistan to wait out the cold, recruit and train.

However, everyone from the C.O. to the Battalion Commander to the Sergeant Major to some cameo appearances by various Generals from places like CandyLand, Oz, and Mother Goose's Headquarters for the Criminally In-Control, all said we did so much damage during the summer, we'd eradicated the world of all evil. We'd shed so much enemy blood, it would fertilize the ground, so that come spring, the land would be covered with money trees and pussy bushes, bringing a thousand years of prosperity and poontang, to a country that had no lingual equivalent for either. A real revolution was underway.

But then it happened. Though January was so cold we had icicles hanging out our asses (it was like being deployed on Hoth with no Tauntauns to cut open and sleep in), but in February it began to slowly warm. Fighting in the winter had been sporadic, but now a patrol got in contact. Then another. Then the firebase was attacked at dusk, just like it had been practically every sunset during the summer. And as we all heard enemy gunfire, command seemed to say, "Not to worry. That is but the sound of the Security Bubble expanding. That's the noise it makes as it grows."

We all looked at each other scowling, shaking our heads incredulously.

The snow all started melting, the days turned to t-shirt weather, and at night on guard you didn't need gloves anymore. The frequency and intensity of the firefights continued to escalate. Battle 6 had said in January, that this spring we would own Ali Abad. And that this fighting season, Dar Bart (the next village south) would be like Ali Abad was last year.

On March 14th, 2008, an Afghan National Army patrol, with seven or eight Americans attached, marched into Ali Abad to search for weapons caches, which reportedly were being hidden in empty graves on the southern, most exposed part of the cemetery. What little cover there is over there is about knee high. The largest firefight we'd seen since October broke out. An hour or two long coordinated assault from three or four different places. One A.N.A. got shot in the face (Doc Lee dubbed it the "Predator wound"), another in the gut, and a third with five bullet holes in his hands and feet.

I was supporting the patrol from Firebase Phoenix. My comrade in sarcasm, Sergeant Rose, asked me what I had to say about the Security Bubble now.

I said, "It looks like it's shooting back at us."

When I was in the 2nd grade I wanted to see Santa Claus. On Christmas Eve I hid behind the living room sofa all night and watched my parents fill our stockings. So I don't believe in Old Saint Nick. And if I were to secretly pull surveillance behind the KOP's little concrete Headquarters building, I'd most likely see Captain Kearney with a bicycle pump maniacally trying to inflate the entire valley with his gross imagination.

New Blood

Our new Platoon Sergeant was Sergeant First Class David Barberet. Sergeant Barberet had been in 1st Platoon on Battle Company's previous deployment, and by all accounts, he was a pretty squared away Squad Leader. I guess he'd injured his back or his knees, so he'd been spending this deployment doing something chill for Battalion. He wasn't tall, but he was muscley and lean. I think he was from Connecticut or somewhere back east. He very much had a cool-guy vibe goin' on, and he was a fun dude to burn a cigarette with. I remember after he'd been with us a month or so, him giving us a speech about how there was nothing wrong with our Platoon.

Lieutenant Moad was a tremendous upgrade for us, and really made me rethink how I felt about officers (even West Point officers). He was very level-headed and kinda cool. There was one patrol to Donga where he didn't see any sense in all of us going up to the village. So he just took the Headquarters element with him. I thought that was remarkable, because it involved him taking a much larger risk with his own life, and he did it to protect us.

In addition to our new Platoon Sergeant and P.L., we needed Squad Leaders. Earlier in the winter, we got a Squad Leader from 1st Battalion, Staff Sergeant Parfitt. Parfitt was witty and hilarious. He was assigned to 3rd Squad.

Company had recently taken Staff Sergeant Navas from us (Weapons' Squad Leader). Staff Sergeant Rice, who had formerly been with 2nd Platoon, but had been shot on Rock Avalanche, returned to the valley, and took Sergeant Navas' place. Rice had been with Battle Company for a long time. He was well-respected. A big ole boy, heavy into Mixed Martial Arts, and he'd been around. Not the kinda guy you wanna play fuck-fuck games with.

We also got Specialist Art Brown and he came to my Squad.

Brown had been with 1st Platoon, but then took on the job of being Captain Kearney's R.T.O. Brown was from Sacramento. He was funny, loved to talk about guns, and was the kinda guy you wanted to have around. (So naturally, Sergeant Miller hated him.) You'd never met somebody so in love with being Airborne. He dropped the phrases "high ground" and "fire superiority" every chance he got.

To Quell The Korengal

Ali Abad After Dark

A couple of nights before, the Scouts had gone into Ali Abad en route to 1705, to do some sort of scouting I assume. They entered the village somewhere past midnight local time, when they came across about four Taliban who were just as shocked as the Scouts were to see armed enemies at that hour. They traded fire, but the Taliban managed to escape back into the darkness.

This left us the question of whether or not it was normal for our foes to be combing the so-called streets of Ali Abad at all hours of the night, or if this was just a freak one-time incident. So we had to find out. Really, the only way to do that was for us to go into Ali Abad, sit in the dark, and wait.

I should explain that under our Rules Of Engagement (R.O.E.) there was some stipulation about how we could only do so many night missions. I can't quote the exact percentage or anything, but it suffices to say it was really limited, which is why we didn't do more of it.

Around 2300 we set out—a patrol of twenty Paratroopers—highly motivated to hangout in complete silence and enshrouded by pitch black in what we all considered to be one of the deadliest villages in the world. The patrol started off kinda janky, as some patrols are wont to do.

In an attempt to reach Ali Abad undetected, it was decided we'd take the narrowest foot trail you've ever seen through the corn terraces. The trail was a ways below the school trail, and not something you'd ever want to be on in the daylight, as there was absolutely no cover.

In Afghanistan, there are foot trails, and then there are tight ropes, and this was the latter. I mean it was barely wide enough for your boots, leaving very little room for error. On one side of the trail was a 3-foot deep irrigation ditch, and on the other side, it dropped straight down about ten feet to the next corn terrace. Which was perfect for guys walking around in the dark with night vision that gave them no depth perception. I think pretty much everyone got their right foot wet at least once. But V., who was carrying the 240 (machine gun), stepped a little too far to the left, and vanished off the face of the trail. Falling ten feet's not good for anybody. It's especially not good for someone loaded down with combat gear and a 4-foot long, twenty-seven pound machine gun strapped around their neck. God bless him, V. was alright. V. was in no danger of evolving into a super Soldier, but that dude put forth more effort than any man in the Platoon.

When we arrived at the edge of the village, I guess it hadn't been predetermined where each element would set in. And, in the P.L.'s defense, it was just one of those missions where you get there and then you improvise. The real problem was, A) Ali Abad, though small (maybe 35-50 houses), was kinda spread out, B) we had limited manpower, and C) you wanted to cover as much of the village as possible. But at the same time, if the shit went down, you needed to be able to reassemble everyone with reasonable ease, and not have some guy way out by himself with no means of communication. And D) we didn't want the villagers to know we were there, which meant staying away from this one house in particular that boasted a dog that would never quit barking if he caught scent of an American.

Well all this involved us scouting around (quietly), and setting in, then being told to move, and setting in again, only to move again. A routine if not amusing, at least familiar. After our last merry-go-round of set-in, pick-up, set-in again, I was assigned a locale. As a SAW gunner, you were always gonna get a likely avenue of approach. Because you had the goddamned machine gun. So I set-in at kind of a fork. Like a triple fork actually, only I had my Team Leader watching my back, though he was about twenty meters away, and out of sight.

Straight down to my east, was a pathway that ran between a 3-story house and a horseshoe shaped field enclosed by a rock wall on the right. I knew that not far past where I could see, was The Stair Master. The Stair Master was a grueling manmade staircase that led down to the Korengal River. Thus, anyone traveling down or up the riverbed, could very likely come right down that corridor on my left.

On my right and to the southwest, was a large walkway between two more big houses that pointed directly at 1705. So anyone walking the road, say from such dubious places as Dar Bart, 1705, Honcho Hill, Landigal, or even worse, Qalaygal, could very possibly walk straight into this opening. The really bad thing as far as I was concerned was, there was an overhang that bridged the two houses, and made for some really nasty dark shadows for my imagination to run away with.

I had no idea where anyone else was. Only that they weren't anywhere near and I'd be on my own if I got into contact. If an armed someone(s) came down one of these two corridors, I was gonna have to blast the crap out of them myself and make damned sure that they were dead.

The thing that worried me the most was, I didn't have the SAW charged. The 173rd's S.O.P. for SAW gunners is, you don't carry a charged SAW. Since a SAW is fired from the open-bolt position, if you had it charged and say you slipped and fell, the bolt could ride forward and A.D. The problem is, it's noisy as fuck to charge it. And, in the Korengal, at night, you've never heard such quiet.

There is no traffic, there is no noise from anything that involves electricity; it's just complete and utter silence. (Unless the monkeys and dogs are going nuts, and they were conspicuously absent this night.) Inside the house in front of me, someone kept walking back and forth through the window from time to time with a candle. I didn't wanna give away my (our) position, so I didn't charge the SAW. But all I could think about was, *I wish this goddamned thing was charged.*

Then the other thing I started thinking about was how much I wanted a cigarette. I knew before we left we weren't gonna be able to smoke. (There was no smoking on a night patrol.) So I brought some nasty apple flavored Skoal along with me. But it was in my left calf pocket, which was fastened with velcro. Velcro is probably the least tactical invention ever devised. Which explains why the U.S. Army uniform is lousy with velcro. So I was sitting in the dark, and I'm looking left, straining through the blackness, then I'm looking right. But with my left hand, I'm slowly peeling velcro back one little prickly strip at a time. This goes on for probably twenty godforsaken minutes till I finally get the can of dip out. The results however, were worth the toil. I was much more satiated with a dip in, peering through the paranoid darkness than I would have been without any tobacco.

After a while, you just start to imagine things. You think you see something. Your heart begins to pound. You think about charging the SAW, all the noise it will make, and then having to mow down everyone coming your way by yourself before Hajj gets you first. I prayed they'd come from the 1705 direction from which I had that 2-foot indentation of cover. From The Stair Master direction, I had absolutely no cover. I would just have to go cyclic till every enemy ceased moving. It was nerve-wracking shit. I wasn't scared, but the realization of my predicament would make any sane person nervous.

I sat there spitting and straining my eyes for hours. At least I wasn't in any danger of falling asleep. Once or twice my Team Leader came to check on me, but for the most part, we didn't wanna make noise so everyone stayed in their respective solo positions.

Then as I peered down the 1705-facing corridor, I saw a dog coming. *Oh shit*, I thought. *He's gonna fuckin' bark when he sees me and everyone in this stinking village is gonna know we're here if they don't already.* I figured the dog would smell me when he was several meters away. But this damned thing didn't know I was there till he was six inches from my face. Then he stood there, staring at me, and me at him through my NODs. I thought about trying to pet him, thought about whispering something to him, but ultimately decided to sit there like a statue. It felt like this staring contest went on forever, but after a few minutes, he walked slowly away down towards The Stair Master. It was a huge relief.

For all the nervousness, and diligence, and driving yourself crazy thinking the shadows were something that they weren't, it was an uneventful night. If the badguys were moving through Ali Abad after hours, it wasn't on this night. To be absolutely honest, at that point I didn't care if they got together and played all-night games of strip-Twister with 10-year old boys while making plans to stage attacks against us the next day. I just wanted to go home, get in my filthy sleeping bag and rack the fuck out. But it would've been sweet to light some Taliban up as they cruised through the village in the middle of the night.

F.R.G. Sends Out Their Bi-Weekly Notices of Death

In the Army they have an organization called F.R.G., which is an acronym for Family Readiness Group. When your unit's in the rear, this group of catty wives is really more of a nuisance than anything, wanting everyone to donate money for this, or attend a meeting about absolutely nothing pertaining to anyone, etc. But when you're deployed, it's a vital link for spouses to get information about what's going on in their husband's unit. And what happens is, the F.R.G. appoints a number of "leaders" who disseminate whatever they're told, down to the wives in their 10 to 15 person group. Which, in theory, sounds like a pretty good idea, right? You wanna not worry the loved ones, and I'm sure they're semi-desperate / curious to know what's going on.

Well one function of these F.R.G.s is to send out what's called a Redline Message. And a Redline Message is always about some Soldier who's been injured or killed. (They only send these out after the immediate family's been informed of course.) I can understand this I guess. But what happened to us was, our families (in my case my wife) was getting a Redline Message for every Soldier who was W.I.A. or K.I.A. in the entire 173rd Airborne Brigade. And the unfortunate truth was, people I didn't know in places I'd never heard of were getting killed or wounded twice a goddamned week.

My wife would get all of these messages and every time I talked to her she'd say hey this guy or that guy got killed, and I would be like, "Never heard of 'em," and you could hear the concern in her voice, exacerbated every time she got another Redline Message. I for one could not understand why the message wasn't filtered down to at least just my Battalion, or even better, just Battle Company. Why did my wife need to know if someone from 1/91 or 1st Bat., or someone a hundred miles from here got killed four days ago? It was driving her and thus me crazy. Sure guys were getting whacked all over the place. But is that something your spouse really needed to know? Come the fuck on, F.R.G.

Make Offer

    Up top at Phoenix we had a for real for sale sign someone had requested in a care package from America. It said "FOR SALE" in big red letters, and beneath it was a white field, which had YEAR and MODEL. This same mysterious someone took a sharpie and wrote, "2007 FIREBASE" very boldly with smaller letters under it that disclaimed, "Only minor damage!!!" followed by a smiley face. This unknown individual, being of relatively sane demeanor, and with at least some knowledge of Korengali real estate, knew it might take a little bit of time to find a buyer. I think that's why this guy went so far as to wrap 100-mile per hour tape (a.k.a. Army duct tape) around the edges of his for sale sign; he was aware it might be on the market a while and thus the sign needed to last.

    I mean, we never exactly had open house or anything, but would you believe not even one person would come to look at the place? I don't understand why people can't appreciate Phoenix. Why it's the most bullet-riddled, amenity-free, unapologetic, needlessly sprawled out, porously perimetered, ballsy, comradely, home I ever had. I suppose if Phoenix had a face, it'd be the kinda face only a Soldier could love.

    Hm. Well maybe we should think about doin' a lease to buy.

Charlie In The Wire

    Some guys were constantly comparing Afghanistan to Vietnam. I can recall Sern't Slo repeatedly declaring, "Man, this is some straight-up Vietnam shit here." The analogy always bothered me though I never said so. No way was Afghanistan the war that Vietnam was. For instance, in November 1967, 2nd Battalion (ours) of the 173rd Airborne went up to take Hill 875. In a matter of about four days, they took 87 dead and 130 wounded. Here, we were losing guys in onesies and twosies. In Vietnam, entire Companies could get wiped out. Even a whole Battalion.
    The casualty and death rates aside, in Vietnam those guys humped all day, whereas we did our patrols, then got to come back to our firebase, which despite its lack of amenities and precarious position on the verge of enemy territory, really did give you a twisted version of comfort and home. I read that guys in Vietnam carried something like 1200 rounds of ammunition in addition to everything else they had strapped onto their backs, walked from sunup to sunset, then had to dig foxholes every night to sleep in. Don't get me wrong, we definitely did our share of digging. But still, an Army cot gets to be pretty comfortable during deployment. However, when they weren't in the bush, Soldiers in Vietnam did have access to beer and hookers. Beer and hookers would definitely make downtime not so down and more of a time.
    When guys returned from Vietnam, sometimes people threw water balloons full of pig blood at them. I couldn't imagine that. When I came back on mid-tour leave, the entire airport at D.F.W. gave us a standing ovation.
    Of course there were valid similarities, too. We were fighting for a populace that didn't want us there. It was difficult to distinguish who the enemy was, and who was on our side. There was more

fighting going on than the American public was aware of. Both countries boasted different but challenging terrain. Whereas the Viet Cong could take refuge in Cambodia and Laos, the Taliban did so in Pakistan, where we weren't allowed to go.

Another gigantic difference was, none of us were drafted. Sure, there were a few guys who were stop-lossed, but we all volunteered to fight this war. But ultimately I think you have to come back to the death toll. Over 58,000 for Vietnam. Not even a fraction of that for Afghanistan.

But ya know, we all grew up watching and idolizing Vietnam era movies like *Full Metal Jacket*, *Apocalypse Now*, and *Platoon*. And there's no doubt that these movies excited and inspired us, and probably had at least a little influence in our enlisting. I guess guys just wanted to be part of the legacy of the American Soldier. And there ain't nothin' wrong with that.

To Quell The Korengal

Big Hair Band Day in Ali Abad

We'd already been in Ali Abad for over an hour and a half. Any Taliban who wanted to shoot at us were well setup by now. The P.L. was having trouble locating the village elder who normally met him in the center of the village. So we laid in our security further in town than usual and the P.L. went knocking on the red beard's house and went inside. (The edlers dye their beards red over there. It's like a status symbol. Sometimes they wear eyeliner too, but I don't know what that's about.)

It seemed like the P.L. had been in oldboy's crib for an eternity. I was getting especially bored, not to mention concerned about how long we'd been in town. Sitting in one place for this long ensured an ugly ex-fill.

I was positioned at the corner of the elder's house with good fields of fire on 1705 and Honcho Hill, and had a couple of houses covering me from Marastana and Donga. Roberts, then the R.T.O. (radio geek), had gotten kicked out of the house for whatever reason, and plopped down next to me. "Are we getting out of here anytime soon?" I asked.

"Nope," he said.

One thing that always seemed to pass the time and calm the ole nerves during deployment, was singing. And on a good day I could get Roberts to join in. That day I was feelin' big hair bands of the '80s and I think I started off with Bon Jovi's "Living On A Prayer."

I'm the absolute worst singer you've ever heard and I specialize in singing loud and off-key. Roberts was almost as bad as I was.

We were there so long, me and Roberts had time to perform almost an entire concert. Motley Crue's "Don't Go Away Mad," a little "Just A Gigolo" by David Lee, took it on down for Poison's "Every Rose Has It's Thorn", brought it back up with some

Cinderella on the ole "Gypsy Road", then mixed in some "Once Bitten Twice Shy" remade by Great White.

It didn't take more than a couple songs to draw a crowd. Though the Afghan children generally shunned us, in a country where Allah and Rock 'n Roll don't go, a couple of filthy Americans wearing assault weapons and putting on a concert is a pretty entertaining thing. I guess it beat watching goats graze.

So one kid came over, then another, then a couple more, till we had about a half dozen groupies, and that turned into ten. One of them was even a little girl. And that's a good turnout for Ali Abad. Though neither one of us had any concept of rhythm or what it really meant to be tone deaf, we just kept rockin' out courtesy of Quiet Riot's "Cum On Feel The Noize."

I can't remember where Sergeant Miller was exactly. Had he been within earshot, he most definitely would've pulled the plug on our little concert. He must've been down on the southeast side of the village somewhere. And the P.L. apparently was in no hurry. Which gave us time to get in some "Too Late For Love" by Def Leppard, followed closely by a very bad rendition of "Dr. Feelgood" (the Crue again).

We were about halfway into our tribute to Poison's "Talk Dirty To Me," when the untimely emergence of Lieutenant Moad put us back on the clock. We immediately stopped singing, slung our weapons, and the kids quickly dispersed. We'd been in Ali Abad for damned near three hours. We all knew we were in big trouble.

The patrol re-grouped and began to ex-fill. The lead element (my Squad) didn't make it to the schoolhouse before machine guns rained down on us. Took us an hour and a half to fight our way back to Phoenix. I silently sang "Heaven" by Warrant the whole way home.

Band of Brothers

Eddie would lean over to me and say, "Man, they used to tell us this same shit last deployment. Band of Brothers, Band of Brothers. This ain't no goddamned Band of Brothers. Someone needs to come up with some new shit."

Every pep talk in the Korengal Valley had to include the C.O. or some candyass general or goddamned Admiral Mullen, sayin' some shit about how great we were, how great the work we were doin' was, and about how, this was undoubtedly, the next Band of Brothers.

You know what? Fuck your band of brothers. And fuck you, you insolent piece of shit, in your dry cleaned ACUs. Band of Brothers my ass. This ain't World War Two. And it ain't Vietnam. This is the 'Stan, man. And the 'Stan don't give a fuck 'bout no band of brothers.

The Stan'll light your little hagiography up with a big barrage of seven-six-two, and blow a couple of holes in your buddies, while you try to shrink behind some six-inch tree. This is the Korengal, bitch. And the Korengal don't take no prisoners. It might shoot you in the face, and drag your dead or dying body off to steal your fuckin' sensitive items. It might wanna saw your head off on the Internet with a dull machete. But it sure as shit ain't gonna quit while there's an American in the valley. And it don't care if you're in no Band of Brothers or not.

E.O.D.: Support Gone Awry

    E.O.D. is an acronym for Explosive Ordnance Disposal. They're the guys who, when you come across an I.E.D., are supposed to come out with all their high-tech training and equipment and diffuse the goddamned bomb for you. As an Infantryman, all you know about I.E.D.s is that A) they're bad, B) they're often accompanied by a secondary and / or an ambush and C) the best thing to do is clear the hell away from it.

    I'm not gonna sit here and roast the entire E.O.D. program. The same way I'm not gonna knock the entire concept of air support coming to save you like they should. All I can tell you is that, in the Korengal Valley, if you were expecting air support or E.O.D. to come out and do their job, you were in for a long and disappointing wait. And by long I mean, all they do is get you shot at while you wait for them to not show up. I can only remember maybe two or three times when E.O.D. actually flew into the KOP and came out to take care of an I.E.D. Maybe in Iraq that shit worked. But in Afghanistan's Kunar province, you could forget about it.

    There was this one time at the very beginning of the deployment when my Platoon was still out at Firebase Michigan, we received some intel about a cache up in the mountains. We stepped off a few hours after dark. Captain Kearney and his entourage including First Sergeant Caldwell drove down from KOP to accompany us. It was funny 'cause we were standing around getting our patrol brief and Captain Kearney was all pumped up and at its conclusion, he yelled, "Yippie-kai-yay, motherfuckers!" and then hopped in a Humvee and rode behind the patrol while the rest of us walked.

    We combed up and down these mountains (which is what always ends up happening when you get intelligence about a cache—it's never accurate and it ultimately turns into a gigantic suckfest).

Eventually we did find this little cave. And inside this cave there were a lot of bomb making materials (fuses, det. cord, etc.) and these two pressure cooker I.E.D.s. And I mean they had like, some kinda nitroglycerin bullshit in 'em or something, 'cause the steel containers they were in were sweating. We were no experts, but just from having seen movies, you knew that was some seriously unstable shit.

So we pulled back, set up security, and called up to Battalion that we needed E.O.D. to come out and take care of these bombs. I couldn't tell you exactly what was said, but it was something to the extent of, "No way. What you're gonna do is police up those mercurial I.E.D.s, walk them all the way down the mountainside without blowing yourselves up, put them in a Humvee, drive them down Pesch River road with all of its ruts, washouts, 4-foot potholes and its endless supply of bumps and rocks, and in the event those suckers haven't detonated taking out the truck and the three Soldiers manning it, E.O.D. here at Camp Blessing will take a look at them."

It was what you might call a tense experience. We did exactly what they said, I mean, what else could you do? No way were you just gonna leave two I.E.D.s sitting there for the enemy to plant in the roads later. I don't know why we didn't just blow them in place with a Claymore or something, other than, we were ordered to bring them in by higher.

I don't recall who got the honor of carrying the bombs back to the road. I know it wasn't me. That is one messed-up circumstance to be in. Knowing your very next step could well be your last. There's a lot of pressure there, to not slip on a rock and fall. The things were heavy too. Walking down that steep mountain in the dark, with your NODs on and no depth perception? That's awesome.

I believe it was Bunnell who got to drive the kegs-o-death to Blessing. He was a good driver and thus an obvious choice. He was also an incessant complainer and I could imagine he was thrilled to have something very credible to bitch about. We did get 'em there without the contents exploding. But Jesus, the things you're asked to do on deployment.

That's not the only instance where E.O.D. failed to report for duty. I can remember one winter day I was on guard, watching 2nd Platoon on the Table Rock spur. They had discovered an I.E.D. on the road below (later to be dubbed "the I.E.D. site"). So 2nd Platoon was on the radio asking what they should do, and Captain Kearney suggested they try to detonate it with a 203 (a rifle-mounted 40mm grenade launcher). The first shot missed and went into the Ali Abad cemetery (which isn't a big deal because there was already so much shrapnel, bullet holes, and detritus in that cemetery you could probably start your own iron factory down there).

The second shot hit the target, but the bomb didn't detonate. I was in awe. Complete awe. 'Cause, and maybe I'm a retard, but even if they did hit the I.E.D. with the 40 Mike Mike, if it's a large bomb, wouldn't it send shrapnel out all over the place and possibly injure the patrol?

Then someone on the radio suggested they try throwing frags on it. Which I thought was an even worse idea. At least with the 203 you could keep your distance from the thing. But to throw a grenade on the I.E.D., you'd have to be 25, 35 meters from the thing? I mean it's not like 2nd Platoon had goddamn Tom Brady out there lobbing grenades.

And this shit went on for almost an hour. (I have a great video of it.) It's a clear case of needing E.O.D. to come out and take care of the I.E.D. However, they weren't about to do that, with 1705 staring them straight in the face just a few hundred meters away. Which, you'd have to give 'em: if the Taliban saw a buncha crazy lookin' dudes who they'd clearly recognize as not being us, they'd go to town on 'em. It'd end up in a gigantic firefight, E.O.D. would get all shot up, and we'd have go down there and put the Taliban back in their place. Messy. So in the end, we just left the bomb where it was. I guess it wasn't goin' anywhere.

Not long after we returned from deployment, a movie called *The Hurt Locker* came out. It was about an E.O.D. team portrayed as this hardcore element out operating independently at times (E.O.D. never went anywhere without at least a Platoon of Infantry to cover them), conducting counter-sniper operations behind a Barrett .50 cal (yeah right), and even leaving the wire without telling anyone (which happens, like, never). As I said, I never deployed to Iraq, but that movie was about as true-to-life as Obama riding into Afghanistan on a My Little Pony leading a full frontal assault on the Taliban.

Pre-Patrol Song

It never seemed to bother Sern't Hunt, but Sern't Barberet (our new Platoon Sergeant) couldn't abide my singing before practically every patrol. Personally, I think he found my renditions of Rihanna unnerving. And probably he thought it was a little weird too. I never really thought about why I did it, but it just took your mind off of everything. Like the fact that once you walk out that wire, you might not come back.

Song choice was key. The dumber and light-hearted the song the better. Nobody wanted to hear you sing "Free Bird" before patrol. I did love me some Rihanna though. Of course, "Umbrella" was my favorite song of hers. But you couldn't ignore "S.O.S." either. And sometimes a little J.T. suited me better.

I mean, how could you go wrong with "Cry Me A River?" Especially since Roberts would get in on that action, and accompany me on the "the damage is done so I guess I'll be leaving" part. Beyonce? Yeah, sometimes. That "you must not know 'bout me, you must not know 'bout me" is some catchy shit. I don't even really listen to that much hiphop, yet nearly all my pre-patrol songs came from that genre. I don't even know what that means.

Sern't Barberet informed Sern't Miller that this little practice of mine was immature and did not reflect well on my leadership potential. I liked Sergeant Barberet most of the time. But I'd be damned if I wasn't gonna sing my jam before we walked out into the great unknown just so he would recommend me for E-5.

Test Fire Gone Wrong

We cleaned our heavy weapons every week on Wednesdays. I enjoyed breaking down .50 cals and got really damned good at it thanks to Roberts. So good at it, the two of us were usually the ones who had to do it, which led to us fighting over who got to break the bitch apart.

I like breaking down weapons, seeing how they work, cleaning 'em up and putting 'em back together. So it wasn't like a punishment to me or anything. I will say, there are certain things in the Army it behooves you not to learn. For instance, if you're fool enough to learn too much about radios, at some point they might make you R.T.O. And that just ain't my kinda job.

So we finished cleaning the .50 cal and the Mark (an automatic grenade launcher), and the standard operating procedure for after you'd finished cleaning the heavies was to test fire the things so you know they work for next time. You called up to the KOP, got permission to test fire, then shot some shit across the valley. You just picked an unpopulated spot and popped off a few rounds.

Bullets be blowin' up all over this motherfucker all the time so it wasn't a big deal or anything. But this particular day, when we went to push on the ole butterfly trigger, I suppose the Taliban must've thought we had eyes-on and were targeting ragheads at 1500 meters, 'cause I'll be damned if they didn't start shooting at us. "Oh my god!" Roberts smiled, "What the hell are they thinking over there?!" I blasted a good seven round burst their direction.

"Well," I yelled, "at least we didn't have to throw all our shit on and run up the hill!" I rocked the .50 some more. There was the crackling of enemy gunfire all across the valley. Our guys came tearing out of their hooches, armed to the teeth and ready for war. Or, at least ready for another annoying firefight. Before I knew it I'd chewed through 500 rounds. "Roberts!" I yelled. "I'm gonna need some more ammo, buddy!"

"Hey just take it easy!" he yelled back. "I don't wanna have to clean these bitches again!"

You Know You've Been Deployed Too Long When...

Everyone in the Platoon rotates into your hooch twelve times a day asking if you have any "new porn."

You've been told to expect a massive attack in the next 24 to 48 hours, about four times a week for the last 11 months. So you can spare me the massive attack announcement already.

There are a couple of loose fragmentary grenades underneath your cot somewhere, along with a Claymore Mine at the foot of your cot, which your buddy in the next cot keeps stepping on. And your quarters are so cramped, no one thinks this is an issue that needs to be addressed.

Every movie you see comes courtesy of Hajj and his pirated $1 DVDs, and you're lying on a filthy cot in the middle of B.F.E Afghanistan watching a film that just came out in American theaters two weeks ago.

You can't remember what ice tastes like.

When you go home for leave, you can't seem to find the piss tube anywhere.

You question whether the Brigade Psychologist has come to your firebase to treat combat stress or to receive his Combat Action Badge.

The taste of Pine cigarettes actually starts to agree with you, and you look down on those that smoke Pleasures.

On guard late at night, you've grown accustomed to taking the instant coffee packets out of M.R.E.s, dumping them into your mouth and swallowing it down with a big gulp of water.

You recognize everybody in the Platoon by their voice alone.

Your Platoon Medic insists you give him your Hem-Con bandages.

When you unzip your first aid pouch to give your Medic the Hem-Con bandages, you find the I.V. you've been carrying around this whole time to be flat and empty of all life-saving fluids.

You're about one mag away from wearing out the chrome lined barrel on your M-4, which you know to be good for 40,000 rounds.

The neck around your I.B.A. (body armor) is solid black.

Fragging the C.O. is discussed openly and with a great deal of enthusiasm and intricate planning.

The most prized possession in the Platoon is the generator. But nobody wants to fill it.

You start to think *burkas* make a girl look sorta sexy.

The last time you called home you felt as though you were speaking to some sort of pampered extra-terrestrials. In a language that neither party understood.

You view the Internet as something used monthly to acquire things the Army neglected to issue.

Upon checking your bank account online, you actually believe there might be too much money in it.

You'd walked so much, the hair on the outside of your calves was worn bald.

Five-five-six Can Suck My Balls

The most common round used by the U.S. military is NATO 5.56 mm. To all you hunters or gun enthusiasts, that translates into a .223 caliber. It's what's known to the hunting community as a "varmint" round. And while I don't dispute that Hajj is a varmint of sorts, he is considerably larger than your average woodchuck, jackrabbit or weasel. Thus, common sense would dictate the use of a bigger bullet.

But back during the Vietnam era, when everyone was so in love with the concept of all rifles being fully automatic, some military genius decided that five-five-six was indeed the perfect round. The logic being that a Soldier could carry twice as many five-five-six as he could seven-six-two (a .308).

After Vietnam, it was recognized that automatic rifles had their place, but it didn't need to be in the hands of every single Soldier. In fact, the Department of Defense estimated the average American Soldier had to expend 50,000 rounds to kill one Viet Cong soldier.

That's obviously less than ideal. Which is why the rifles we currently carry (the M-4) are semi-automatic (though you can set the selector switch to fire a 3-round burst). Now, the M-4 is like a shortened version of the M-16 used in Vietnam. The M-4 has a 16" barrel whereas the M-16 sported a 20-incher, and the M-4 has a collapsible buttstock so you can adjust it to your personal reach. But the point is, today's Soldier is taught to actually aim and try to hit a specific target rather than just spraying bullets all over creation. That's what your SAW gunners are for. (And the SAW also fires five-five-six by the way.)

Now the other issue that needs addressing is this: supposedly five-five-six is a really lethal round because when it hits its target, it tumbles, which has the effect of turning the human body into its own sort of shrapnel. Five-five-six is also supposed to be frangible, meaning it hits the target then splinters out into several pieces doing traumatic damage. However, as anyone who's ever actually shot somebody with the U.S. military's standard issue five-five-six ball (a.k.a. M855) can attest, what normally ends up happening is, the bullet shoots right through the badguy like a goddamned icepick. The would-be victim then continues to operate as if he'd never been shot.

 I once saw Eddie pop this guy in the leg from a few hundred meters out, and the dude didn't even break stride. Sergeant Brennan was shot in leg by someone in 2nd Platoon (1st and 2nd Platoon had more than one friendly-fire incident) and he was able to walk down the mountain, ford the river, then up the other side and finally to the KOP with little medical attention. He was barely even bleeding they said. And he was R.T.D. (returned to duty) the very next day. And I've spoken with any number of veterans from both Iraq and Afghanistan with stories of having to practically empty half a 30-round magazine into an insurgent to get him to drop.

 After we'd been in country a few weeks, each Squad was issued one Vietnam surplus M-14. The M-14 is a descendent of the M-1 Garands used in World War II, but fires a seven-six-two round (.308). And you don't have to hit somebody but once with that badboy. It's admittedly a heavy rifle, and more expensive than an M-4. But it has the range and stopping power required to fight the war we were in. In my opinion, every American in Afghanistan should've been carrying either a SAW or an M-14. (Except for Weapons Squad of course. The M240 Bravo also fires seven-six-two. It's as solid a machine gun as it gets. Even the Afghans like it, and they think all our other weapons are crap.)

 It just does not make any sense to me. The whole reason we went to five-five-six in the first place was because everyone carried automatic rifles and thus needed to hump more rounds. So they gave guys smaller bullets. But when we recognized all we were doing was wasting ammo, and that a better strategy is to teach guys to be marksmen, then simultaneously, wouldn't you give them a larger round back to get the job done? I mean, in World War II, our grandfathers were using thirty-ought-six for Christ's sake. 'Cause now what we have are Soldiers and Marines trying to kill fully grown men with a round better suited for gophers.

Too Easy

You've probably noticed, but the Army is not without its own jargon and catchphrases. From hooah, to roger, to Company, Battalion and Unit mottos, to an infinite number of acronyms. But the one that always irritated me the most, was "too easy." Any time your superior told you to do something, without fail some douche bag would say, "Too easy." That shit was like fingernails on a chalkboard to me. 'Cause ain't nothin' in the goddamned Army "too easy." In fact, everything is fucking hard. Most times, it's made immeasurably harder than it needs to be, by the very guy that said "too easy." Had I been allowed to execute anyone and everyone who ever muttered the words "too easy," the Army would've been a much more tolerable organization. "Too easy" my ass.

Conflicts of Interest

Specialist James Chico tried everything from sleeping in a bug net to dousing his clothes in cancer-causing Permethrin to scratching himself till he bled, all of which conflicted with the sand flea's obsession with their favorite chew toy—his legs.

Sergeant Marcus Miller had as much interest in body-building as he did in soldiering. A deployment could really get in the way of one's life. Though Sergeant First Class David Hunt and his wife had graced our firebase by giving us some free weights, our meager weight lifting facilities apparently were not adequate for a 240-pound man. So soldiering was most definitely conflicting with Sergeant Miller's fantasy of looking like Mr. Universe.

In a desperate attempt to return his sleep patterns to some semblance of normalcy, Specialist Richard Lindley (a.k.a. Mino) began popping whatever kind of pills he could find, which conflicted with his ability to wake up in the middle of the night for guard or, at the crack of dawn to go on patrols. One morning when we woke him, he walked out into the hall and after ten minutes we went to investigate why he wasn't getting his kit on, only to find him standing in a dark corner by the door talking gibberish (possibly speaking in tongues, but since no one spoke in tongues we couldn't make an accurate assessment). The general consensus: he was going slightly insane. But since everyone else was far from par themselves, who were we to say? Thus, it went largely unnoticed and definitely untreated.

When he wasn't watching every last episode of *Rescue Me*, all Sergeant Jason Slomiak (a.k.a. Slo) really wanted to do was sit in his hooch and play *Guitar Hero* on Mino's 12" tv, which conflicted with our patrol schedule, deployment as a whole, and his roommates questioning whether Slo would ever be able to get "Bark At The

Moon" right. Still, his unheralded effort to spend every free second in front of a television the size of a loaf of bread was nonetheless remarkable.

For football fans such as myself, Specialist Timothy Hoff and Specialist Jerry Barnard, this whole war thing was a crushing conflict with our interest in seeing the Dallas Cowboys win another Super Bowl. Of course, ever since the mid-90s, the Cowboys kinda conflict with themselves when it comes to that endeavor.

And speaking of hopeless endeavors, despite the defeat of Alexander The Great back in the day, Russians in the 80s, and the British before that, Captain Dan Kearney had dreams of conquering the unconquerable Korengal, which conflicted with his men's desire to live. Regardless, he still changed his MySpace name to Kaptain Korengal.

Farewell to Phoenix

 The rumors and speculation had been abuzz for a month or more. Destined Company, who I think was down around Chowkay (wherever the fuck that is), was opening a new firebase, and they needed their Platoons back to do so. See, Destined had attached its 4th Platoon to Battle Company and loaned its 1st Platoon out to Able Company, and now they were calling in their cards. We were already shorthanded. The last thing we needed was to lose an entire Platoon.

 Instead of about 120 of us doing the dirty work, now there were only gonna be about 90. And someone had to cover down on Destined's duties behind the wheel of those Humvees. As Paratroopers, most of us hated trucks. We were way more comfortable just walking everywhere.

 And then there was Dallas. O.P. Dallas gossip had been circulating for months now. It was allegedly going to be built either on top of Table Rock or the I.E.D. site. Someone was obviously gonna have to build and man Dallas. And the rumors were, it was gonna be 3rd Platoon. The thought of this made us anxious, and as Belgarde once told Captain Kearney, "Sir, if we're gonna build this thing, I'd rather do it now while it's winter, than wait till it's spring when the Taliban's back in full force."

 So who was it gonna be? Tactically speaking, you couldn't abandon Restrepo or Vegas. Vegas being our only outpost on the east side of the river, and the furthest north, and plus their A.O. was so large. And Restrepo was the furthest south, had respectable high ground, and was probably Captain Kearney's favorite thing in the fucking world. Which left us.

 We really couldn't fathom how you could just leave Phoenix. The place was important. Even with Restrepo now being the southern tip of the spear, Phoenix was a justifiable firebase and still received plenty of attention from the Taliban. I mean, who was gonna patrol to Donga, Marastana, Babyol and Ali Abad? Besides, this was our home. Sure it was a shit hole, and anybody in their right mind would gladly pack their bags, set that place on fire and never look back. But what we felt for that dump was a certain twisted love. I think, when you fight for a place for so long, it kinda becomes a part of you. Leaving that firebase was like losing a member of the Platoon.

Leaving Phoenix was also like leaving our independence behind. We felt like this was less about Destined being recalled and some new O.P. in the works, and more about Company wanting to keep closer tabs on us. We were gonna be the KOP's bitches. This was like taking a double-tap to our pride.

Ultimately it was decided that we would handover Firebase Phoenix to the A.N.A., who would stay there with the two-man E.T.T. (which must've scared the bejesus outta them—not to mention we were pretty good company compared to the average Afghan National Army Soldier). And that this would be looked upon by higher, as part of the transition of getting the Afghans on their feet and fighting for their own country. It just sucked it had to be us.

So on March 25, 2008, we loaded all of our belongings onto jingle trucks, took one last picture as the free, fuck-everybody-else Platoon that we were, and grudgingly began walking to the KOP, defiant every step of the way.

The KOP Life

As much as we all resented leaving Phoenix, the KOP did have its perks. For instance, you could take a shower, do laundry, call home, or screw around on the Internet, almost daily. There was also at that point two hot meals served a day. Sand fleas weren't anywhere near as bad at the KOP. But it wasn't all roses either. All these, what we considered to be luxuries, honestly made us feel like lesser Soldiers.

Instead of being in our old Platoon hooch, Company conspicuously made us move into the hardstand building about four doors down from the TOC. So guess what? Any time a detail needed to be pulled, the first place they came was our hooch. Which we knew; we knew they wanted us close, and we knew they wanted to punish us. But goddamn. This entire time we all felt like we acquired this reputation we didn't deserve.

I know how it started out: Sergeant Hunt is the kind of N.C.O. who doesn't suck the C.O.'s dick, and, yeah probably Lieutenant Wells and Lieutenant Gillespie weren't the greatest P.L.s in the world. And yeah, Briggs got busted with some alcohol. I guaran-goddamn-tee you, practically every guy who served in Iraq or Afghanistan had a little sip now and then. It's not like we were doing beer bongs out on patrol.

Point is, we did our jobs. And we did them just as well as 2nd Platoon, or 1st Platoon did theirs. You told us to go on patrol, we went on patrol. Sure, we had an attitude. But never, ever did 3rd Platoon conduct itself in an unbecoming manner. I don't care what anybody says or writes; they don't know shit. They weren't there. Not with us they weren't. How any other Battle Company Platoon was better than us, we had no idea.

But back to our new assignment. Then there were the trucks.

These trucks were at the very least on their second 15-month deployment, and they were a mess. That road just chewed them up. It was rocks and ruts, ditches and 500 meter drop-offs, hairpin turns and Taliban ambushes and I.E.D.s around every corner.

Our Company S.O.P. or whatever was that the road had to be patrolled once a day. Tactically speaking, this seemed like an awful idea. I bet Rogers' Rangers wouldn't've patrolled it every day. I mean, how predictable could you be? But that's what we were told to do so we did it. Our Platoon from Destined was long gone. Thus, mounted operations fell on 2nd and 3rd Platoon. (They did it one day, we did it the next.)

But there was a distinct difference between how 2nd Platoon went about their mounted patrols, and the way we conducted ours. Namely, speed. 2nd Platoon hauled ass. One day, as Sergeant Miller and I were manning O.P. Three (we were responsible for manning said O.P. twenty-four/seven), I said to him, "Look at how much faster they drive. Why the fuck can't we do that?"

Reason #1: Outside of myself and Bunnell, no one in our Platoon could drive worth a shit. I mean, come on, yall. Sure, the Humvee's a little wide and the road's a lot narrow and there's a sheer drop-off on the other side, but it's a goddamned truck, not some alien spacecraft. Still, dudes drove like they'd never been behind the wheel of a car before. Oh my god, have you ever seen Skaines drive a Humvee? I'm pretty sure my long-dead grandmother would be cursin' at him for goin' so slow.

Reason #2: Sergeant Barberet. I'm sorry but to me, this was an obvious speed-is-our-security situation. It took an hour to an hour and a half for the enemy to setup on you. Now the Taliban knew these patrols were going out every day. The only variable, was when. So in my mind, what you would wanna do is, from the very second you rolled out the front gate of the KOP, you would wanna reach the turnaround point (which was this little village just south of Firebase Michigan—can't remember the name of it) in thirty minutes, so as to be back inside the wire in around an hour. Which was not an easy feat with all the switchbacks and 3-foot potholes, but doable with the right drivers.

But the problem was Sern't Barberet insisted we bound through every, single, draw. Bounding through a draw means, one truck drives through a draw from which they might be ambushed, while the truck behind and in front of them, comes to a complete stop and covers that draw with its weapons till the truck is safely through. Then the next truck moves through the draw, while the truck behind and in front of them, comes to a complete stop and covers that draw with its weapons till the truck is safely through, etc. etc. etc. Which is good security in a sense, but it also takes for fucking ever. I wanna say our mounted patrols took about three hours. 2nd Platoon would conduct theirs in less than half that.

There were no recovery assets in the Korengal. No giant Army tow truck was gonna come out and save the day. If a truck broke down while out on patrol, that patrol had to get that truck back to the KOP. And they broke all the goddamned time. So then you're out there, exposed on the road, tryin' to hookup a tow rope, then you were pulling that thing back doing two miles per hour. I think we started out with five or six trucks per Platoon (meaning between us and 2nd Platoon, we had about a dozen).

Within about a month or so, out of those twelve trucks, we were lucky to get five to roll out the wire. It was always the half-shafts, or the A-frame cracked, or the alternator wasn't charging the battery, or this or that. We had three mechanics on the KOP, but they refused to do much other than let you borrow a tool here and there. They said maintaining the trucks was our responsibility. It really made you appreciate the simplicity of just walking everywhere.

When we weren't doin' the truck thing, we had to cover down on Destined's foot patrols, which consisted largely of going to this village northeast of the KOP called Oginau. Not much ever really happened there. But then too, we were still expected to patrol our old A.O. Meaning, Donga, Marastana, Ali Abad and Babyol, which, from the KOP, was a long goddamned ways. And since we weren't doing as many foot patrols anymore, we weren't in as good of shape as when we were at Phoenix.

The whole thing just sucked. Yeah, we all liked being able to call our families more often. The food was nice. Showering was good. But there wasn't a man in 3rd Platoon who wouldn't've traded our current conditions for being back at Phoenix.

Rattlesnake Appreciation Day

We were just chillin' out on O.P. Three, pullin' some more guard. When you were on the O.P., you didn't get many visitors. Sometimes if someone's coming out, they'd call it up on the radio. But other times, say if First Sergeant Caldwell for instance, wanted to make sure everyone was doing things to standard, you might get an unannounced guest. (Those visits didn't usually end well for us, 'cause even if you were at your post and doing everything right, First Sergeant could always find something that didn't agree with him. Don't get me wrong; we all loved the guy. But a lotta times, you just didn't wanna see him coming. A simple derelict cigarette butt on the ground could send him into a lengthy and painful harangue.)

A Black Hawk had landed and taken off about an hour ago but I didn't think anything of it since birds were in and out of here all damned day, every damned day. So I was in the pit pulling proper guard and in pops this Major. One that none of us had ever seen before. A Major is kind of a big deal. So as a good Soldier, you're gonna be like, *Oh shit. I got a goddamned Major up in my O.P.*

"Afternoon, Sir," I said.

"Hey, how you guys doing out here?"

"Good, Sir." I noticed he had a rather big camera in his fat, clean hands. "What can I help you with?"

I don't remember the dude's name or what unit patch he was wearing, but he said he was from The Department of Homeland Insecurity or the Detachment For A War-Free Afghanistan or the Blue Oyster Brigade or some shit like that. And I felt skeptically better after he assured me that he was out here to do nothing in an official capacity. But there was still a lingering sense that maybe I was being tested and that this could go bad if not handled properly.

He asked me to show him around and kind of orient him to the place. "Well, you see all that?" and from the eastern gun position I pointed and swept my hand from as far west as I could see to as far east, "That's bad, Sir. Indian country," I reflected as I squinted and scanned the valley.

He was older, large and overweight. The uniform he wore had not a speck of dirt or grime on it. The digital camera was bulky and expensive looking, like the kind you can change out the lenses on (whereas we all carried the cheap light ones you can put in your pocket). As many pictures as he took, you would've thought he was with Combat Camera or a Japanese tour bus, but it became more and more obvious that he was in fact who he said he was and possessed no motive other than accumulating 79,461 shots of the Korengal for his personal collection. I thought it was weird, but because of his rank I humored him.

So, I thought to myself, *this guy is the quintessential combat tourist, eh?* That sorta thing killed me. It was hard to understand. Not to be melodramatic, but he was risking his life just by being here. He could've gotten waxed walking the exposed spur you have to cross to get to O.P. Three. And I bet he didn't even walk down low like you're supposed to. People that came just to see the valley usually had zero tactical knowledge, and even less of an idea of the real danger they were putting themselves in. But I guess in certain, small military circles, the Korengal was already considered an infamous curiosity. And perhaps it was becoming some watered-down version of The Red Badge Of Courage, just to say you'd been here.

Deep down, I think every man in Battle Company realized that where we were and what we were doing was something exceptional. Something that most people would never get a shot at (so to speak) if they lived twelve lifetimes. That this would be one of the most if not THE defining experience of our lives. At the time, we had nothing but disgust and contempt for our current circumstances. But I guess we were pretty badass.

Anyway, the Major wanted to know if we could go up on the roof, so I took him. On the roof of O.P. Three we had an L-RAZ (a very large (about the size of a filing cabinet turned on its side), heavy and really expensive thermal optic that could see, in detail, to the very end of the valley, but chewed through batteries so quickly we could only use it for limited periods of time). I explained all this to him after he asked about it. We also had, not exactly a camo net, but a sort of parachute looking thing strung up on the top of the O.P. to give us some semblance of concealment while you were up there in the daylight. But there wasn't any real cover up there whatsoever, so frankly it wasn't a good place to stand if you didn't have to. While this nitwit was snapping away at his camera, I had one foot pointed back to the roof ramp in case someone decided we made for juicy targets.

He just kept going on and on about how gorgeous the valley was. "It's just stunning," he would say.

And I would be like, "Uh, yes, Sir," which is what any E-4 would say to placate an O-4. But since this concept was so off-the-wall to me, I took what he said into consideration and attempted to judge the valley on its tree-hugging merits alone.

The mountains jutted up from the valley floor like they were in a race to get to Allah. But each promontory with its own unique shape and direction. The whole cauldron was covered with trees and the river rushed through the ancient panorama in a hurry to get somewhere else.

"Just so beautiful," the Major repeated.

I guess the place was beautiful. But in all honesty I'd never ever thought of it like that. I mean, one could say a goddamned rattlesnake is beautiful. But I'd probably be too busy not getting bit to conduct a proper photo shoot.

PEZ People

Partially in the interest of building goodwill with the Afghans and partly in the interest of us having more work on our hands than we could handle, the KOP employed a large number of "local" workers. I put local in quotes because none of them came from the Korengal due to the fact that a true local who decided to work for us would undoubtedly be executed on his way home from work one day (like Trash Man). Thus these guys came from all over the country with the better part of them coming from places like Asadabad, Jalalabad and Nangalam. They were paid $10 a day, which was rich considering the average salary in Afghanistan was but one or two dollars per day. These were guys who were just trying to provide for their families, just trying to get ahead. But if anyone ever found out that they worked for us when they got home, them and their families would be in mortal danger.

The jobs they performed varied from kitchen help, to downloading Chinooks, to taking supplies to the O.P.s, to collecting and burning garbage. You know, glamor work. But, we couldn't house them inside the wire because of the security risk. I mean who's to say that one of them isn't working for the Taliban. So at night after being searched, they would walk out the front gate, where there was an establishment of hodgepodge hooches—the workers' shantytown. It was none too pretty to be sure, but I couldn't honestly say it was much worse than the firebases other than we had electricity, personal electronics, bottled water and military-issued sleeping bags with cots. And in the morning they would line up at the front gate, to be searched again, in their manjams, before they began their shifts.

Well this one day after work, a guy came by our workers' hooches, claiming to be from the nearby village of Oginau. "I have a goat for sale, real cheap," he told the workers. Two of the workers said, "Wow. That's a really good deal for a goat," and you know how Afghans love goats. "But the goat's in Oginau, you have to come get it." So these two workers of ours took off with this stranger to go get their goat.

They made it about 150, 200 meters from the KOP, before they got jumped by a few of the alleged seller's buddies, who like him, were Taliban, wanting to send a message to the rest of our workers, that being employed by the Americans is punishable by grizzly death.

Right after dusk, we got spun up to go retrieve the bodies of our two dead workers. Since it could've potentially been an ambush, we treated it as such, though we knew Hajj didn't like to fight after dark. We fired up the Humvees and took the winding road north towards Oginau. I guess the workers are the ones who had originally found the bodies and reported it to us—I don't know. Probably they went looking for their buddies or something. Maybe they just heard the screams. Grunts aren't given details concerning how things came about. Grunts just get orders from their Squad Leaders to dismount the vehicle and, "Bring the body bags."

So we walked up to the site of execution, or whatever you wanna call it, and there were these two gentlemen, and someone had taken a knife and cut their throats, from the spinal cord, all the way over to the other side of the spinal cord. It was the foulest thing I've ever seen in my life. Blood in general does not bother me. But when a person has emptied their entire body's worth of blood onto the ground, it stinks. I don't care who you are. It stinks just like puke, or shit, or anything else that leaves the human body. It's nauseating. But it had to be done. They weren't the easiest guys to put in a body bag, what with their heads practically lopped off. You had to have one guy lift the dude's feet, another guy assigned to the shoulders, and a third Paratrooper designated to hold oldboy's all but lopped-off head. The gore was indescribable. Some things you just weren't meant to see the insides of.

After the deployment was over and we were back in Italy, I caught Doc Sanchez somewhere casual. (Can't remember if it was on or off-duty or on or off alcohol.) He was the head Medic for Battle Company. I asked him, what's the absolute worst thing you saw or had to do during our deployment. He told me, "When I had to sew those two workers' heads back on."

O.P. Dallas Con-Op

March 26, 2008

The decision had been made, and the time had come to build O.P. Dallas. The night before we were to start construction, some crazy monkey business must've gone on between Sergeant Rice and Sergeant Barberet. They had come to agreement that Sern't Rice would take a mounted patrol consisting of himself and elements of Weapons Squad and 2nd Squad, and they were gonna make some sort of preliminary fortifications. And they were gonna keep all of this secret from the guys that actually had to build Dallas—namely us. The Taliban had noticed this little charade at first light and had tossed asunder the wood that the patrol had set into place.

When Sergeant Miller filled me in on this while I was brushing my teeth the next morning, I was like, "Are you fucking serious?!"

I could not believe two guys with as much time in the Infantry as Sergeant Barberet and Sergeant Rice could have come up with something so dumb.

"They might as well have put up a billboard saying, Coming soon, O.P. Dallas: to the top of an Ali Abad Cemetery near you," is what I told Sern't Miller. So much for the element of surprise.

But we knew what we had to do and knew it wasn't gonna be easy. The general consensus was we'd probably lose three to four guys puttin' this place up. I suggested we take a picture as a Squad before we left. With Belgarde and Mino on mid-tour leave, and I can't remember where Eddie was, there weren't but five of us in 1st Squad: Sergeant Miller, Sergeant Fuller, Brown, myself and McLauchlan.

Considering how few people are on the KOP at any given time, we had a large group of guys not going on the Con-Op show up to see us off. But it wasn't a hey-good-luck-we'll-see-ya-later kinda thing, though they may've said that. What their faces were saying was, *Goddamn we're never gonna see some of these dudes again—some of these guys are gonna die.* We could see that. We could feel it. This could very well be our last night to live. But we didn't really talk about it.

It's funny. When you got a mission like this, sure guys would bitch about how this or that was a stupid idea, and why aren't we doing it this way instead of that way, and thank God I have a lotta cigarettes right now, and if you die can I have your iPod—shit like that. But no one ever said, *I don't wanna go I'm scared.* Guys just did shit. Whatever they were told, whatever the mission, however they felt about it, no one ever refused. No one ever cowered.

Me? Fuck yeah I was worried. I didn't wanna be one of the four dead dudes everybody was predicting. There were only gonna be about twenty of us working the site, which meant five to one odds, and that ain't great. I sure as shit didn't wanna become O.P. Shadix. But when the time came, I slung my assault pack and walked out the front gate just like everyone else.

We humped down to Firebase Phoenix and held there till dark. We used that time to take every SMAW-D, A.T.4, and Claymore Mine we could get our hands on. It wasn't that far of a walk, so weight wasn't a concern. As soon as the sun descended, we stepped off. 2nd Platoon also took part in this. They S.P.ed to 1705 where they'd wait in a blocking position, thus, hopefully keeping the enemy a little further away from the O.P.-to-be.

We reached the site, spread out on the road, started to pull security, and immediately the disorganization began. I couldn't even tell you what the holdup was. All I do know is we were sitting there for somebody to make up their mind about something.

After a while, Roberts came up to me with a metal detector, and said I somehow had been designated the I.E.D. Setter-Offer, I mean, the guy who was gonna sweep the site to make sure it was clear of bombs. Which, okay, fine. Somebody's gotta do it. That can be me. But why the fuck didn't you tell me about this earlier? 'Cause he was trying to show me how to operate the damned metal detecting thing, it's dark as Satan's sphincter, and if I could've messed with it for about ten minutes in the daylight, we wouldn't've been having any of these problems.

Roberts was trying to show me all this shit, as if I needed to know how to work every single feature: "Okay and so you flip this switch 90° to detect 14k gold, and then to 180° for 24k gold, and if you're in a primarily sulfur based area you want to...," and I'm like, "Goddammit. Just turn the fuckin' thing on and leave it on!" and it had a little trigger you pull and I don't even know what.

What I did know was, if there was an I.E.D. down there on a pressure plate, my new assignment as Master Metal Detector would be very short lived. I could not've felt more betrayed by Sern't Rice's little "Let's get there a day early and start building shit so they know we're gonna build something bigger" act last night. Nothing in combat feels much creepier than knowing the enemy's expecting you.

Still I went down there. People made fun of me later. Saying how professional I looked and how I went over every inch. I don't know anything about that. I just had this vision in my head of some commercial with a dude walking on a beach with a metal detector finding everything from lost car keys to gold necklaces. And I adhered to the goddamned vision.

Problem was, the entire site was lousy with little pieces of metal. And every last thing set the mine detector off. Every single time I'd be like, *Oh shit this is it, they buried a goddamned bomb and it's right fucking there*. And then Roberts would start digging on the spot with his bare hands and it would turn out to be a piece of tin foil, or a spent A.K. round. And we'd move onto the next one. This was taking way too long, and before I was even finished the site was declared clear. I had my doubts but I had my orders too.

We immediately started to rebuild the wooden fortifications that Sergeant Rice and company had put in last night, the majority of which had been tossed too far down the mountain to retrieve. We setup our Claymores in the draws, drove pickets into the ground around the perimeter, and laced the whole thing with razor wire.

The concept for building O.P. Dallas was fairly unique, and I think you have to give Captain Kearney a lot of credit on this one. See, there existed somewhere within the theater of Afghanistan these gigantic reinforced concrete slabs called Texas Barriers. Each one of them was about five and a half feet tall, probably five feet wide and about a foot thick at the top, and three feet thick at the bottom. I think each of 'em weighed about two tons. In addition to these standard barriers, we had three barriers shaped like an upside-down U. They were about five feet tall, four feet wide and about a foot thick. And we were gonna use these for our three heavy weapons positions.

So in the preceding weeks, one by one, we had these things flown into the KOP by Chinook, till we possessed about twenty of them. Obviously, moving these by hand was impossible, which necessitated the use of a Hajj truck with a crane on the back of it. Thus, a couple of days before the Con-Op, they managed to get this crane up that insane road of ours. Which must've taken some doing, considering you can barely get a Humvee up that road.

But now, here we were, in the dark, waiting on the crane. Jingle trucks had been pre-loaded with the barriers, so once the crane was in place, a jingle truck would pull up, the crane would take the barrier off of it, the truck would go back to the KOP, and the next truck would bring another barrier out. In the meantime, we would work our asses off filling sandbags and Hescos.

About three hours had already passed and we had very little progress to show for it. Everyone knowing, if we didn't have at least three walls with overhead cover and the three heavy weapons in place by first light, we were gonna die.

Eventually, the crane showed up and began to lift the first barrier. As it turned out, the crane wasn't quite heavy duty enough for the weight of these barriers. When it went to lift one, it struggled and made all sorts of ugly noises that suggested it wasn't capable of these kinds of loads. But it did finally manage to lift the barrier off the jingle truck.

Then when it went to swing the barrier around, the back wheels of the crane would come off the ground, and it looked like the whole thing might bury the front end of the truck into the dirt. But after much ado, this little-crane-that-could got the first barrier in place, and even managed to set it down on Sergeant Rigel's foot. (Rigel was the head mechanic for the KOP and a very ornery guy, but he grew on you.)

The first barrier was one of the upside-down U types. Dallas was going to be shaped kind of like a triangle. The tip of the triangle was going to be facing 1705, where a .50 cal machine gun would be placed. We set up four, 4-foot Hesco's in front of the upside-down U and began filling sandbags to place in the Hescos. It was right about then we realized this was going to be some of the hardest digging we'd ever had to do. The ground was like compressed rock with a little dirt in between. Campbell, who was from Kentucky, said, "You know I used to work in the coal mines, and it was a lot easier than this." But knowing you're going to die if you don't dig enough is pretty powerful motivation. So with pickaxes, e-tools, and a few long-handled shovels, we went to work.

The frustrating thing was, there were about a gazillion pre-filled sandbags piled up at the KOP, which was an excellent idea. But thus far, none of the pre-filled sandbags had made it down to Dallas. It was more important to get the concrete barriers in place first.

The work continued. We alternated digging and pulling security. (Pulling security being your break.) One by one, the crane managed to swing the barriers into place, and now we were really rolling. What looked like a total goatfuck in the beginning now started to look promising. And though we all were expecting a hail of R.P.G.s and seven-six-two at any moment, it hadn't happened yet. Lately, we'd been intercepting transmissions from the Taliban on their walkie-talkies, of them complaining about being low on ammo. So maybe we'd caught them with their pants down.

We dug, and we dug, and we dug. One sandbag after another was filled. It sucked ass, but this place was coming together faster than any fortification I'd ever seen. Maybe around 0300 or so, after all the concrete barriers were in place, the first jingle truck loaded with the pre-filled sandbags arrived. We made a human chain and downloaded every precious one. After the truck left, we stacked them into the Hesco's and it really began to dawn; this was gonna work. We weren't safe yet, but if we kept this pace, we might just pull this off.

Not a single round had been fired at us. We had brought our four workers with us from Phoenix and they were helping with the digging too. When we finally had three sides of Dallas erect, it was time for one of the most critical parts of the construction: putting a roof on this bitch. The Afghans, particularly Salaam (our head worker), were instrumental in helping us figure out the best way to arrange the beams and plywood to make a sound roof. 'Cause nobody in the world knows how to make a house out of nothing but bullshit better than Afghans. Then it was a matter of laying sandbags on the roof, three deep. Which was a lot of damned sandbags.

As the sky began to lighten, our fortifications were in place, and 2nd Platoon started to ex-fill off of 1705. About the time they got to Ali Abad, they got into a brief TIC. One of their guys took a round to the helmet, but he was okay and they made it back to Restrepo without further incident. That was like our 3rd or 4th guy to get shot in the helmet. Those things'll deflect anything except a direct hit.

We'd done it. We had cover on three sides, and overhead cover to boot. The northwest end of the O.P. was wide open, but we didn't figure to take contact from that direction. Thus, that portion could be completed the following night.

We all plopped down (minus the guys on guard manning the heavy weapons), exhausted. We listened to Captain Kearney over the radio talking about how there was a lot of I-Com chatter taking place about Dallas, and how the natives were giving it "stern looks."

"Hey, that wasn't there yesterday!" I said, imagining what the locals must've thought about this new concrete monstrosity in their backyard.

"Somethin' seems different," Sergeant Miller joined in. "Can't put my finger on it."

We'd had Humvees up on the road providing additional security for the last few hours. "Are the trucks still here?" Sergeant Miller asked.

"Hell no," I said. "They had to make breakfast at the KOP. Now that everybody's gone they're serving breakfast again." Breakfast had been squashed a few weeks ago, due to shortages.

"Don't they have a lotta precious stones in Afghanistan?" I asked looking around at our new place. "These sandbags could be worth millions."

Sergeant Miller said, "I think it's only at high elevations."

"Well how much higher do we need to be?" I laughed. "Like on Table Rock." We were all just delirious from sleep deprivation. But just then we took a pot shot.

"Hey who had 0600?" someone said. (As we'd been betting on when the first attack on us would begin.) We got to our feet, preparing to return fire. But it was just the one shot, and hardly worth getting up for. We settled back down.

"I got bad news," Sergeant Miller announced. "They're still planting I.E.D.'s in the same spot. Hey look at these crazy white people out in the open," he pointed to the open end of Dallas where Doc Lee and Vietz were attempting to put up some sort of communications antenna.

"It's just our best medic and F.O. Nobody we can't do without."

Someone kept stacking all of these A.T.4s and SMAW-Ds next to me and Sergeant Miller. "We got so many explosives in this motherfucker and nowhere to go. Where we gonna shoot 'em from?" The design of Dallas (for the time being) was such that, if you weren't in one of the heavy weapons positions, you couldn't really do any shooting. "We gonna run up to the road, shoot 'em, and run back in? No one thought this through," he laughed.

"Not knowing is half the battle. 173rd!" I chimed to the tune of the old G.I. Joe cartoons.

We pretty much waited out the rest of the day. Around mid-afternoon though, came a gigantic barrage. If the Taliban really were low on ammo at the time, they must've gathered everything they could get their hands on to welcome our new position. P.K.M.s, A.K.s, R.P.G.s. "Hey watch your ass through that hole," yelled Bunnell, "There's fuckin' rounds hittin' right there on the edge!"

Brown came out of the .50 pit, saying the stupid thing was jamming. Of course our .50 wasn't working. Why would we have a working .50 cal? So him and I went back there to try and unfuck it. We finally got the thing rockin'. But what Sergeant Miller said earlier was right, there wasn't anywhere for most of us to go, besides out the back and into the open to get shot. So you just hunkered down, let the heavies do their work, and waited it out.

It was actually a pretty beneficial firefight in that it demonstrated all those little gaps between the roof and the barriers were seriously dangerous and needed to be sandbagged up. It also showed us our heavy weapons sucked, which we already knew.

The rest of the day was spent digging the floor out. There was maybe five, five and a half feet of clearance inside Dallas (less in places), and nobody wanted to spend the rest of the deployment not being able to stand straight up in there. Then at dusk we did stand-to, as we expected another attack. None came.

Finally it was a matter of waiting for 2nd Squad to come down and relieve us, so we could go back to the KOP and get some real rest. Sergeant Fuller started singing, "You can tell an Airborne

Ranger by his wife. By his wife! You can tell an Airborne Ranger by his wife. By his wife! 'Cause she fucks like a stallion, she's fucked everyone in Battalion, you can tell an Airborne Ranger by his wife. By his wife!"

I imagined trying to sell this place, "7,000 ton bunker. Newly remodeled, plenty of digging for the kids. Bad neighborhood, conveniently located to everywhere you don't wanna go. Make offer."

"You think they'll try and mortar us over here, or you think we're too close to Ali Abad?" Sergeant Fuller asked Sergeant Miller.

He nodded, "No, they'll try. We're on a spur by ourselves. They gonna try. Mortars and everything else."

Then we got into some debate about renaming O.P. Dallas. "How about O.P. Detroit?" suggested Sergeant Fuller. "It's more fitting than Dallas is." My pitches were Castle Greyskull, The Alamo, and O.P. Fish-in-a-Barrel.

We waited forever for our relief. Sergeant Miller said to me, "Hey Shadix, I got good news and bad news."

I said, "I don't wanna hear either one. I know the good news ain't true and the bad news gonna get worse."

Finally, 2nd Squad rolled up in the trucks, we switched out, and headed back to the KOP.

Dallas was still a work in progress. Aside from finishing the open side, we needed Hescos around the entire perimeter, the floor needed to be dug out further, and it would take a month or more to get it all done. But by the time we were finished, it was the most heavily fortified position in the entire Korengal. It was a veritable brick shithouse. And we didn't even take one wounded building it.

V. 2ND SUMMER

The Korengalis

Con-Op labeled "Rock Nitro"
May 14, 2008

There was this giant area west of the Abas Ghar (1st Platoon's A.O.) called the Shuriak. In the Shuriak, there was no American presence whatsoever. Thus it was a breeding ground for Taliban enthusiasts, where the proliferation of red beards and eyeliner, A.K.47s and R.P.G.s, and the desecration of good ole American apple pie, went uncontested.

Well we couldn't have that. This called for a Battalion-scale operation. I believe Chosen Company was the main element (meaning the guys who had the hard work). All Battle Company had to do was setup in a blocking position and wait. We were responsible for protecting Chosen's flank from any evildoers, and also to take care of any squirters who might be fleeing from Chosen's path. Able Company I think had a role similar to ours, on the opposite side of this valley. But the best part was, we were only supposed to be out for 24 hours. Although all Con-Ops carried a propensity for everything to go wrong, we were cautiously optimistic this might be an in-and-out operation.

The night of, we waited in the dark on the L.Z. at the KOP for the Chinook that was gonna give us a ride. (Walking that far would probably take six or eight hours). It was currently somewhere between 2000 and 2200 local time. The word going around was that we would be flying into a hot L.Z. (Don't ask me how the Taliban allegedly knew we were comin'.) Except for machine gunners (due to the open-bolt nature of the weapon), in the Korengal, we always had a round chambered in our weapons, since shit could start flying at any moment. Then everyone started passing along a new order to unload all weapons (as you don't want it going off in the bird—for the well-being of a helicopter always comes before that of a grunt).

Belgarde turned to me, "Hey Shadix, we're flying into a hot L.Z., so be sure to unload your weapon first."

"Yeah I'll get right on that." Fuck a helicopter. We were not gonna unload our rifles. We weren't the fucking A.N.A. who A.D. their weapons five times a day. And we weren't a bunch of brand new Privates who were pissing their pants at the thought of a firefight. We were Battle Company. And we'd been in country almost a year.

They weren't on time, but the Chinooks flew in and we ran up the ramp and took seats. Away we went. You just never knew what to expect on a Con-Op. While I was trying not to think of it, Sergeant Fuller, who was sitting next to me, leaned over into my ear and yelled, "Our job is badass!" with a mouth full of dip and a shit-eating grin.

You had to love Sergeant Fuller. He was always ready for a fight. And he was right. While the average American was fast asleep in his bed, or due to time zones, more likely plodding through another monotonous day at work, here we were, in a helicopter flying high over the mountains of Afghanistan, armed to the teeth, our best friends in the world at our sides, goin' out to fuck somebody up.

When we got to our "hot L.Z." the Chinook pilot determined that you couldn't land a Chinook there for all the trees. Awesome. We then flew around, I think aimlessly, until someplace you could actually land this fatass bird was identified. And of course, this new locale was nowhere near where we had intended to get off. Which necessitated some extra walking.

But it wasn't that bad. We only had to hump for about an hour or so till we arrived at our blocking position. Then we established security, emplaced our Claymores, and began digging in. On this particular Con-Op, every man was required to bring ten sandbags, and every other man had to pack an e-tool (folding shovel). We went to work digging fighting positions. Three or four men in each one. After the sandbags were filled, we started camouflaging our little gun nest. It was then that I realized, the saw blade on your Gerber (multi-tool) was absolutely essential. Almost everyone carried a multi-tool of one brand or another, but since I broke both mine and Brown's building Dallas (in little less than thirty seconds), the new one I ordered off the Internet had a jagged saw blade. And it cut through these tree branches like butter. We broke larger branches too, as supports for our roof, then used the little branches as added concealment. Chipmunks could not have been prouder of what they had built. As the sun rose, we stepped out to inspect what we had done. For that sort of thing can look alright at night, but not so great in the morning.

It was goddamned beautiful. It looked like it belonged there.

Other teams had done well too. But myself, Sergeant Fuller and Belgarde believed ours to be the best. Speaking of, Belgarde and I both had SAWs, and it was not normal to have two SAWs so close to one another. But the position we were given was the most likely avenue of approach. This necessitated extra firepower. And the gunteam was setup just south of us, facing the same direction—east.

While I was reluctant to believe we were gonna spend the entire Con-Op just sitting there, that's exactly what happened. In my mind, I was thinking, *Somethin's gonna go straight to shit, and they're gonna need us, and we're gonna have to pick up, start marchin', directly into hell, and this is gonna be a giant goatfuck, and people are gonna die.* But we sat there, quietly, and nothing much happened. Chosen wasn't even taking much contact. A round popped off every now and then, but that was it.

Though I would never do this on a normal Con-Op, I'd brought along a couple Rip-Its. A Rip-It, if you've never had one, is a cheap-ass energy drink. (The Army's not paying the premium for Redbull, but does recognize that energy drinks have their place in combat.) These were the citrus kind, which are the best. The regulars don't taste so great, and the diets are downright awful. So having been up all night, I started drinking my citrus Rip-Its. I had a Rip-It and a Pine cigarette, followed by another Rip-It and a Pine cigarette.

Then I needed to shit. I was usually happy when I had to take a combat crap. But this was not the best time. We were in serious Injun country. I didn't wanna leave our foxhole to do my business. But I had to go. I rifled through my assault pack, and the best thing I could find was a ziploc bag. But this was not the gallon size which would've made things immeasurably easier. No, this was but the quart size—a real challenge.

Much to the disgust of Belgarde and Sergeant Fuller, I dropped my pants and began squatting over the quart sized ziploc bag. I hadn't taken a shit in about four days, so I had to move the bag, in order to layer the feces, as it came out. It barely fit. And I was told it smelled of spoiled cabbage and rotting unborn fetus. However, I managed to zip it closed. I have a picture of it if you're interested. Sergeant Fuller, who unapologetically and constantly spat and swore and farted like anyone else, was quizzically most offended by this. I'd go so far as to say, appalled. Hell, I didn't care; I was just happy to have taken a crap in a safe place. I tossed the bag down the hill.

Thus relieved, we continued taking turns pulling guard. Then about late afternoon, it happened. What started walking over the hill, but three Taliban carrying weapons. They were straight chillin'. One guy had his P.K.M. with the buttstock slung over his shoulder and his hand holding the barrel. It looked like they were bullshittin' with each other. They had no idea death was upon them.

The gun team (which was the position just south of ours) had the best fields of fire on them. We didn't have any commo, so it was sort of chain-whispered to the P.L. that we had eyes-on, and requested permission to send these fuckers to Hajj heaven. They say every dog has his day, and I guess it was Fimbres' turn. He opened up that 240, and got 3 kills. Awesome stuff.

Almost immediately, there was I-Com chatter (Hajj babblin' on their walkie-talkies). I don't know every last thing that was transmitted, but what I do know is they were talkin' 'bout how their guys just got wiped out, and that they said, "I think it was The Korengalis!"

We all thought this remarkable. Prior to this, the Taliban in the Korengal were The Korengalis. Now, they addressed us as The Korengalis. We had a reputation. We fought so fucking hard, they respected and feared us, and we'd stolen their call sign. This was a victory and a realization that made you feel nothing but teeth-grinding pride. That's right, motherfuckers. We are The Korengalis.

Pride aside, we now knew our position was compromised. We no longer had the element of surprise. That machine gun fire announced our location. And we were just hours away from picking up and leaving. Rock Avalanche was what was on everyone's mind. In killing those three guys, had we assured there would be an ambush waiting for us on our way out?

The sun began to set behind the mountains. To me, the obvious thing to do here was to wait for complete darkness, then go retrieve the Claymores, and ex-fill. But *a la* Captain Kearney, Sern't Barberet didn't see it that way. He wanted us to get the Claymores now. It didn't make any sense when we could just wait ten or fifteen minutes and get 'em under the cover of darkness. But orders are orders. "Alright," Sern't Fuller said, "I'm gonna go get this bitch. You fuckin' cover me," he told me.

"I got ya, Sern't," I said as I repositioned the SAW so that if necessary I could light up the entire mountainside.

"Ready?"

"Hooah." I scanned the terrain, SAW charged, safety off, ready to go cyclic on any evildoers. He dashed out of the foxhole, ran like a rabbit, grabbed the Claymore, and hauled ass back.

"That was fucking stupid," Sergeant Fuller said as he caught his breath.

We waited for it to get completely dark, then everyone sliced their sandbags open and destroyed their foxholes, so as to not give the enemy fighting positions to work from. Then it was time to move. Again, first and foremost in everybody's mind, was Rock Avalanche. We were anticipating an ambush. And we (1st Squad) had point.

"Just stay behind me," Sergeant Fuller said. "Like a good 25 meters or more. There's no sense in both of us getting chewed up if we do walk into an ambush."

I didn't wanna argue with a consummate arguer such as Sergeant Fuller. So I said, "Roger." I really respected that he was looking out for us, but no fuckin' way was I gonna let him walk that far in front of me. I trailed him by about ten meters, which was our normal interval. If the shit went down, I wanted to be there; I wasn't gonna leave my Team Leader out there by himself. I had the SAW charged, but the safety on.

Like I said before, SAW gunners never patrol with the SAW charged. Being an open-bolt weapon, it has a higher likelihood of A.D.ing (accidental discharge). But I felt circumstances necessitated me taking that risk. If we got lit up, I wanted to be able to return fire immediately, and not have to reach over while the bullets are flying and charge the SAW.

It was goddamned nerve-wracking is what it was. You scrutinized every last bush, tree and rock. Every shadow seemed to move. And if nothing seemed to move, it was instantly suspect for not being suspicious looking. It was a creepy feeling. We didn't have to walk that far to the L.Z., but it felt like a fucking eternity.

Finally, we linked up with the Scouts, and then the other Platoon from Battle Company (I don't remember if it was 1st or 2nd). Then we felt pretty safe. Because there were about forty-five of us. And all we did was push out to form a perimeter around the L.Z. I don't remember having to wait that long. Thirty, maybe forty-five minutes, before the first Chinook arrived. Of course, we weren't on the first flight out, but the next one wasn't too far behind. We loaded the bird without incident and went home.

It had become apparent that the Taliban decided to alter their strategy. Rock Avalanche had taught them a lesson. No longer would they engage us when we were on a Con-Op (and thus out in force). Which made sense for them, tactically speaking. Why even try to fuck with us when you have a quarter of a Battalion, or even half of a Company out there, with designated air and artillery assets? Why not just wait and attack individual, Platoon-level patrols who aren't as well supported. But too, these guys knew U.S. Army units rotated in and out. So they had to be thinking that our time in the Korengal was coming to a close. So why not wait these aggressive, seasoned, live-for-the-fight motherfuckers out till the new cherry unit comes in, and then kind of, reinstate our *jihad*?

This was all fine and interesting, and complete speculation. I did not give a fuck. All I cared about was everyone made it outta there, and I was gonna get to sleep on my comfortable cot tonight, and call my wife tomorrow.

Combat Promotion Board

Sergeant Fuller had been reassigned back to 1st Platoon, which created a vacancy in our leadership. As in, we needed a Team Leader to replace him. I'd miss Sergeant Fuller. Even though we butted heads from time to time, I enjoyed having him around. When I asked him how he felt about goin' back to 1st Platoon he said, "Yeah it's cool. I'll probably live longer over there."

I'm not sure how it happened, since I knew Sergeant Barberet (my Platoon Sergeant) wasn't my biggest fan. It's very possible Sergeant Miller pushed for it. All I knew was I had been recommended for promotion, and that I would attend the last combat board of the deployment.

To explain: Promotion from E-1 (Private) to E-4 (Specialist), is mostly just based on Time In Service (how long you've been in the Army). But to be promoted to E-5 (Sergeant), takes two things. First, Time In Service and Time In Grade (how long you'd been in the Army, and how long you'd been in your current rank). But second and most importantly, your leadership within your Platoon had to recommend you. (And you weren't the only guy they were considering. I imagine there was a debate, with the Platoon Sergeant and the four Squad Leaders who were each making a case for why their guy from their Squad should be the one from our Platoon who should be sent to the promotion board.)

All I know is, however it played out, I was their pick. I took this very seriously and without a trace of sarcasm. If someone was gonna recommend me for the promotion board, no way was I gonna prove them wrong by going in there and blowing it.

The way this worked was, about four to six weeks prior to the board, you were given a list of topics to study, which could range from weapons, to first aid, to awards and decorations, to Army programs, to field sanitation; there were dozens of topics, always of course prefaced by unit history. A combat board differed from a promotion board in the rear, which would involve you meticulously preparing your dress uniform. In combat, the board was conducted in your combat uniform (though a clean one). This made it much simpler.

I got ahold of a board study guide, and began making note cards of every single question I might be asked. I studied that shit day and night, till as soon as I saw the question, I could instantly rattle off the answer verbatim. And still I went over it and over it. I felt my Platoon had laid a responsibility upon me. And the last thing I wanted to do was let them down.

A couple days before the board, I hopped on a Black Hawk bound for Blessing (our Battalion Headquarters) wearing a brand new uniform, got my billeting, and continued going over my note cards. Everyone who was attending was put in the same hooch. An N.C.O. came in that night to give us some advice. I don't remember his name, but the best suggestion he had was to stay loud.

"A lot of guys, when they go in to a promotion board, they start off loud, and as the board goes on, they get quieter and quieter. Stay loud," he advised. I remembered that.

Later that night, I stepped outside to have a smoke. You felt pretty safe at Blessing, and it was a welcomed feeling. While burning one, who walks past but Abad. Abad had been one of the Mortarmen at the KOP. I bet he wasn't five-foot-two, I believe his family was from Puerto Rico, and he had the best demeanor of just about anyone I'd ever met. They'd transferred him out here a couple of months ago to Chosen Company.

"What the fuck?!" I said, "How you been doin', man?" He told me everything was all good. I asked him if he missed the Korengal and he said hell no. And I was like, "Yeah I can see that. Good for you," etc. But then he told me, "Dude, have you heard about this new firebase they want us to put up?" And I said, "What? Why would yall be buildin' a firebase? We're about to go home, man. Let 1st I.D. do that shit." We got to talkin', and the gist of it was this: Chosen Company intended (or was ordered, whatever) to construct a new firebase in this very hostile region quite a ways south of Camp Blessing. Naturally, none of them wanted to do it, primarily because

A) the deployment was about over, and B) because the place they wanted them to build it on had no high ground whatsoever.

That was the first time I'd heard of Wanat. It wouldn't be the last. I tried to make him feel better. "Man, don't be worryin' about that bullshit. No way are they gonna have yall build a firebase with this little time left."

He shook his head, "Yeah, I don't know. It sounds pretty serious." I switched subjects and we continued to bullshit for another twenty minutes or so. I gave him a handshake and a hug and told him I'd see him back in Italy with a beer in our hands. It was the last time I'd ever see him alive.

The next morning we waited in line outside of a room comprised of our Battalion Sergeant Major (Command Sergeant Major Meyers), and three First Sergeants. A promotion board is like Army *Jeopardy!*. You go in there. They look you over, then they grill you on all these pre-chosen topics. Except you don't get to choose, as in, "Alex, I'll take Weapons for $400." Confidence, they say, is key. I remembered what the N.C.O. from the night before had said about staying loud.

I went in there, and I killed it. I knew and yelled the answer to every single question. I received 149 out of 150 possible points. The next day I jumped on a Korengal-bound Black Hawk. First Sergeant Caldwell was waiting for me on the L.Z. It was the first time he ever personally congratulated me on anything.

First Sergeant said something to the extent of, "Really appreciate you goin' in there and representing Battle Company the way that you did."

I said, "Well thanks for givin' me the opportunity, First Sern't."

It would take a couple months and I'd be back in Italy before the actual orders came through, but I was gonna be "Sergeant Shadix." That the Army or, more importantly, that Battle Company of the prestigious 173rd Airborne Brigade thought I was worthy of becoming a Non-Commissioned Officer? It was one of the proudest moments of my life.

Gonna Miss This

Due to a ton of diligent digging, and the inherent human nature to improve one's surroundings, O.P. Dallas had evolved into a not-so-horrible place to spend a week. Yes, inside, the quarters were cramped. The size of it was such that the cots literally touched each other. It was also as dark as a cave in there. Fortification wise, we now had Hescos lining the entire perimeter (to include a few positions you could run out to and return fire). Hescos also ran the length of area that stretched between Dallas and the KOP road. We had a well-stocked A.S.P., free weights were brought down, and we constructed a little gym area outside on Dallas' north side (covered by camo netting). Getting to the shitter wasn't nearly as dangerous as it had been, though a Dishka round had gone through the shitter right at eye level, meaning, if someone had been doing their business there when that round came through, they would've been killed on the pot (the last way anyone wanted to die was while taking a crap). The food situation still sucked, and there still wasn't and never would be any electricity at Dallas, but that wasn't something we expected anyway. And needless to say, no running water.

Dallas became a nigh-impenetrable position in the Korengal. You could shoot it with small arms, R.P.G.s, Dishkas, to no avail. So the Taliban took to setting a guy or two in the Ali Abad cemetery, and having them fire up into the gun positions. Primarily the eastern facing .50 cal. About half of 2nd Squad received purple hearts from this very tactic. Luckily, none of them were severely wounded, so they just received an award with free license plates and college.

Anyway, if you were doing your week-long rotation down there, and you weren't presently on guard, you either slept, read a book or worked out. (I did a lot of Sudoku. Great way to kill time.) But from time to time, you got sick of being in all that darkness. So this one day, I went outside to burn a cigarette, just to see some sun.

Sergeant Barberet was also out there. Sern't Barberet was always a cool guy to have a smoke with. He was good to bullshit with and you couldn't help but like the guy. So anyway, we were speculating on when we'd be going home, which nobody knew the answer to, but we did know we were getting short.

"You know what the funny thing is, Shadix?" he asked me.

"What's that, Sern't?"

He looked at the ground, rubbed his bottom lip with his thumb. "After this is all over, you're actually gonna miss this shit."

I shook my head, "No way, Sern't. No way will I ever miss this place."

"Yeah," he exhaled. "We'll see."

To Quell The Korengal

Replacements to the rescue?

The dichotomy of combat is intensity and boredom. There are firefights with bullets flying through the air, bombs exploding, mortars and machine guns, planes and helicopters shooting missiles, the roar of an A-10's gatling gun, moments where you're running for your life, or you're pinned down, your brothers at your side, and you don't know but whether this is your last day on earth.

Conversely, combat can dull you to death—just an endless cycle of patrols, guardshifts, shit burning, downloading resupply trucks, 4-hour blocks of sleep, fucking sand fleas and filth. It gets so monotonous. All you want is for it to end. And it doesn't seem like it ever will. But then, finally, the new unit comes to relieve you. Just onesies and twosies at first, but you can almost see that last great bird, coming down from the sky, to take you back to the Promised Land.

In July 2008, some of the guys from 1st I.D. out of Fort Hood, Texas began to show up. Now you'd think logic would've told the Army, "Hey, the Korengal Valley is the worst place in Afghanistan, site of some of the heaviest fighting in the entire War On Terror. So what we ought to do is send one of our best units to replace the 173rd." Right? Uh, well, not what happened. These 1st I.D. guys up until very, very recently were a heavy unit (heavy meaning mechanized and mechanized meaning they rode around in Bradleys, which are armored personnel carriers). They were a new unit too. I mean, 1st I.D. is supposed to be out of Fort Riley, Kansas, not Texas. These guys were some sort of transition unit. They said they didn't even know if they were going back to Hood after the deployment. They said they might be going to Fort Carson, Colorado or, it's possible they'd disband the unit after their deployment. So already when you hear this you're thinking to yourself, *What the fuck? This sounds like some seriously pieced together bullshit.*

On top of that, they were the fattest Army unit I'd ever seen. In the 173rd, we had, on average, two guys per Platoon who were a little on the chubby side. (I'm talkin' to you V. and Wilson.) These 1st I.D. dudes had two guys per Platoon who weren't big fatties. They told us they did a lot of rucking before they deployed, but I mean you could just look at 'em and tell, no way were they gonna be able to hump up these mountains. Now, it's Army tradition for the unit being replaced to try and breakoff the incoming unit as you take them out on your patrols. When we ripped out with 10th Mountain, yeah they tried. But despite the elevation, we were some in-shape motherfuckers. Running six to twelve miles three times a week and doing 90-pound ruck marches before you deploy will do that to you. But with this 1st I.D. unit? You didn't even have to try to run them into the ground—they just fell out.

We had one of their guys fallout going downhill. How the fuck you gonna fallout goin' downhill?! 1st Platoon said they went out on one of their patrols (and all of their patrols were long and grueling—way worse than anything us or 2nd Platoon had to do), and one of the 1st I.D. guys took nothing to drink but sodas with him. It's July in Afghanistan, yall. It's in excess of 100°. We're slogging between 60 and 85 pounds up the Hindu-Kush mountains. If you're not drinking water, you're not gonna make it.

We were about to S.P. on this one patrol when one of 1st I.D. raised his hand and asked, "Should I bring my NODs?" We all looked at him like, "What the fuck?! Where the fuck are your NODs?! Yes! You bring your NODs! Yes, your NODs are supposed to be on your person at all times!" Sure, it's supposed to be a three-hour patrol. But once you walk out that wire, there is no telling what's gonna happen. We could be out for nine hours. We could end up being out there for two fucking days!

Most of these guys didn't even know to tie their NODs down. Which I thought had been explicitly covered all the way back to basic training. (In the Army, anything considered a "sensitive item," meaning something valuable that you don't want the enemy getting his hands on, is tied down to you or your weapon with five-fifty cord (nylon parachute cord - super strong). Nobody expects joe to be anything but green. It's your first deployment, got it. But with this unit, even most of the N.C.O.s seemed very inexperienced.

To Quell The Korengal

They were ill-equipped too. Almost none of them had a rhino mount (the NODs attach to your rhino mount, the rhino mount attaches to the base plate on your helmet, and some of 'em didn't even have the base plate). I don't think any of them had a headlamp either. Or had even seen a headlamp. I mean, yeah the Army doesn't issue 'em, but a Petzl with a red lens is something you used constantly (we use red light because it's the least visible to the human eye; white light is a combat no-no). Hell I'd worn mine so much the elastic on the headband was sacked out.

We were down at Dallas and we had a couple of the 1st I.D. guys with us, showin' 'em the ole ropes and all. Well, 2nd Platoon went down to Ashat or Lui Kalay or wherever-the-fuck, and a firefight kicked off. As I've said before, Dallas was a brick shithouse—easily the most fortified American position in the Korengal. Unless Hajj scored a direct mortar hit on the roof, you were probably gonna live. I wasn't pullin' guard at the time and neither were our 1st I.D. counterparts. So when Eddie yelled from the gunpit, "I need more seven-six-two!" I hurried back to the A.S.P. to grab a couple cans.

The 1st I.D. dudes had the two bunks adjoining the A.S.P. and when I went back there, they were both standing in front of their cots, with very lost looks on their faces. And their knees were literally shaking.

"Yall don't have nothin' to worry about here," I said. "This place is as safe as it gets."

The knee-shaking really stuck with me though. I suppose we were just so accustomed to bullets flying everywhere all the time; we just didn't think nothin' of it. Then again, my knees didn't shake in my first firefight. I was excited and nervous, but no knee wobble at all.

Look I don't mean to slam these guys. They were good guys. And I'm sure they had some experienced N.C.O.s, but I just didn't have any contact with them. And of this I have no doubt and am living proof of—if you don't have combat time, the Korengal will make sure that you do. The Korengal will square you away. It will see to it that you have experienced more fighting than practically anyone since Vietnam.

Or it will bury you. One or the other. But still, a unit deploying without providing its guys with rhino mounts for their NODs? If that ain't complete and utter failure on your command's part, as well as an inauspicious beginning to a deadly deployment, I don't know what is. Assed-up though they were, I felt for those guys. But my time was almost done and I was so ready to go home—this was their fight now.

Trouble In The Ranks

1523 local time

    All was quiet on the southern frontier. Down at O.P. Dallas, Specialist Brown pulled guard in the western gunpit, cleaning his fingernails with his favorite 12" knife. He was almost an hour and a half into a 2-hour shift. Bored out of his brain. He couldn't wait for it to end so he could get back to sleep for 4 hours before having to wake up for guard again.

    Suddenly, he heard the high-pitched staccato of enemy machine guns. He knew the routine: he charged the .50 cal, pulled the bullet case that sufficed as a safety, shrugged, and opened fire on 1705. He didn't see shit, but we took fire from that mountain all the time, so you couldn't go wrong shooting it up. There was the habitual yelling and exchanges on the radios that accompanied every firefight, but after several minutes, O.P. Restrepo reported they weren't receiving any effective fire. O.P. Dallas called the KOP and said the same: There were no bullets coming our way. "Cease fire!" Sern't Miller yelled to Brown, "Cease fire!" Restrepo too ceased fire.

    However, the enemy continued to shoot. The American Soldiers looked at each other, puzzled. To the southeast, they could distinctly hear two different groups of fighters. Then they saw an R.P.G. fired. They could see the signature from where the rocket propelled grenade was launched, and they also saw where it impacted—about 400 meters due east. There weren't any Americans anywhere near there. That was seriously deep in enemy territory. "Are they shooting at each other?" the Soldiers asked. "They sure as hell are."

    Over the next ten days or so, the fighting amongst the enemy continued. "Hey!" yelled Sern't Miller, "You can't be having firefights without us!" Obviously, someone wasn't getting along.

Boredom: The Ultimate Combat Blessing

A lot of times I tried not to say anything. But always when somebody declared that they were bored, I wanted to butt-stroke them in the mouth. As much action as we'd seen, as much as we'd been through, friends we'd lost—to me, if things were nice and quiet, that's as good as it ever got. But if we'd gone two or three days with no contact, some-asinine-body would always go off on how they wish something would happen.

"Man, I'm bored. I almost wish we'd get in a firefight right now." At that point I'd been in enough firefights that they'd gotten annoying. It had grown into a hassle, a chore. The best thing you had to look forward to was some downtime. Watch a movie on your iPod, listen to some music, read a book, play some P.S.P., write a letter to your wife or family, or just get some good old-fashioned sleep.

Between details, patrols, guard and firefights, you were doing something all the goddamned time. So if Hajj couldn't organize a decent offensive for a few days, Amen! I'd like to watch *Iron Man* and *Superbad* sometime this deployment. Keep up the peace, my Taliban bitches. A boring day in the Korengal is a good day.

Of the Atrocities of 2nd Squad and the Resignation to Pop Tarts

With almost two months left in the deployment, higher had decided we didn't need any more mail. That care packages provided much of our diet, was either not taken into consideration or dismissed by some General eating ice cream in one of Bagram's two 24-hour Chow Halls. Thus, there was nothing to eat at Dallas but M.R.E.s. To the untrained palate, M.R.E.s aren't so bad. They taste alright. But after about thirteen months, they start to get a little old. And you have to take into account, M.R.E.s are renowned for their butt-plugging abilities; one could eat M.R.E.s for several days and never take a shit. They take constipation to a whole other level. But it was what it was, and we ate what we had.

So you headed outside where we kept our food and water, and what did you find but a bunch of rat-fucked M.R.E.s. Courtesy of 2nd Squad, of course. In the unpredictable world of combat, there are some certainties: 1) Your Commanding Officer is in fact trying to kill you, and he will do everything he can to see to it you are neutralized. 2) The country you are fighting in, sucks. 3) 2nd Squad will never burn their shit barrel after re-fitting on the O.P., and they will rat-fuck every M.R.E. they can get their hands on at Dallas.

I liked 2nd Squad—as individuals. Chico and Barnard were two of my favorite people in the Platoon. But as a collective entity? They were awful. My thing was, why did we follow 2nd Squad in every rotation anyways? We were 1st Squad. They should come after us, then 3rd Squad could come in and clean up after 2nd Squad. Keep things numerically straight is what I'm saying. Order.

But let's back up a minute. There are probably those among you that are unfamiliar with the crime against humanity known as rat-fucking. To explain: There are twenty-four varieties of M.R.E.s. Each comes with a main course, a snack or some shit, and a desert. As wrong as it is, there are those "Soldiers," who will rip open every M.R.E. in the box just so he can get his grubby little claws on a vanilla poundcake or a package of peanut M&Ms. Leaving behind everything that no one particularly wants to eat. And for the next guy to come along, and see nothing but a box full of Veggie Omelets, red hots and moist towelettes is something that should fall under the jurisdiction of the Uniform Code of Military Justice.

Fuck it. I'll eat another goddamned Pop Tart.

Officers: Fact vs. Fiction

Hollywood is so full of shit when it comes to its portrayal of officers. If you've never served, you probably don't know what I mean. But let's take Lieutenants for example. What's the difference between a brand new Lieutenant and a Private First Class? The Lieutenant graduated from college, and he went to Officer Candidacy School (a 12-week course). So besides being able to do some admin things like writing up an Op Order and possibly quoting some Shakespeare, the honest to God answer is, very little. Except, the Lieutenant's supposedly *in charge*.

Fast tracking, it takes most guys three to five years to make Sergeant, six or more for Staff Sergeant, and the Platoon Sergeant's been in for ten plus years. So how is some college educated, cherry little twerp supposed to come in and tell veteran men how to do things? It's preposterous.

Now back in World War II, battlefield commissions were given out. That is, Non-Commissioned Officers (Sergeants), who performed at the most amazing levels, were made into Lieutenants. Most notably, Staff Sergeant Audie Murphy (credited with over 240 kills and more acts of valor than him or anyone else can probably remember). These days, any ole college boy will do.

Look, I'm not sayin' they don't mean well (in most cases), but there is no substitute for experience. So for every movie I watch and book of fiction I read, to portray an officer as some hardcore character who knows exactly what to do in any given situation (because he's been in every fathomable scenario dozens of times), makes me wanna fuckin' choke some writers out.

These guys don't know shit, yall. Officers are normally more of a hindrance than a hero. They often have a different agenda than us enlisted guys. Especially during deployment. I'm not gonna lie; in the

Korengal, we were just trying to get us and ours back home alive. I mean, we never backed down from a fight, but we fought as smart as we could. And when it came to patrols, we wanted to execute them in a manner that mitigated as many risks as possible. As in, "Okay, we gotta go to Marastana today. We just went to Donga yesterday. So if we take the school trail into Ali Abad, go down the Stair Master and ford the river, the Taliban won't be as likely to guess where we're actually going."

Officers? Dude, most officers are always thinking, "What can I do right now that might help me get promoted?" They were always sucking up to Battle 6, who was probably always sucking up to Rock 6 (Lieutenant Colonel Ostlund), who was sucking up to Sky Soldier 6 (Colonel Preysler), who was sucking up to some General.

So to summarize, don't believe the hype, yall. Officers are overpaid frat boys who ride on the backs of enlisted men, who do the actual work, who actually know their jobs and honestly don't need some snot-nosed school boy wearing a butter bar getting in the way.

O.P. Paulson

Since being relegated to the KOP's bitches, 3rd Platoon was also moved from O.P. Three back to O.P. Four. Even though O.P. Three was more in the fight, it didn't offend most of us, as after thirteen months, we were getting pretty fought out. Plus, O.P. Four was just easy. It was really close to our hooch, and it had electricity.

Paulson had been a SAW gunner for 3rd Squad as long as I'd been in the 173rd Airborne. But the weight of these weapons and the harshness of this terrain was really starting to break guys off. Especially the SAW Gunners and the 240 Gunners. By the time we got back, every single one of us would have back and / or knee problems. And Paulson's back just couldn't take it anymore. So instead of patrols, he was permanently assigned to guard O.P. Four, which meant, as a Platoon, we only had to send one guy up there every four hours to help him out.

I never really hung-out much with Paulson in Italy—other than the inevitable beer-pong in the barracks. But besides sporting the largest head in the Company, he was a pretty cool dude. He knew a lot about guns, which was one of our favorite topics. He could take a single strand of guts from 550-cord and use it to make an M-4 fully automatic.

As this was no longer just an O.P., but Paulson's billeting as well, and since none of our N.C.O.s wanted to be anywhere near anything that involved pulling guard, Paulson began taking certain liberties. His first order of business was to install a door that you could actually lock from the inside. In this case, a piece of plywood was the door and 550-cord served as the lock (we didn't exactly have a Home Depot over there).

The whole reason there was never a door was so First Sergeant or whoever could roll up into the O.P. unannounced and catch you pulling guard with your helmet off or reading a magazine. But the thing was, the Taliban could sneak in there and slit your throat just as easily. The absent door was neither practical nor tactical.

Then Paulson started assembling furniture out of ammo crates, ammo cans, anything he could get his hands on. Before you knew it, the inside of the O.P. looked more like a lounge. He'd rigged up a 120mm mortar can coffee table and things that served as couches and chairs. Don't get me wrong: the gunpit (where you actually pulled guard) was still the gunpit. But the living quarters was now livable.

"I like what you've done to the place," I said.

He nodded, "I know, right?"

Eventually I reached the point where if I didn't have anything duty-related going on, I'd head up to the O.P. just to hang. This cut down on the number of details I had to partake in. Like I said before, when we left Phoenix and moved here, 3rd Platoon had been relocated from our former hooch into the end of the new hardstand (cinderblock) building, which was hot as fuck! (I swear to God, I sweated less in my rack at Phoenix.) And, it was probably a 25-meter walk from the TOC to our front door. So anytime anyone in the TOC needed anything, and I mean anything done, they came directly to us. They had a detail to do every frigging five minutes. And with the deployment winding down, the number of details multiplied exponentially—especially inventories. Which meant taking serial numbers from every little last piece of equipment and checking them off on a spreadsheet. Fuck that.

Whoever was in our hooch did the details. Whoever was harder to find got off. 'Cause no way were those TOC monkeys walking up to O.P. Four to make you do a detail. Shit, they'd probably fallout about halfway up the hill. Where Paulson and I would be kicked back, smokin' Pine cigarettes, bullshittin' about guns and life in the rear, while watching a Hajj copy of *I Am Legend* for the two hundred and ninety-ninth time.

To Quell The Korengal

Sky Soldier 6 on the High Ground

Our Company guide-on (flag) was tattered and faded from the sun. We'd been in country for over a year, so I guess our Brigade Commander (call sign Sky Soldier 6) decided it was high-time to put in an appearance. Anyone who wasn't gainfully employed had to go to this formation in front of the TOC. Although by this point we had managed to erect a 10-foot rock wall around that portion of the KOP, we still didn't care much for having to line up in front of the enemy in broad daylight. But that's what happened when we had high-profile visitors.

Colonel Preysler came out and gave us the standard *Hooah Speech*. Keep driving, you're doing good work out here, I'm proud of everyone, etc. Given that he was a Brigade Commander, it wasn't too windy of a speech. At its conclusion he wanted to come by, shake each of our hands and bullshit with us, while still in formation. We opened ranks. I was in the first rank, and the third guy he talked to. I can't remember what he asked me or how it started, nor was I anticipating a lengthy conversation with him, but somehow Bella came up.

Bella was an isolated outpost in Chosen Company's A.O. It had been abandoned a couple weeks earlier, and some of the guys from my Platoon (2nd Squad specifically) had gone there to help tear it down. Anyway, so somehow me and the Colonel got on the topic of elevation. He told me something to the effect that Bella was at a higher elevation than the KOP, and therefore Bella should've been safer. To this day I wanna believe I totally misunderstood the guy. I just nodded my head and said, Yessir. But what I was thinking was, *Sir, are you a total moron? The elevation of a Combat Outpost is completely irrelevant. What matters is the elevation of your position relative to the elevation of the surrounding ground.* I mean, that's gotta be the most rudimentary principle in all of mountain warfare: high ground. Bella was in a bowl, for Chrissake. Chico and Barnard said the mountains around that place were 500 to 800 meters higher than the firebase. It doesn't matter if your little base sits at 25,000 meters, if the mountains around it are 26,000 meters tall. Or even 25,500. But here was a Full-Bird Colonel, telling me the most important thing was the elevation of the firebase. And we were all about to pay big for this misperception.

What Happened in Wanat

Over the course of several months, Chosen's C.O., Captain Myer, had *shurra* after *shurra* with the village elders of Wanat in an attempt to get them to agree to let him build this new firebase. Of course, the elders didn't wanna give the Americans permission for fear of Taliban reprisal, nor did they wanna turn their town into the inevitable battlefield it would become simply because of the American presence. For it has been well-documented in Afghanistan, that Americans attract bullets. Lots of bullets.

The *shurra*s also made clear to the enemy Chosen's intention to build there. For some reason, we just did not value the element of surprise. Of later importance, there was an A.N.P. (Afghan National Police) garrison located in Wanat. The Chief of which wasn't the kind of guy that made you feel all warm and fuzzy inside.

As a prelude to the construction of Chosen's new firebase, there was an unfortunate accident a few days prior (on July 4th) and not far from Wanat, involving two Apache attack helicopters and a couple of Toyota Hi-Lux pickups. Among the seventeen people killed was the staff of the local health clinic (the only one in the area). As evidenced by Rock Avalanche, locals tend to get a little pissy when civilians are killed, and that in turn tends to escalate into a *jihad* in which a bloody revenge is dealt.

With only two weeks left in the deployment, Chosen Company (based out of Camp Blessing) reluctantly set out to build a new firebase to replace Bella, which they had been ordered to abandon about a month or so prior. What we were told was that 1st I.D. (the incoming unit) wanted it there. But no one ever said why 1st I.D. couldn't build it themselves.

The whole idea here was to construct a firebase close to the local populace that could be resupplied by trucks. (Since there was a shortage of helicopters to fly supplies in, logistics was always a concern.) In turn, you could also control the Taliban's use of the road. Wanat was the District Capital for the Waygul valley, thus it was a good place to setup shop and provide legitimacy to the local Afghan government.

So on July 8th, 2008, a Platoon from Chosen Company set out in 5 Humvees. A "Vehicle Patrol Base" (a circling of the wagons, if you will) was established adjacent to the Wanat Bazaar to provide cover while fortifications were dug. (The bazaar being a focal center of any Afghan community.) The area the trucks occupied was an open field about 300 meters x 100 meters, with the C.C.P, A.S.P., and C.P. (Command Post) all located in stalls in the bazaar.

In official Army documents, COP Kahler (as it was to be named after one of Chosen's fallen Platoon Sergeants) is almost always referred to as nothing but a Vehicle Patrol Base, rather than the Combat Outpost (firebase) it was intended to be. (I guess that's what you call backpedalling.) "Vehicle Patrol Base" isn't even recognized as being a legitimate Army term.

Anyway, as soon as Chosen arrived in Wanat, it started dumping rain, which does not bode well for constructing a new firebase. Within the Army, we have this little section called S-2, that is responsible for intelligence. Among their duties is reporting things such as the weather. One would think before Chosen ever left Blessing that S-2 would be like, "Uh, hey there's gonna be a torrential downpour tonight, so maybe you should push your operation to the right one day." But I guess for whatever reason, that didn't happen.

Chosen setup an O.P. called Topside (a reference to the 503rd's notorious assault on a Philippine island in WWII). The site sat among the corn terraces and was selected because it had several large boulders to offer cover. What it did not have was much high ground. It had been decided that the O.P. would be better off if it were closer to the firebase, so it could be resupplied and reinforced easier. The better high ground was determined to be too far east.

A Chinook flew in with 24 A.N.A. and 2 E.T.T. (bringing total manpower up to about 70) and also delivered additional ammo, mortars, sandbags, Hescos, shovels, a Bobcat with a fuel blivet, and some engineers to oversee construction of the firebase. In theory, a

Bobcat sounds badass when it comes to constructing a new firebase. Problem was, the Bobcat's bucket could not reach to the top of the 8-foot Hescos to fill them. So it could only do 4-foot Hescos. Which, last time I checked, the average height of an American Soldier is well over 4 feet. And then, the Bobcat ran out of gas because the equipment sent to transfer fuel from the blivet to the Bobcat was the incorrect type. So that was that. Anyway, the supplies the Chinook brought in were only meant to last a short while.

A Hajj construction company had been contracted, which was supposed to arrive on July 10th, but didn't get there till the 13th (and even then not carrying a fraction of the supplies they were supposed to bring). They refused to drive from Blessing to Wanat without proper combat escort, insisting that the Taliban were watching the road. Among the supplies the contractors were supposed to bring with them was additional food, water, sandbags and excavation equipment. Chosen quickly ran out of sandbags to fill, and even ran out of water. July in Afghanistan is hot, yall. And digging there is hard work. Without water, there's no way you can do it. So for three days, very little was accomplished at Wanat.

With only two weeks left in the deployment, air assets were tied up with the business of flying the 173rd Airborne out, and flying the incoming 1st Infantry Division in. Likewise, command's attention was, if not entirely devoted to, at least distracted by, the RIP (Relief In Place—a month or two long process through which the outgoing unit shows the incoming unit the ropes, then hands off the reins).

Also, with only two weeks left in the deployment, Chosen Company must've been thinking, *What the fuck?!* As if they hadn't shed enough blood in this godforsaken country. (Chosen already had six K.I.A.s prior to Wanat.) Who the hell wanted to do something so dangerous with two weeks left? At that point in time, we were all into doing our patrols as cautiously as possible and not taking any crazy risks. In fourteen days most guys saw themselves having a nice Italian meal then going out to tittie bars to do body shots off Romanian strippers. We were so short it was ridiculous and all anyone could think of was going home. Alive. And preferably with your legs intact.

In the days that preceded the attack, Chosen noticed there was an unusually high amount of foot traffic in the village, and that some of the hoodlums were getting as close to the American positions as possible. There was even a group of fighting age males that would do nothing but sit there and watch Chosen work and draw diagrams on the ground.

A large number of people were spotted in the mountains carrying things, but since Chosen couldn't positively identify any of it as being weapons, under our R.O.E. they weren't allowed to open fire. Several of the locals actually told Chosen that an attack was imminent—but when isn't it? One dude told them that he was moving his family to another village. He wasn't the only one who left. In fact, the Taliban moved into the village the night before the attack, ordered the locals to leave and set in—a feat that went completely unnoticed. Chosen had no air support whatsoever, not even a Predator (Unmanned Ariel Vehicle), which conceivably would've seen all the enemy fighters moving into place. Also, the day before the attack, water started pouring through an irrigation ditch near the O.P., making it difficult to hear anyone who might be approaching the position.

At about 0420 local time, the Taliban launched their assault. It was a coordinated strike from multiple positions, some only 50 meters away. They knew what they were doing. They targeted the mortar pit and the TOW Humvee first. They fired R.P.G.s and small arms into the mortar pit, wounding Specialist Abad with shrapnel, and fired three more R.P.G.s at the TOW truck, setting it on fire. The crew had to abandon it and pull back to the C.P. (Command Post).

The Taliban was everywhere. They littered the mountains, but they had also infiltrated houses and buildings in the immediate vicinity, showing preference to those that were 2-story so as to fire from elevated positions (such as the mosque and the hotel). They went so far as to climb trees just to get some high ground. In some cases, they were as close as five to ten meters. That's ballsy. They were climbing the walls and getting so close, the guys in the mortar pit were throwing grenades at them.

The gunners on the other trucks continued to empty can after can of ammunition. The remaining trucks were armed with .50 cal machine guns and Mark-19 automatic grenade launchers. The Taliban attempted to approach the firebase from the road, but the truck stationed there as a Traffic Control Point managed to repel the enemy, till it took so much fire the .50 cal was disabled.

The O.P. was also receiving heavy R.P.G. and machine gun fire. The Taliban's main support by fire position was a house about 900 meters to the southeast that offered plenty of high ground on the O.P. Meanwhile, a horde of Taliban moved in on the O.P. from every direction. The Paratroopers there began going cyclic to gain control of the battle tempo. But in doing so, started to run out of ammo and their weapons malfunctioned. (A machine gun, or a rifle for that matter, can only maintain a certain rate of fire before the barrel and internals overheat.)

Three minutes into the attack, our guys began getting fire support from the one-five-fives (155mm cannons) in Blessing. A total of ninety-six 155mm mortars were launched to clean the mountains of the Taliban infestation.

Chosen was maintaining the perimeter of the firebase proper, but the O.P. was taking a beating. Lieutenant Brostrom (Chosen's P.L.) took a group of guys to go reinforce the beleaguered position, which was in danger of being overrun. It didn't help that their Medic was shot just as they left the C.P.

The mortar pit managed to get their gun up, despite taking continuous heavy fire, and began launching rounds, till an R.P.G. started a fire in the attached A.S.P., forcing the mortar crew to withdraw to the C.P. (dragging the incapacitated Abad behind them) where the TOW team and the Headquarters element were putting all that first aid training we went through prior to deployment to good use. Medevacs were en route, but Specialist Abad (who had already taken shrapnel from an R.P.G.) died before they could get there. His pregnant fiancée would never see him again.

The E.T.T. with their charged A.N.A. occupied the north end of the firebase (er, I mean, "Vehicle Patrol Base"), and were engaged from the tree line and buildings to the north. However, they mostly took small arms fire since I guess the Taliban didn't want to waste an R.P.G. on something that wasn't American.

Then the 9 rounds inside the TOW truck, which had been on fire for some time, began to cook off. A TOW is a missile, and missiles tend to make for big explosions. Four A.N.A. were wounded and another seriously burned when the TOW truck exploded. Two of the TOW missiles landed in the C.P., and the Soldiers there heard the missile's motor spinning up. Sergeant Phillips quickly grabbed a couple of sandbags to use as oven mitts and escorted the burning missile outside, while Captain Myer heaved the second missile over the C.P.'s wall.

Finally, air support began to arrive and decided it was high time to drop some precision-guided munitions on these fuckers. In turn, the volume of enemy fire decreased enough to start staging casualties for medevac, while a couple guys sprinted through the bullet bath lugging ammo to resupply positions that were going black on ammunition.

However, the O.P. received no such lull. Within the first 20 minutes, all nine guys initially manning the O.P. were already injured or dead. All but one was injured by the initial R.P.G. volley. They fired their weapons till they jammed, lobbed grenades, blew the Claymores, and shot pretty much every round they had while administering first aid and tourniquets to themselves and their wounded. Several of the Claymores had actually been disabled by the Taliban or turned to face the O.P. Once all their ammo was spent, they shot a LAW rocket at fighters just 15 meters from the O.P. Now virtually helpless, the Taliban ran right up the C-wire and fired more R.P.G.s and threw grenades at the Paratroopers. The first wave of reinforcements led by Lieutenant Brostrom was pretty much wiped out as soon as they arrived at the O.P. The Taliban were throwing rocks into the O.P. in hopes that Chosen would mistake them for grenades and thus expose themselves. A second wave of reinforcements went to the O.P., but was met by another volley of R.P.G.s, wounding everyone.

Over an hour into the fight, Apache attack helicopters finally arrived to turn the tide of the battle. They ran danger close gun runs using Hellfire rockets and 30mm cannons. One final group was sent to the O.P. and with the help of the Apaches, was able to hold their ground once again.

Chosen spun-up a Q.R.F. (Quick Reaction Force) from Blessing. They mounted Humvees and began driving north. Because they knew their brothers needed them, the Q.R.F. pushed straight through the traditional I.E.D. sites along the way, ignoring the very real possibility that the Taliban knew they'd come and could have an ambush setup.

Throughout the fight, the firebase itself was never breached.

About an hour and a half into the fight, the first medevac arrived and began flying casualties out of the war zone. Shortly after, Chosen's mounted Q.R.F. element reached Wanat with an additional nineteen Paratroopers and four trucks. They pushed up to the north side of the base and repelled a flanking movement.

Q.R.F. elements from Able and Battle Company were also spun up to join the fight and secure the area, arriving at 0720 local, and 0855, respectively.

Estimates of enemy strength vary, but it is believed that no less than 200 Taliban launched the assault led by foreign fighters to include Al Qaeda, Pakistanis, and the Kashmir-based Lashkar-e-Taiba. Final numbers were nine Paratroopers killed in action, twenty-seven wounded. It was one of the bloodiest attacks in the entire war in Afghanistan.

To Quell The Korengal

Wanat

    We'd just returned from a mounted patrol to the six-seven-two gridline. It was still morning but already damned hot. After we squared the trucks away, everyone headed to the chow hall for breakfast. As soon as we got in there, everyone was talking about how Chosen Company had been hit while building this new firebase. The initial report was four or five dead and nine wounded. I sighed and decided I'd hit the gym instead of eating 'cause I wanted to get a workout in, as I knew exactly who they'd choose to go help Chosen out.

    I'd managed to pack on some pretty serious muscle in the last couple of months, replacing much of the twenty-five pounds I'd lost in country. As much as I hated living on the KOP, it had its advantages. I hadn't even finished with my workout before I was told to start packing for Q.R.F.

    I pulled back the mosquito net on the door, and walked in our hooch (the hottest on the KOP), took my assault pack and a Claymore mine off the wall, tossed in some pre-loaded spare mags I had under my cot, walked outside to the water bin, decided on taking six 1.5-liter bottles, went back to the hooch, filled the camelbak bladder up with two of the bottles, and put the other four in the assault pack. I already had a few field stripped M.R.E.s ready to go—tossed those in their along with a handful of protein bars, then thought and re-thought, about how many packs of smokes to bring along. 'Cause this could really turn into one of those drawn-out things in my mind. I packed the better part of a carton. My weapon was constantly clean and ready to go, but I put a little extra oil on the bolt carrier and chamber, then changed out the batteries in my NODs for some fresh ones.

    Like a good Team Leader, I asked Brown how many rounds he

was carrying for the SAW and took a 200-round drum off his hands. (I'd seen Rose do that once before a Con-Op, and I'd thought, *That's what a good Team Leader does. Help your guys out, ya know?*) I didn't do too much checking to make sure Brown and Lindley had everything. They knew as well as I did what needed to be done and I trusted them to do it. We'd gone through this kinda thing so much, everyone was staged outside in probably ten minutes.

We were taking the entire Platoon except for 3rd Squad. (Someone had to stay back and cover down on the O.P. and the trucks). We tried to sit in the shade while we waited on the word. Eventually, we saw Captain Kearney exit the TOC and walk towards us. I started singing the *Imperial March* and a lotta guys joined in. Captain Kearney half-smirked when he heard it, but he looked all business.

"Guys," he started, "look I really hate to do this to you with only two weeks left in the deployment." We were all a little taken back. This was the first time in fifteen months we'd heard Captain Kearney not get excited about sending us into the shit. It was equal parts weird, gratifying and alarming. He continued, "But our brothers in Chosen Company need our help. The latest numbers are nine dead and twenty-seven wounded."

Our stomachs sank. With two weeks to go, Chosen had nine guys dead? Captain Kearney kept talking, mostly just reiterating brotherhood and how much he didn't want to send us, but at the end we moved down to the L.Z. and waited for the Chinook, which arrived in under twenty minutes (which was a goddamned record I think).

I was always worried when I got on a bird. Afraid it was gonna get shot down. It's that same helpless feeling you had riding in a Humvee with the ever-present possibility of hitting an I.E.D. and burning to death inside the truck. Completely powerless to do anything about it. One R.P.G. into a helicopter's rotor, and you would come crashing to the ground.

Normally, leaving the valley was a good thing. But if Captain Kearney was already sorry about this, you knew it was gonna be bad. And as we rode in the chopper, you couldn't not stare at all those body bags we loaded on the bird. We were flying straight into the proverbial belly of the beast. We wouldn't've liked it under any circumstances. But with just fourteen days and a wake up left in the deployment, nobody was lookin' to get posthumously promoted right about then. The bird touched down briefly in Blessing, and picked up three guys from the 101st. I don't know who they were and I never saw them again once we got to Wanat.

It wasn't a long ride from there. I don't think it was more than five minutes. Lieutenant Moad started shouting stuff no one could hear. I'm sure he was saying something to the extent of, "As soon as this thing hits the ground, get the fuck off. And someone unload the supplies."

And indeed as soon as she touched down everyone was scrambling out as fast as they possibly could. I realized guys were either gonna just not think about, or not want any part of, unloading the ungodly amounts of ammo, water, M.R.E.s and let's not forget, body bags, that was our cargo. So I stayed behind with Eddie and Lieutenant Moad to make sure there was enough help. That shit was heavy too. I was suckin' before I ran down the ramp and into this goatfuck called Wanat.

The Chinook had landed in the middle of these low-rise farm terraces. There was no cover. We didn't know shit. We didn't know how hot this A.O. still was or was not. If the Taliban were still hanging around, and if so, did they feel like taking a shot at a Chinook and a bunch of fresh reinforcements? Our guys had dismounted the bird, and with cover nowhere close, they just set in behind about an 18-inch terrace. Eddie had the presence of mind to realize this was not the place you wanted to be in if some shit broke out, and ordered everyone to take cover behind this enormous tree. It was a freaky big tree for the Kunar. For twenty-nine guys it wasn't much, but it still beat the hell out of sitting in the open waiting to get rolled up.

From our tight-interval positions at the tree, you couldn't not be in utter awe at what a horrible spot had been chosen for this firebase-to-be. There was this mountain immediately to the east (not 200, 300 meters away) that was a bad 1300 meters higher than the ground we were on (over 4,000 feet!). It was covered in spurs and draws and there was a smaller mountain in front of it that would give the enemy endless positions from which to fire at you. It was staggering. It was like looking up at a skyscraper. Either Colonel Preysler couldn't read a topographic map, or he deliberately picked the lowest point in the entire village for Chosen to build on.

What was even more appalling was the blatant lack of work that had been done in the five days they were blessed with before the onslaught. (We didn't know anything about the supply shortages that had gone on, so we were in total disbelief.) Five days is ample time for a driven Platoon to emplace some serious, life-saving fortifications. My Platoon built Restrepo in a couple of days. With Dallas we had cover on three sides and overhead cover before the first sunrise.

But our first order of business was to get all the supplies we'd brought with us off the L.Z. That by itself was going to be an enormous chore. We'd brought the three staples of combat: food, water, and plenty of ammo. The L.Z. was on a crop terrace, three or four terraces below the actual compound (such that it was). And so we started carrying everything by hand, in full body armor, in the July sun. I don't even know what a case of .50 cal weighs, but I'm guessing in excess of 100 pounds. And I don't even know how many we brought, but I don't think anyone even fired a .50 cal the entire time we were there (as all of Chosen's .50 cals were shot to shit).

Simultaneously, Sergeant Barberet and Lieutenant Moad linked up with whoever the senior-most man was in Chosen (Captain Myer, I presume, as they'd lost their P.L. in the attack). They quickly established a new A.S.P. and a C.C.P. These were just located in stalls in the bazaar, with the C.C.P. a good distance away from the A.S.P.

As we humped all of these supplies off of the L.Z. you just, you couldn't help but be struck by the rampant and well-placed havoc that had been wreaked. Taking the most direct route (which you weren't gonna go on some scenic tour with a 100-pound crate of ammo on your shoulder), you had to pass a Humvee (the one that had the TOW launcher on it). It had been one of the first targeted by the Taliban, and they had decimated it with R.P.G.s.

Then of course, the TOW missiles inside had cooked-off. It was amazing to me, when you consider the thick armor on one of those Humvees, all that was left of this thing was the actual wheels, the radio antennas, and sparse parts of the frame. Everything else had burned away. It looked like a smoking animal carcass. In order to get the ammo to the new A.S.P., you also had to pass what was the mortar pit. And there was blood splattered all over the wall behind it. We knew that one of our former Mortarmen from the KOP, a hilarious Puerto Rican guy named Abad, was one of the guys who had been in there and died. Every building was riddled with bullets. It was complete carnage.

Two hours had passed. We finally took a break, but there was still a shitload of equipment left on the L.Z. We rested in the shade of a tree near the new C.C.P. A Humvee was placed in front of the stall to provide cover for it. All of the Humvees had been shot all to hell. This one I was looking at, the bullet proof glass around the turret had been received so much fire it was all cracked. But looking at the truck got me to thinking, "Do any of these trucks still run?" I asked to no one in particular. "'Cause if they do, why the fuck are we walking all these supplies up, when we could just drive a truck down there, load it, and bring everything back? I mean, we can't get the truck right to the supplies, but we can carry everything to the highest terrace, and just drive it back from there." That raised eyebrows.

The survivors from Chosen were in this, shock, is the best word I could use to describe it. They didn't talk to us. They didn't really talk to each other. They didn't move. They looked like ghosts. So we just let 'em alone.

But now we needed one of their trucks. Whoever was left in charge of them decided that we weren't qualified to drive one of their shot-all-to-hell vehicles, but said they'd supply the driver, and we'd load the truck. Fine, whatever, dude. We got all of the remaining supplies in one trip.

That was good, but now we were on to grimmer issues. Able Company had arrived before we did. And I guess they had removed the actual bodies down from O.P. Topside (where seven of the nine K.I.A.s came from). But there was still the matter of the K.I.A.'s belongings.

I'd never seen anything like it. If you were into pools of blood, and pieces of bone and flesh, it was the place for you alright. And do you have any idea how many flies something like that attracts? Finding something that didn't have a bullet hole in it was just... I mean their weapons were shot to pieces. The 240 had a bullet hole through the barrel, and there was an M-4 that was so wasted it was barely recognizable. But the Army wanted those weapons for accountability of course. There was also an L-RAZ up there (a super high-tech and bulky piece of thermal imaging equipment), that the enemy had shot to shreds. R.P.G. tail fins were everywhere.

The O.P. fortifications themselves just left you shaking your head more. For the most part, the sandbags were just one deep, and barely over knee-high. So that if you were crouching low enough, it would cover your torso. Like everything else in Wanat, it was exposed to practically the entire valley. It was a 360° killzone.

Some body armor and RACKs had been cut off of the wounded with medical shears, and they were drenched in blood. Carrying them down to the L.Z. meant your lower body was soaked in red. On one trip, carrying the fallen's hundred pound rucksacks and equipment, I passed Sergeant Miller, and I said to him, "This place is indefensible." I didn't do it on purpose, but we were within earshot of where a group of Chosen guys were. He took me aside and chewed me out. Rightfully so, I guess. Told me these dudes didn't need to be hearing that.

After I don't know how many trips, we finally got all of Chosen's gear off the O.P. The mess was officially cleaned up. And now came the really serious part. We had to man this bitch. We had to do whatever was necessary to ensure we could hold this "indefensible" ground. And no one really thought it was possible.

We all gathered back down at the C.C.P. It was probably 1530, 1600 local. I don't remember where 2nd Squad and Weapons got assigned to, but Lieutenant Moad told me, "Shadix, take your fireteam and man the O.P."

It was my least favorite order of the deployment. "You mean The O.P. of Death, Sir?"

He got upset with me. I wasn't about to refuse an order, but I wanted him to know what I thought of it. That place was retarded. We went anyway. The first order of business was to make this into someplace that could actually protect us. That meant digging. As Brown and I manned the O.P., I sent Mino down to retrieve some sandbags, a pickaxe and, if possible, a long-handled shovel. He came back with sandbags.

"They don't have any shovels, they don't have any pickaxes," he said. That was bad news. All we had were e-tools. Though all the blood had softened the ground some, it was still really difficult digging. Without a pickaxe, I bet we weren't filling one sandbag every ten minutes. One guy pulled guard while the other two dug. We did have a few hours of daylight left, but it quickly became apparent that the idea of having sandbags two to three deep with overhead cover by dawn was impossible. I'd say the ground at Wanat was just as tough as it was at Dallas. But we kept digging. Because it was the only way we thought we'd survive the next sunrise.

While Mino pulled guard, Brown and I dug. "I need a smoke break," I told him. I lit up a Pine and took in the scene. There was this burning house about 900 meters to our southwest with probably about 100 meters of elevation on us. Obviously the O.P. had been taking a lot of fire from it, and they'd done their best to eliminate the threat.

"In this location, it's just hard to setup," Brown said, "Everything has high ground on us."

"Five days," I muttered. "Yeah but, if you were here, for five days, wouldn't you like, build something to protect yourself from all that?" I waved my hand at the skyscraper of a mountain to our west.

"I would," Mino nodded. "Iwouldn't even put it down here in the first-fucking-place. I'd put the O.P. on the fucking high ground."

"Yeah this is the lowest O.P. I've ever seen," I agreed. "I mean, you've got that behemoth back there," referring to the skyscraper, "You've got that whole ridgeline to our northeast, I mean that burning house even has high ground on us. There's nothing that can't shoot down on you except for the river, which we don't even have eyes-on. Five days..." We were in a bad spot.

As we continued to dig, a cow snuck up on us. Don't even know where it came from. The river below us was loud and it concealed noises. But a cow just materializes out of nowhere?! What if it was a team of Taliban who were actually trying to be quiet? It further illustrated how terrible a position this was.

After an hour or two, a Scout team led by Lieutenant Piosa (2nd Platoon's old P.L.) showed up to help us man this bitch. Sern't Barberet was with them. Sern't Barberet had joined us less I think to help out and provide guidance, but more because one of his good buddies was on the Scout team and they wanted to do some catching up. Considering our current circumstances, that really irritated me. Good God—that fucking sun comes up, and we're all sitting in these same piss-poor fortifications, and we are gonna die come dawn, same as Chosen.

There was this dead Hajj one terrace below the O.P. It was strange because, this guy had B.D.U.s (our old woodland camouflage pattern) on underneath his manjams. As if he was a real Soldier who was trying to look like a local. He also had a chest rig with several A.K. mags. He had tiny hands and white teeth and his dead eyes looked straight up at the sky. He also stunk. Sergeant Barberet got sick of it, so he grabbed a picket, wedged it underneath oldboy, and started rolling him till he fell down to the next terrace. He didn't smell good before, but moving him definitely did not help. Lieutenant Piosa sniffed, "What is that? Did somebody fart?"

"That's the smell of death, Sir," I told him. And it was heinous.

Eventually Sergeant Barberet told me, "Hey Shadix, keep digging, but come dusk, the plan is to relocate." That made me feel an almost a false sense of hope. As in, thank God we're not gonna be here at dawn, but what if that changes, like it always does, and we're still here when the sun rises?

At dusk, there was a mandatory stand-to. Everyone hunkered down behind their weapons, waiting for a possible onslaught. Nothing happened. After the sun set, we mounted NODs and picked up. I could not overstate my sense of relief. There was this compound of a house a couple hundred meters higher to our southeast. The plan was to go in there, fortify the crap out of it, and that would serve as the new firebase for the incoming unit.

It wasn't a bad place. Still didn't have a lot of high ground, but nothing so poor as where Chosen was told to build. It was farther away from the skyscraper mountain (which was a plus), but sat in much closer proximity to the southeastern ridgeline (from which you'd no doubt receive constant fire). But in these parts, this was about as good as you could expect, yall. It wasn't perfect, but it was doable.

One thing was for sure: we weren't getting any sleep. Though the compound offered some protection, it was far from fortified. 1st Squad was assigned to this smallish room that had windows facing south and east. That portion of the house was elevated with kind of a sub-story beneath it (for housing goats or whatever), which we did not have eyes-on. Obviously the perfect place for the Claymore. The next order of business was gun positions. We didn't have any sandbags, so we needed rocks. Lots of rocks. One guy pulled guard while the rest of us went on a scavenger hunt. The glass-less windows in our room were huge. Huge is bad. You wanted just a large enough gap to give you maximum fields of fire, but you didn't want a hole so large you were likely to be shot through it. And for the moment, rocks were the answer.

We were isolated in this little room, and while we tended to our tasks, other Squads did likewise. Weapons Squad was closest to us. Headquarters of course was in the center of this labyrinth of a compound. The Scouts were building a foxhole on the northern end (facing the burning house, which we now had a little high ground on). A few hours into the night we took about four potshots from the burning house (though who would enter a burning house with the sole intention of shooting random rounds at us is beyond me). I do believe the Scouts killed the lone shooter though. We worked relentlessly all night. A lot of guys were simply tasked with carrying supplies up from the village. With the corn terraces to climb, it was not an enjoyable detail.

Earlier, at about 1930 local time, a group of Afghan Commandos guided by a team of Army Special Forces arrived on scene. They went directly to the district center, and disarmed the twenty members of the A.N.P. (Afghan National Police). Though the entire town was laid to waste, the A.N.P. station remained remarkably untouched. The station was not within line of sight of the firebase, but it was in full view of the avenues of approach used by the Taliban. Also curious was the fact that the A.N.P. donned brand-new uniforms, when the norm was for them to have but one uniform, which was typically well-used. Inside the station were over a hundred weapons, thousands of rounds and R.P.G.s, many of which were dirty and appeared to have been recently used. That's way too many guns for twenty guys.

Working with S.F. (Special Forces) has its perks. Notably, the amount of support you get. They brought an AC-130 Spectre Gunship with them. Being Airborne, we were familiar with C-130s as that's normally what we jump out of. But this was a whole other beast. It's armed with two 20mm Vulcan cannons capable of firing 2,500 rounds per minute, one 40mm Bofors cannon set to fire 100 rounds per minute, and one giant 105mm Howitzer. It also has this enormous

I.R. (infrared) light on it, capable of lighting up an entire mountainside. So that while I was on guard and looking out my NODs, it was bright as day out there.

Roberts walked into our room and told me not to shoot, as S.F. and the Afghan Commandos were about to recon the mountains I was staring at. The Afghan Commandos were quite a departure from the A.N.A. They actually looked and moved like serious Soldiers. About an hour passed, then there was some shouting in Hajj to my east. A call on the radio said the Afghan Commandos had found four insurgents. Thirty minutes later I heard four distinct gunshots. Executions were in order. And nobody ever said shit about it.

Late in the night, Able Company, who was manning some houses in town, got eyes-on a few badguys trying to sneak up the riverbed. They called it up on the radio, said the dudes had weapons, got permission, opened up with the 240, and made short work of 'em.

Shortly before first light, everyone was at stand-to, bracing for another morning like the one that had befallen Chosen. There was nothing but eerie silence. An hour later, we were back to work. We now had sandbags, and sandbags need filling. One guy pulled guard while everyone else dug. It was hot and it was hard work. We took just the wire baskets from a couple of 4-foot HESCOs, laid them flat, and secured them against the windows to act as R.P.G. barriers, then completely walled up the south-facing window (as someone else had eyes-on that area).

After that was done it was one trip after another from the COP to our new abode, carrying as many supplies as possible. By about 1400 local, everyone was satisfied with their positions and their stores of ammo, food and water. So at long last it was time to implement a sleep schedule.

We did stand-to again at dusk. Again nothing happened. We didn't wanna put too much stock into it. But it seemed like the A.O. had gone quiet. The Taliban are opportunists. They hit you when you're weak. Not when you've got virtually two Companies of hardcore combat killers dug in and ready for a fight. Still, this was no time for complacency. We were all on edge. We just wanted to go home. Alive.

The next day a bulldozer was brought in. It carved a road through the corn terraces, to our new firebase. The original idea here was to have a firebase that could be resupplied by truck. Now you could. Though it wasn't as close to the populace as command had wanted, it was someplace you could actually fight from and survive. And honestly, it'd be better to have the firebase somewhat removed from the populace, so when you took fire you didn't have a bunch of collateral damage. We'd done a lot of digging, and though the place was far from finished, here was COP Kahler. All we needed was for 1st I.D. to come in here and relieve us.

We waited another day. No one came. On July 16th, 2008, the order came to pull out. We were pissed. How could you let these guys die for nothing? Just send a Platoon in here to man this bitch and it'll all have ended in some sort of positive closure. Some visage of victory. This was a complete waste. It was hard to take. Even though we missed the real battle, Wanat would haunt us all for the rest of our lives.

We destroyed our fighting positions, everything we'd worked so hard to build the last few days, and moved to the west end of the compound. Me and Mino guarded this short corridor, waiting to move down to the L.Z. Mino decided to make a movie.

"Alright. This is Specialist Lindley and Specialist Shadix here," (I still didn't have my orders promoting me to Sergeant), "waiting at this valley called Wanat."

I interrupted, "I think the town's Wanat, I don't know what the valley's..."

"We don't know where we are," Mino continued. "Either way we're waiting to ex-fill, but we've been delayed an hour. I think we're doing some sort of tactical withdrawal."

"First thing we have to do is wait for everyone else to leave," I said. "See, that's what happens. You show up to help, you don't get to, you gotta be the last to leave, is the way it works."

"Yes. But, we wait in anticipation for Chinooks, and for the first time in our lives, we cannot wait to get back to the Korengal Valley." He was right about that. It is a sad state of affairs when everyone is dying to get back to the Korengal.

A Day 15 Months In The Making

We returned to the Korengal with less than a week and a half left in the deployment. We stayed on the KOP for a couple days doing mounted patrols, participating in more of those oh-so-fun inventories, and pulling guard on the O.P., till it was our time to rotate down to Dallas. Already some of Battle Company was loading on Chinooks, making their way to Bagram to rendezvous with that final bird back to Italy.

But of course we had to stay till the very end. The Chinooks that flew our guys away also dropped off more 1st I.D. guys. They were everywhere. We now had four or five of them at Dallas. They were all cherries. One of 'em was named Knight. He was a tall, thin black kid and he kept talking about how he couldn't wait to get into the shit. He'd be dead in a couple months. Died in Ali Abad. Been a long time since anybody died down there. But for now, very little was going on in terms of enemy activity. Speculation was, the Taliban knew we were leaving, so why try and fight a salty adversary when you could just wait till next week and go toe-to-toe with their inexperienced replacements?

So we laid in the cave-like confines of Dallas, pulled guard when it was our turn, went outside to lift weights when it wasn't, and otherwise talked about what we were gonna do when we got back to good ole Caserma Ederle (the name of our post in Italy).

"All I want is to eat a really nice Italian dinner and a drink a big cold beer," Belgarde declared. "Followed by another big cold beer. And then another, and then another... What're you gonna do there, Brown Bear?"

Brown laughed, "Dude," he shook his head, "I just wanna be with my wife, ya know?" To call Brown's wife, Maritza, a head-turner, would be an injustice. So I'm sure he was more than ready to get back to that.

Sern't Miller's plans were more aloof. They involved a train to Milan, and the never-witnessed-but-always-"bad", Samantha.

Eddie was leaning towards getting really drunk and stirring up shit at a strip club. And I was sure he'd have plenty of company.

"I'd just like to sleep a whole night without having any guard," Mino said. "But a beer might be nice. And a real pizza."

The days dragged by like nails on a chalkboard. There'd been maybe only two TICs the entire time, and both of them as our guys showed 1st I.D. the routes across the river (Donga and Marastana, and maybe Lui Kalay out of Restrepo). We saw and/or heard as one Chinook after another flew our friends out of the valley. But still we remained. Everyone started getting frustrated. They kept pushing our flight date to the right. Every morning we were told, "You're leaving tomorrow."

Then one night, the prophecy came true. "The trucks'll be here at 2000. Be ready." And in fact the trucks came. I remember the gunner in the truck I got in still had no NODs mount. He was holding his NODs in front of his eye with what I hoped was his non-dominant (non-firing) hand. As unlikely as we were to get ambushed at night, it sure didn't make you feel good. In retrospect, I might shoulda given him my rhino mount, but I think my logic was, if we take contact I can dismount and still fight, or kick him out of the turret, plus I wasn't sure that bozo behind the .50 cal would even pull the trigger. Anyway nothin' happened.

We were under the impression that we weren't leaving till tomorrow, since we hadn't packed a single thing. Come to find out we were flying out in two hours. We had immediately gone from long-and-drawn-out to, hurry-the-fuck-up mode. It was a rush to get everything we had consolidated into a rucksack and a duffle bag. Though we'd already mailed a ton of crap home, guys still had a lot of belongings.

Finally, with everyone's shit secured, we staged on the L.Z. and waited. We were the next to the last to leave. With only Captain Kearney, his R.T.O. and a couple Headquarters guys left behind. Eventually, we heard a Chinook. We crouched impatiently against the Hescos as the 1st I.D. guys downloaded the bird. Then we hauled ass to get us and ours onto it. A couple of the Chinooks leaving in the daylight had been shot at. I think one even got mortared. I felt better about leaving at night, but I never felt good about getting on a bird in the Korengal. Once wheels were up, my heart was about to beat out of my chest. It felt like it took forever, but once we made that hard right into the Pesch and out of the Korengal, I knew we'd made it.

Hard to hear inside a Chinook, but guys were laughing and screaming, givin' each other high-fives. It was almost surreal, and probably the biggest relief in our lives. We'd survived the Korengal.

From "The Light Brigade"

Storm'd at with shot and shell,
While horse and hero fell,
They that had fought so well
Came thro' the jaws of Death
Back from the mouth of Hell.
-Alfred Lord Tennyson

Home Psychotic Home

Home had seemed like such a distant dream. We'd been gone so long, it had been built up to fairy tale proportions. But when you get back, a lot of things just aren't what you thought they'd be. And maybe more importantly, you're not who you were.

Each man carried the psychological equivalent of a hundred pound ruck stuffed with issues. I guess we'd all been crazy for quite a while, but we were in a realm of crazy called combat which made that 100% acceptable. However, Vicenza is a civil, somewhat quiet town in northern Italy. The citizens there had spent the last 15 months going to work, mowing the lawn, and eating pizza in a Paratrooper-free environment. But when we got back, guys went absolutely apeshit. It was akin to unleashing the barbarian hordes upon a benign and unsuspecting populace.

Now, we partied hard on a regular basis prior to deployment. I've always said, there's not a college in the America that parties harder than the U.S. Infantry. But this was different. This was some sort of angry, I've-got-a-beef-with-the-world-that's-been-pent-up-for-15-months-and-we're-gonna-go-round-and-round-till-I-passout-or-I'm-in-jail kind of partying. We were violent. We should've disembarked the plane, surrendered our weapons and been admitted to an asylum.

Instead, madmen who hadn't had real sex since mid-tour leave, each one armed with a powder keg of aggression, their combat blood brothers at their sides, and tens of thousands of dollars worth of accumulated combat pay each, swarmed upon the town like insatiable locusts. We brought the war home with us. The national military police of Italy, the *Carabinieri* (or, the Carbs, as we called them), responded frantically all night. Their sirens never ceased. We fought Italians, Nigerians, cinderblock walls, turned on each other, then bought more shots. There wasn't an eastern European stripper in town who didn't have her pockets full and her vagina stuffed with 173rd Airborne.

There were incidents that suggested we weren't right. A dude from Battle Company stabbed a guy from Able Company (or was it the other way around?) for shooting him with an airsoft gun. Someone within the Brigade tied a hooker to a telephone pole and beat her profusely. There were more domestic calls than a TIC Tuesday. For about an hour, we'd come home heroes. Now we were just making a mess of it and could not tarnish our own reputation fast enough.

In addition, the Army wanted to reintegrate us into the Army. Whereas, we believed ourselves to be Battle Company, which was like a separate entity that did whatever the fuck it felt like. Mostly, our purpose was destroying things. Regardless, the Army demanded haircuts, clean uniforms, bloused boots—even the American flag patch we wore on our right shoulders bothered us. In combat, that patch is black and grey. In garrison, it's red, white and blue bordered by gold. It just looked wrong and felt wrong.

There was a 0900 formation every day, for which a third of the Company would be out of ranks (as in, not there for roll call). Normally, not making formation meant you were in deep shit. Now? Not so much. Of the guys that did fill the ranks, 80% had a Blood Alcohol Content somewhere between lava and this-guy-should-be-dead-right-now. When at the position of attention, it was not uncommon for dudes to stumble trying to hold their balance. In my eventual seven years with the Army, it was the only time that being intoxicated in formation was not just a seemingly-acceptable thing, it was the norm.

For the first 90 days after a deployment, no one goes on vacation because we're under evaluation. Although the evaluation obviously did not take into account our off-duty activities, as far as the "evaluation" went, we didn't have a full duty day or anything (though that might've helped keep guys in line). Normally we got off around noon, which meant at 1201 everyone was double-fisting it again. But we did have to go through certain medical this-and-that's.

When I went to my mandatory mental health screening, I walked into a small office containing a female full-bird Colonel. She was there to talk to us one-on-one. She asked me about my experiences in Afghanistan, and I was reluctantly about to tell her some shit that was gonna blow her mind. So I started to tell her about this one firefight, but then she asked me, "What?" And I said, "You know, a firefight. A contact. A firefight. Ya know? A firefight. We were in this firefight…"

I repeated the word firefight at least five more times. And it was totally lost on her. I could see cricket chirps in her eyes. And it dawned on me: this woman, this certified Army psychologist, had no idea what a firefight was. In retrospect, I should've adjusted my terminology and said gunfight. But that's not what we called it. This officially offended every fiber of my Paratrooper being. I mean my God, you'd think the Army would at least have the courtesy to ensure their shrinks were familiar with our basic jargon. I could not believe it; this is who they send to talk to the most combat proven Company in the United States Army? Unbelievable.

"I'm fine, Ma'am," is all I kept repeating till she let me leave.

The usual result of our mental health visits was a prescription: Citalopram, Wellbutrin, Zoloft, Trazadone… Pills. Pills was the Army's answer and I never found one that worked. Really, the only cure is time. The first 90 days you're back, no one is right. You still jump at loud unexpected noises, you don't like being in crowds, you're constantly looking around for badguys, your temper can snap without a moment's notice, and alcohol tastes better than you ever remembered. But after six months goes by, you still do those things only not as bad. When a year passes, things are much improved, but still not right. And finally after about three years without a deployment, you can actually enjoy the 4th of July again.

Once the 90 days of being back are up, leave is in order. Most guys take thirty days since we'd saved up so much leave during combat. Then you have to face your family, who you're thrilled to see, but your family expects you to be who you were 15 months ago. And you aren't. You're colder. More distant. Parts of you are dead and can't be brought back to life. Other more primal things within you are for the first time awake and will never know sleep again. Still, regardless of either party's expectations, being home again is something.

However, it's so bizarre to watch society in motion and think,

Right now guys are slugging it out in the Korengal. Everyone is so oblivious. The world as the average person knows it seems so staged and out of touch. And none of it feels the least bit natural. The paradox is, you're happy you have access to your family, beer, girls, clean clothes, showers and the amenities that come with civilization, but when you've been fighting so much for so long, all these day-to-day things just seem so preposterous. Neither world is right. Neither world is real. And now neither world is home.

At first you don't wanna go back to war but you don't wanna be in this mess either. But the funny thing is (just like Sergeant Barberet told me), when you're deployed, all you can think about is going home. But once you've been back for 90 days, all you can think about is goin' downrange again.

Epilogue

    Two more units pulled deployments in the Korengal Valley after us: 1/26 of the 1st Infantry Division out of Fort Hood, and 2/12 of the 4th Infantry Division from Fort Carson. In April 2010, with forty-two dead and hundreds wounded, the decision was made to pull out of the Korengal in favor of the "new population-centric counterinsurgency strategy," which meant to hell with the rural areas and focus on the cities. This left those of us who'd been there to ponder, *What the fuck were we fighting for?* The resounding sentiment was, what a waste.

    Though none of us wanted see another American die there, the thought of them just abandoning that place made us sick. All that digging and patrolling, blood and sweat, fighting and dying... all for nothin'? There were videos on Youtube of the goddamned Taliban smiling and strolling across the KOP uncontested, walking in and out of the hardstand buildings which I couldn't believe they left intact. You'd think they would've at least had the common courtesy to bomb everything we built off the face of the earth in the interest of not giving the guys we fought against a nice warm place to live. You could tell from the videos, they knew they'd won. I wanted to puke, I wanted to scream, I wanted to throw something expensive... this was an outrage. And there was absolutely nothing I could do about it. Fuck it. Just give up, huh? I guess that's what you call American resolve.

    I've been asked, and asked myself, and we often asked each other, what we were doin' in the Korengal. One thing we were unquestionably doing was holding the enemy at bay. It didn't take goddamned Alexander The Great to figure out that with no American presence in the Korengal there was nothing to stop the Taliban from attacking the Pesch, which was a major supply corridor for that area.

Well, sure as prayer call five times a day, that's exactly what happened. All these articles started surfacing about how the Taliban were using the KOP and the Korengal as a staging area to launch attacks on convoys coming up the Pesch river road. 'Cause there were no Americans between the Pesch and Pakistan. Firebase Michigan, a place we manned the first six weeks of the deployment and rarely saw any action at, became the new Restrepo, the new tip of the withdrawn spear. I guess it is what it is.

Not to get too self-congratulatory, but our deployment did not go without a little publicity. The Army Times would publish several articles about us. In one issue we got about an 8-page spread. Another article was published about us titled "Brilliance In Battle." We made The New York Times (thanks to Elizabeth Rubin) on several occasions. Sebastian Junger and Tim Hetherington made a documentary about 2nd Platoon called *Restrepo*. Tim also published a book of photographs (*Sleeping Soldiers*), while Junger published an article in Vanity Fair (January 2008) called "Into The Valley Of Death," then penned a novel simply titled *War*. And our Medal Of Honor recipient, Sal Giunta, wrote his own book called *Living With Honor*. And some Italian chick quote-fucked me in the Italian Vanity Fair (good luck gettin' a copy of that).

All this aside, with no physical legacy remaining in the Korengal, all we were left with was what we carried inside us. And if one were to sift through the pain and hardship, you'd find a bulletproof layer of pride and camaraderie. You would find regret, but only in certain instances on certain days when things had gone wrong. You would find sadness. The kind of sadness that only sacrifice knows. You would find brothers. Brothers that can only be made in the forge of combat. And you would find a man. Who would not trade these experiences for the world.

THE END

APPENDIX

GLOSSARY:

Acronym, Abbreviation & Jargon Decoder

The Army is lousy with acronyms, abbreviations and jargon. This secret acronym, abbreviation and jargon decoder will help you make sense of it all. Please note, acronyms with periods in between mean each letter should be read individually, whereas acronyms that do not have any periods should be pronounced as a word.

A

A-10: An attack plane built around a 30mm Gatling gun capable of lighting up an entire mountainside. It's really designed to knock out tanks, but works incredibly well as Close Air Support for ground troops. It's one of the baddest things in all of combat.

A-COG: Advanced Combat Optic Gunsight. Depending on the model, a tough, 3 to 4 power compact scope typically mounted on the M-4 rifle. It has a bullet drop compensator and a Tritium illuminated reticle. Tritium being a radioactive compound, and Sergeant Miller being a neurotic, he continuously insisted the scope was leaking radiation into his eyeball.

A.D.: Accidental Discharge. When a round goes off without the shooter intending it to. See A.N.A. (Afghan National Army).

A.C.U.s: Stands for Army Combat Uniform. It's this digitized bullshit that according to regulation, functions in 3 primary combat environments: desert, urban & woodland. The reg. goes on to say that, though it is not optimal for either one, it is functional in all three.

Which is another way of saying, the shit doesn't work anywhere. It's also probably the worst camouflage fielded since the Red Coats. Added to which it's lousy with this cheap-ass velcro. I think our uniform is a disgrace to the Army's uniform.

Apache: An attack helicopter capable of kicking a lot of ass.

A.N.A.: Afghan National Army. The bozos who are supposed to be fighting for their country. In reality, they're a bunch of paycheck collectors whose primary function is self-preservation.

A.O.: Area of Operations. The place your Platoon, Company, or Battalion is assigned to kickass in.

A.S.P.: Ammo Supply Point. Where you keep your ammo consolidated. Ideally in a location away from troops so that if the enemy were to hit your A.S.P. it wouldn't kill your guys.

Assault Pack: Basically it's just a tough camouflage backpack.

A.T.4: A bazooka designed to knock out tanks. (The A.T. stands for anti-tank.)

B

Battle 6: Captain Kearney's call sign on the radio.

B.C.: Battalion Commander. In our case, that meant Captain Kearney's boss, Lieutenant Colonel Bill Ostlund, who was nicknamed "Wild Bill" and was known for giving some really entertaining speeches as well as being a fine officer in most of his men's opinions.

Bob: The center of the solar system, also known as the sun.

BUB: Battle Update Brief. At 1700 Zulu every night, all Battle Company elements would get on the radio and send up their respective reports.

Burkha: It's a giant blue sheet that women have to wear over there. Covers their face and their entire body, all the way down to their feet.

C

C-130: A 4-engine turboprop airplane, and the most common aircraft that a Paratrooper jumps from. But they can also be used as a cargo plane.

C-17: A huge military cargo jet that can be reconfigured to carry personnel.

C.C.P.: Casualty Collection Point. When you take a number of casualties, you pick a safe spot to consolidate them, administer first aid, and prepare for medevac.

Charlie Mike: Continue Mission.

Chinook: A giant Vietnam-era helicopter with twin rotors and twin turbines. It's the workhorse of Afghanistan, responsible for long troop movements, and resupplying firebases that don't have any road access.

CLU: (Pronounced like "clue.") Stands for Command Launch Unit. It's a large clunky, infrared device. You're supposed to use it as an optic to fire a Javelin missile, but we used them as a giant pair of NODs most of the time.

C.O.: Commanding Officer. For a Company, the C.O. is a Captain. In our case, one with an exceptionally large ego and no shortage of wild ideas.

Con-OP: Quizzically stands for Concept of Operations. I believe this is because those who put it together want those of us out executing it to think that someone actually put some thought into this shit. In all fairness, no matter how meticulously planned, at some point the Con-Op is gonna go to complete hell, at which point you just improvise. I sincerely suggest the term "Goatfuck" replace the term "Con-Op." Though it may be less professional sounding, it gives the Soldier on the ground a better idea of what he'll be doing.

COP: Stands for Combat Outpost, a term that for whatever needless reason was chosen (half way through our deployment) to replace the word Firebase.

C.P.: Command Post (a.k.a TOC, or Tactical Operations Center). A place where those in command and other assorted booger-eaters consort to make a grunt's life more miserable, whilst sitting in reclining chairs in a climate controlled office, eating jelly donuts with sprinkles on top.

D

D.T.V.: Damn The Valley. A phrase coined by Thomas Hunter from 1st Platoon. The rest is pretty self-explanatory.

E

E.T.T.: Embedded Tactical Trainer (a.k.a. Afghan National Army babysitter). Typically, they consisted of 1 Marine and 1 Navy Corpsman (Medic), although I met a few Army guys who did it as well.

Ex-fill: Ex-fill means you are leaving the place your patrol intended to go, and are now headed home.

F

Firebase: A Platoon-manned outpost.

Firefight: A gunfight. (That's for all you Army shrinks out there.)

Fireteam: The smallest element of the Infantry, ideally consisting of 4 men (though we never had more than 3), comprised of a SAW gunner, a grenadier, a (theoretical) rifleman, and a Sergeant to serve as Team Leader.

Five-five-six: 5.56 mm. The round fired by our M-4s and SAWs. The civilian equivalent of a .223. Not a round ideally suited to killing people, but we shot what we got.

F.O.: Forward Observer. This is a critical job in Afghanistan. The F.O. calls for fire, directing the rounds of the mortar team & aircraft, onto enemy positions. If you didn't have a good F.O., you were in deep shit.

H

H.A.: Humanitarian Aid, or welfare. We gave the Afghans food, shoes, school supplies, and coats in the winter. We also had projects such as trying to pave the road, built a bazaar in Babyol that they never used, and tried to get a pump in Ali Abad so they didn't have to walk all the way down to the river every time they needed some water. And they couldn't give two shits about any of it.

Hesco: Giant baskets used to fortify a perimeter or position, composed of hardened strands of wire running vertically and horizontally (forming little bitty squares). They come in different heights (4-foot, 7-foot, etc.) fold down flat, and when it comes time to fill them, you simply raise it, unfold it, then (the hard part) fill it. It has this tough fabric lining to keep all the dirt and sandbags inside.

Hooah: Hooah can mean a lot of different things. In the affirmative it can mean: I understand, it will be done, fuck yeah!, you're retarded but since you outrank me I'll do it anyway, etc. As an adjective, for example, "That was pretty hooah," or, "These mean are hooah," it means motivated, dying to kill, badass, hardcore, and so on.

Hooch: A hooch is the off-duty habitat of the deployed Infantryman. It can consist of a green Army tent, a Hajj house, the living quarters of an O.P., or a bunch of lumber stacked together to form a square with a tarp thrown over it for a roof. Basically, it's where a guy chills and sleeps when he's not on patrol, on guard, or otherwise defending America's freedom.

Humvee: To get technical, it's really written HMMWV, which stands for High Mobility Multipurpose Wheeled Vehicle. But to the layman, it's a Hummer. Now as an ordinary guy, I love American pickups and S.U.V.s. But as far as the military is concerned, I hate trucks. I would way rather walk, so don't expect me to talk these things up. They were fucking 15-month old garbage. Getting them to roll out the wire and back under their own power was a lot to expect.

H.V.T.: High Value Target. The badguys you really wanna get.

I

I.B.A.: Interceptor Body Armor (a bullet-proof vest to the layman).

I-com: Armyspeak for walkie-talkie.

I.E.D.: Improvised Explosive Device. Also known as a roadside bomb. Or in our case, a trail-side bomb.

I.O.T.V.: Interceptor something-that-starts-with-an-O Tactical Vest. The allegedly new and improved version of the I.B.A., which very few of us used 'cause it took too long to get on. When the sun sets, and the enemy starts lighting up your firebase, the last thing you need is body armor that requires 12 steps to put on.

J

Jihad: Hajj for "holy war."

Jingle Truck: The semi of Afghanistan. Though not nearly as long (they didn't pull a trailer). They really look more like dump trucks, minus being able to dump things. But the Afghans won't just roll in an impotent dump truck. They have to pimp it out. So they paint all kinds of crazy Hajj shit on the sides, then hang all of these jingley things from the undercarriage, so as the truck plods along the mountain road, it makes this jigley noise which gives the vehicle its name.

Joe(s): Joes are enlisted men who have yet to attain the rank of Sergeant. They are Privates and Specialists. If shit rolls downhill, these guys are neck-deep.

K

K.I.A.: Killed In Action. When a badguy kills a goodguy.

Kickdown Box: Normally a large black plastic chest into which a Soldier places his overflow of goodies. Being reunited with ones kickdown box can at times be likened to opening a xmas present or discovering buried pirate treasure.

KOP: Korengal Outpost. Also known as Battle Base when on the radio. This was the Company Headquarters, home of Kaptain Korengal, and safehaven of phones, internet, 1 or 2 hot meals a day and washing machines. (Not to be confused with COP which stands for Combat Outpost, a term that for whatever needless reason was chosen to replace the word Firebase.)

L

Lima Charlie: Loud and Clear

L-RAZ: (It's actually LRAS, but that's not how it's pronounced.) The L-RAZ is a very very expensive thermal optic, that is very very large, and very very heavy. No one will dispute its effectiveness. I could get behind that thing at night and zoom in on a goat 2 kilometers away. And you could tell it was a goat. But it stands on a tripod, and I'm guessing its dimensions are about 4' x 4' x 2'. And weighs enough that 2 guys wouldn't wanna carry it very far. It also chews through 6 radio batteries at a time.

Lume: Short for illumination; how much moonlight you have on a given night. A full moon is 100% lume.

L.Z.: Landing Zone. Where a helicopter sets down.

M

M240 Bravo: A 7.62mm, belt fed machine gun that fires from the open bolt position.

Mark 19: An automatic, 40mm grenade launcher. (This is a heavy weapon, not something someone can carry around.)

M-Dub:see M.W.R.

Meter: Think of it as a European yard. (1 meter = 3.3 feet)

M.R.E.: Officially stands for Meal Ready to Eat. Whether you're ready to eat it or not, is entirely another matter. They come in a nigh-impregnable brown plastic bag about 2 feet by 1 foot. Each M.R.E. contains a main course, a side of something, and a dessert. Main courses range from such delicacies as Chicken Fajita, to Spaghetti, to Pseudo Beef Patty.

M.W.R.: The official acronym for Morale, Welfare & Recreation. But when you're deployed, it's just the place that has the phones and internet.

N

N.C.O.: Non-Commissioned Officer, also known as Sergeants.

NODs: "Night Optical Device," or simply, night vision goggles.

O

O.P.: Overwatch Position. Two definitions: one being a machine gun element that overwatches the main element while on patrol. Or, one of the five somewhat fortified fighting positions that guarded the KOP.

P

P.I.D.: Positively Identify. Meaning, you see someone carrying a weapon, and you are thus clear to engage them.

Pine: A brand of cigarette imported to Afghanistan from Korea costing anywhere between 50 cents a pack to $3 a carton depending on where they're purchased. It's some of the finest bark to ever leave the Korean peninsula.

P.K.M.: I haven't the slightest idea what P.K.M. stands for, though I suspect it's an acronym for Pre-Millennia Killing Machine. It is a Russian designed light machine gun, 7.62mm, belt fed, and the preferred weapon of the Taliban with which to open up an ambush or contact. It could be considered the enemy's equivalent to the SAW.

P.L.: Platoon Leader. A Lieutenant in charge of a Platoon. Normally, a man of no experience, with poor instincts, foaming at the mouth to please the C.O. while forgetting to have any regard for the life of his men.

Platoon: An element of 30-42 men, composed of four Squads.

POG: (Pronounced "pogue" as in, rhymes with rogue.) Stands for Personnel Other than Grunts. Essentially, anyone who doesn't have a real combat job.

P.S.P.: Play Station Portable. A little handheld video game system made by Sony. Almost everyone had one as it was an awesome time killer.

Q

Q.R.F.: Quick Reaction Force. Although under certain circumstances (such as a Con-Op), a designated unit or element will be assigned to Q.R.F. (and thus prepared), the more likely scenario is as follows: some Platoon (maybe in another Company) gets unexpectedly chewed up bad. So bad, Battalion needs someone to plus them up / secure the area / repel the enemy / clean up the mess. So there you are, chillin' on your cot, not a worry in the world, when your Squad Leader busts in and starts yelling for everyone to pack their shit for a possible 3-day mission. The next thing you know, you're on a helicopter, flying to God knows where to do Satan knows what.

R

Rack: Your bed, or cot, or whatever you've got.

RACK: Ranger Assault Carrying Kit. A modular vest you put on over your body armor. It holds all of your ammo, your NODs, and whatever else you're carrying. It's also referred to as MOLLE, L.B.E. (Load Bearing Equipment), L.B.V. (Load Bearing Vest), or simply, your kit.

R.O.E.: Rules of Engagement. Directives stating when and how it's acceptable to fire upon the enemy.

R.P.G.: Rocket Propelled Grenade.

R.T.B.: Return To Base.

R.T.D.: Return To Duty. Refers to one's status after they've been wounded. In the Korengal, unless you were dead, you were usually R.T.D. in 0 to 3 days.

S

SAW: Squad Automatic Weapon. A 5.56mm, belt fed light machine gun that fires from the open bolt position.

Sern't: How "Sergeant" is actually pronounced in the Army (if you wanna sound cool).

Seven-six-two: Referring to the 7.62mm projectile, which is fired by the majority of Hajj's weapons, but also by our M240 Bravo and M-14 (though the cartridge length is much longer on our weapons). The civilian equivalent is a .308.

S.F.: Special Forces. More commonly known as Green Berets (though they don't refer to themselves as that).

Shurra: Hajj for "meeting."

Singay: Pashtun for, "What's up?"

Smoking: *(Also, "to smoke" or, "to get smoked.")* A time-honored tradition in the Army, whereby an N.C.O. will make his joes do pushups till he reaches complete muscle failure. At which point the N.C.O. chooses a new exercise, such as flutter-kicks or mountain climbers, then goes back to pushups. This can go on for 5 to 10 minutes or more. If you were in 3rd Squad, it could be more like 30 minutes to an hour. The premise of smokings is that a joe has done something wrong, and must do penance with pushups. But the thing was, most of us rarely did anything wrong. But the other thing was, a crafty N.C.O. can imagine that you've done something wrong and smoke you all the same.

S.O.P.: Standard Operating Procedure: how things in a certain situation are supposed to be done.

S.P.: S.P. actually stands for Starting Point. However in the context of a patrol, S.P. means the time that the patrol is leaving the firebase. And it also takes on a verb form, as in, "We are S.P.ing for some village you don't wanna go to."

Squad: An element of 7-9 men, composed of two fireteams.

T

T.C.P.: Traffic Control Point. In our case, it was just a little shack on the KOP road outside of the KOP that would search vehicles coming in and out of the valley.

'Terp: Short for Interpreter. Each Platoon was assigned an Afghan Interpreter who followed us out on patrols and lived in Headquarters' hooch. They got paid $900 US a month, which I was told was more than President Karzai made (before embezzlements of course).

T.H.T.: I asked everyone but the T.H.T., and exactly no one knew what the acronym stood for. I will therefore assume it to be Tactically Hapless Turds. They're supposed to be military intelligence, though the quality of intel ours provided fell far short of being intelligent.

TIC: Troops In Contact (just another term for a firefight)

TOC: Tactical Operations Center. A place where those in command and other assorted mouth breathers consort to make a grunt's life more miserable, whilst sitting in reclining chairs in a climate controlled office, eating jelly donuts with sprinkles on top.

W

W.I.A.: Wounded In Action. When a goodguy is injured by a badguy.

Z

Zulu: Note: To make it easy for the reader, all times in this book reflect local Afghan time, which is not what we used. We went by Zulu time which is an old World War II thing. Zulu is what time it is in London and we still utilize it today to avoid having to do time zone calculations. Battle Company used it because all of the birds used it and it was important for us to be on the same page as them. Just in case they weren't too busy to give us some air support.

1-2-3...

203: (Pronounced "two-oh-three.") A 40mm grenade launcher that attaches to the bottom of our M-4 rifles.

240: (Pronounced "two-forty," also M240 Bravo.) A 7.62mm, belt fed machine gun that fires from the open bolt position.

.50 cal: A.K.A. M2 .50 cal. It's a huge .50 caliber machine gun. If you've never fired one, you're missing out.

550 Cord: (Pronounced "five-fifty" cord.) Parachute cord capable of supporting 550 pounds per line. It has a multitude of uses.

5.56: The round fired by our M-4s and SAWs. The civilian equivalent of a .223. Not a round ideally suited to killing people, but we shot what we got.

7.62: Referring to the 7.62mm projectile, which is fired by the majority of Hajj's weapons, but also by our M240 Bravo and M-14 (thought the cartridge length is much longer on our weapons). The civilian equivalent is a .308.

Bibliography

Cubbison, Douglas R. "Cubbison Report on the Battle of Wanat"
http://the.honoluluadvertiser.com/specials/wanat/wanat_thefullstory

Combat Studies Institute Press "Wanat, Combat Action in Afghanistan, 2008"
http://usacac.army.mil/cac2/cgsc/carl/download/csipubs/Wanat.pdf

I also used to have an official U.S. Army report covering the incident that was published shortly after Wanat, but I can't for the life of me find it. It had all the names taken out of it and was a pain in the ass to read. I've read and watched everything related to Wanat over the years—including the saga of awards to reprimands which were overturned. I also had conversations with one of the survivors from O.P. Topside, Tyler Stafford.

About The Author

Darren Shadix served in the U.S. Army for 7 years. He joined at the ripe old age of 33 and was immediately assigned to the 173rd Airborne (for which, his jealous Drill Sergeant smoked him). Between Army deployments and government contracting, he has spent 3 1/2 years in the cauldron of depravity known as Afghanistan.

Made in the USA
San Bernardino, CA
29 April 2017